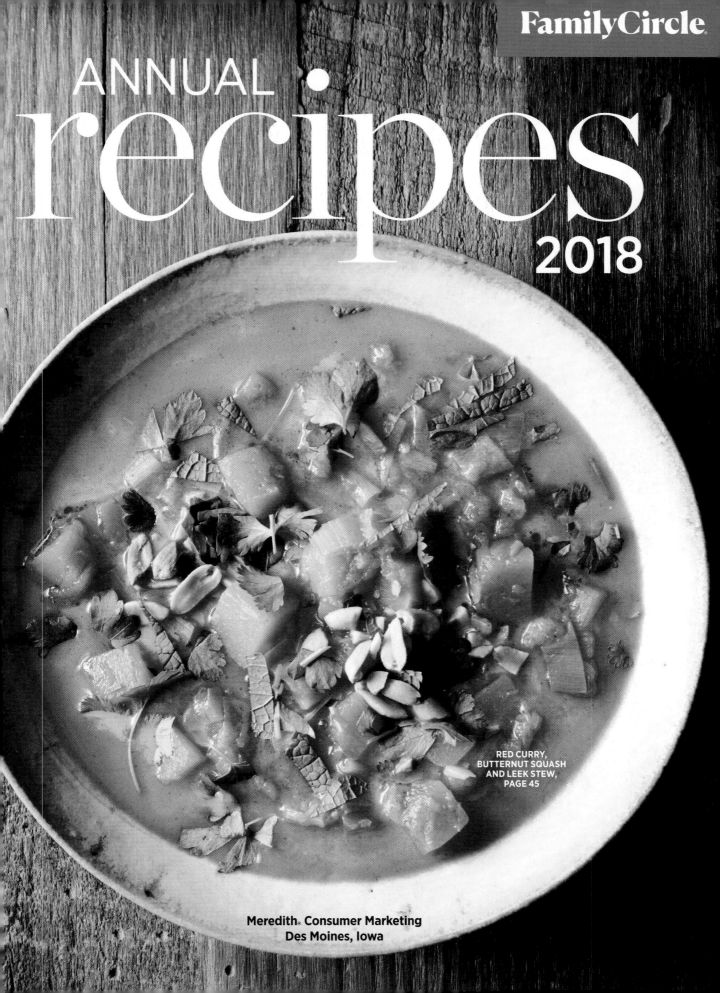

FamilyCircle

ANNUAL recipes 2018

RED CURRY,
BUTTERNUT SQUASH
AND LEEK STEW,
PAGE 45

Meredith Consumer Marketing
Des Moines, Iowa

APPLE BLINI,
PAGE 77

A YEAR'S WORTH OF FABULOUS *FAMILY CIRCLE*® FOOD, JUST FOR YOU.

One of the missions of *Family Circle* throughout the past year has been to engage in conversations with real-life families (such as yours!) about their challenges, joys and dreams—heartfelt exchanges about how to live better in order to serve our readers better. One of the most important aspects of being a family is preparing and enjoying meals together. Eating good, healthy food is not only a necessity, but mealtime also serves as an opportunity to talk to each other, and listen to each other, and to solve problems and express love. Feeding our families well is important to all of us.

At *Family Circle*, we carefully consider the recipes we include. We know quick recipes need to be easy, health- and budget-conscious and—it goes without saying—delicious. The company-special recipes need to be spectacular in some way but still simple enough to make at home. You'll find both kinds of recipes—and everything in between—in this one volume: an at-your-fingertips collection of every recipe that appeared in the 2018 issues of the magazine.

We know busy weeknights present cooking challenges, so the foundation of the food section in every issue is a collection of recipes that helps you get delicious, nutritious food on the table any night of the week. In the September section alone, we included a month's worth of recipes—25 recipes that take 25 minutes or less to make, such as vegetarian Coconut Curry (page 209), Sourdough Turkey Burgers (page 211) and Pasta with Sausage and Broccoli (page 211).

We hope our conversations with real-life families help your families to live, cook and eat better every day.

Cheryl E. Brown, Editor in Chief
Family Circle

Family Circle₍ *Annual Recipes 2018*

Meredith Consumer Marketing
Director of Direct Marketing-Books: Daniel Fagan
Marketing Operations Manager: Max Daily
Assistant Marketing Manager: Kylie Dazzo
Business Manager: Diane Umland
Senior Production Manager: Al Rodruck

Waterbury Publications, Inc.
Editorial Director: Lisa Kingsley
Associate Editor: Tricia Bergman
Creative Director: Ken Carlson
Associate Design Director: Doug Samuelson
Graphic Designer: Mindy Samuelson
Contributing Copy Editors: Terri Fredrickson, Gretchen Kauffman
Contributing Indexer: Mary Williams

Family Circle₍ **magazine**
Editor in Chief: Cheryl E. Brown
Executive Food Editor: Julie Miltenberger
Associate Food Editor: Sarah Wharton

Meredith National Media Group
President: Jon Werther

Meredith Corporation
President and Chief Executive Officer: Tom Harty

In Memoriam: E.T. Meredith III (1933–2003)

Copyright © 2018
Meredith Corporation.
Des Moines, Iowa.
First Edition.
Printed in the United States of America.
ISSN: 1942-7476
ISBN: 978-0696-30276-3

All of us at Meredith Consumer
Marketing are dedicated to providing
you with information and ideas to
enhance your home. We welcome
your comments and suggestions.
Write to us at: Meredith Consumer
Marketing, 1716 Locust St.,
Des Moines, IA 50309-3023.

LET'S EAT! Coming together around the family table at the end of the day to enjoy a home-cooked meal soothes away the day's stresses and satisfies on so many levels. This collection of recipes from the 2018 issues of *Family Circle* makes it easier than ever to serve tasty food you cook yourself—whether it's a 30-minute dinner, a holiday celebration or a special evening with friends. Recipes are organized by month to take advantage of what's in season and to make it easy to find the perfect recipe for any occasion.

VEGGIE ITALIAN HEROES, PAGE 115

BEST-ON-THE-BLOCK
BABY BACK RIBS,
PAGE 139

CONTENTS

SLOW COOKER
BEEF STEW,
PAGE 17

JANUARY

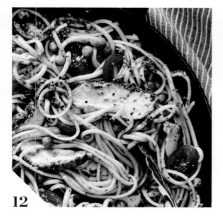

12

18

24

HEALTHY FAMILY DINNERS

Hello, self-checkout lane! Six delicious meals with only 6 ingredients each.

MAKEOVER MAC AND CHEESE

To make this dish a little heartier, add a middle layer of cooked crumbled sausage to each mac and cheese.

Makeover Mac and Cheese

MAKES 6 servings **PREP** 20 minutes **COOK** 8 minutes **BAKE** at 375° for 15 minutes **BROIL** 3 minutes

STAPLES

- 3 **tbsp unsalted butter**
- 3 **tbsp all-purpose flour**
- ¾ **tsp salt**
- ½ **tsp ground black pepper**

INGREDIENTS

- 1 **box (16 oz) medium shell-shape pasta**
- 6 **tbsp seasoned panko bread crumbs**
- 2 **tbsp chopped parsley**
- 2½ **cups 1% milk**
- 3 **tbsp dried minced onion**
- 8 **oz extra-sharp cheddar, shredded**

■ Heat oven to 375°. Bring a large pot of lightly salted water to a boil. Add pasta. Cook according to package directions, about 8 minutes. Drain.

■ Meanwhile, melt 1 tbsp butter in a small skillet. Add bread crumbs and cook, stirring, 3 minutes. Remove from heat; stir in parsley.

■ In a saucepan, melt 2 tbsp butter over medium. Whisk in flour; cook 1 minute. While whisking, add milk, onion, salt and pepper. Bring to a simmer and simmer 3 minutes.

■ Stir 1½ cups cheddar into milk mixture, then stir pasta into cheese sauce. Divide among 6 individual skillets or small pots. Sprinkle with remaining cheddar and the bread crumbs.

■ Bake 15 minutes. Increase heat to broil. Broil 3 minutes and serve.

PER SERVING 599 **CAL**; 22 g **FAT** (12 g **SAT**);25 g **PRO**; 73 g **CARB**; 9 g **SUGARS**; 0 g **FIBER**; 794 mg **SODIUM**

Pesto is a magical ingredient—it adds so much flavor for so little effort, especially if you buy it. Here, it does double duty as a coating for the chicken and as a sauce for the pasta. It's sold in jars on the shelf and in plastic tubs in the refrigerated section. If you can find it, opt for the refrigerated stuff. It has a much better, fresher flavor and a more vivid green color.

Chicken Pesto Linguine

MAKES 6 servings   **PREP** 15 minutes   **COOK** 15 minutes

STAPLES

- **1   tsp salt**
- **¾   tsp freshly ground black pepper**
- **3   tbsp olive oil**

INGREDIENTS

- **2   lemons**
- **1   lb linguine**
- **1¼   lbs boneless, skinless chicken breasts**
- **⅓   cup plus 2 tbsp basil pesto**
- **1   pint grape or cherry tomatoes, halved**
- **1   cup frozen peas, thawed**

■ Juice 1 lemon to yield 3 tbsp lemon juice. Cut remaining lemon into wedges. Bring a large pot of lightly salted water to a boil. Add linguine and cook according to package directions, about 12 minutes. Drain.

■ Meanwhile, toss chicken with 2 tbsp pesto, ½ tsp salt and ¼ tsp pepper.

■ In a large lidded skillet, heat 2 tbsp oil over medium-high. Add chicken, partially cover and cook 6 minutes. Flip chicken and cook 5 minutes. Uncover and add 1 tbsp oil, tomatoes and peas to skillet. Reduce heat to medium. Cover and cook 4 minutes or until chicken is cooked through.

■ Transfer chicken to a cutting board and slice on the bias. Toss linguine in skillet with veggies, ⅓ cup pesto, lemon juice and ½ tsp each salt and pepper. Add sliced chicken and toss to coat. Serve with lemon wedges.

PER SERVING 553 **CAL**; 19 g **FAT** (3 g **SAT**); 33 g **PRO**; 62 g **CARB**; 5 g **SUGARS**; 1 g **FIBER**; 703 mg **SODIUM**

CHICKEN PESTO LINGUINE

PORK AND FRIED RICE

BBQ CHICKEN SAMMIES

Pork and Fried Rice

MAKES 4 servings **PREP** 20 minutes
COOK 13 minutes **BAKE** at 425° for 20 minutes

STAPLES

- ¼ **tsp freshly ground black pepper**
- ⅛ **tsp salt**
- 3 **tbsp vegetable oil**

INGREDIENTS

- 1 **pork tenderloin (about 1¼ lbs)**
- 4 **tbsp low-sodium soy sauce**
- 1 **medium onion, halved and sliced**
- 1 **bag (14.4 oz) frozen broccoli stir-fry vegetables (do not thaw)**
- 2 **pkg (8.8 oz each) fully cooked white rice**
- 3 **large eggs, beaten**

■ Heat oven to 425°. Rub pork with pepper and salt. Heat 1 tbsp oil in a large skillet over medium-high. Brown pork, about 6 minutes.

■ Spoon 1 tbsp soy sauce over pork and place on a small rimmed pan. Bake 20 minutes, until temp is 145°.

■ Meanwhile, reduce heat under skillet to medium. Add 2 tbsp oil, onion and frozen veggies. Sauté 4 to 5 minutes, until crisp-tender.

■ Microwave rice per package directions, 90 seconds. Stir rice and 3 tbsp soy sauce into skillet.

■ Push mixture to one side of pan and add eggs. Cook, scrambling, 2 minutes. Stir egg and rice mixture together.

■ Divide rice among 4 bowls. Slice pork and fan over rice.

PER SERVING 562 **CAL**; 21 g **FAT** (3 g **SAT**); 41 g **PRO**; 49 g **CARB**; 6 g **SUGARS**; 3 g **FIBER**; 808 mg **SODIUM**

BBQ Chicken Sammies

MAKES 6 servings **PREP** 20 minutes **BROIL** 11 minutes **COOK** 10 minutes

STAPLES

- ½ **tsp freshly ground black pepper**
- 1 **tbsp olive oil**
- ¼ **tsp salt**

INGREDIENTS

- 3 **large boneless, skinless chicken breast halves (about 1¾ lbs total)**
- ¾ **cup bottled barbecue sauce**
- 1 **large red bell pepper, cut into strips**
- 1 **medium yellow onion, halved and sliced**
- 6 **thin slices cheddar**
- 6 **seeded hamburger buns**

■ Heat broiler. Cut each breast half in half crosswise and pound lightly to ½-inch thickness. Spread out onto a foil-lined rimmed baking sheet and spread 1 tbsp barbecue sauce over each. Season with ¼ tsp black pepper and broil, 3 inches from heat, 10 minutes.

■ Meanwhile, heat oil in a large nonstick skillet over medium. Add bell pepper and onion and sauté 10 minutes. Stir in ¼ cup plus 2 tbsp barbecue sauce and season with salt and ¼ tsp black pepper.

■ Remove baking sheet from broiler and divide veggie mixture among chicken pieces. Top each with a slice of cheddar and broil 1 minute to melt cheese. Transfer to buns and serve.

PER SERVING 554 **CAL**; 20 g **FAT** (7 g **SAT**); 39 g **PRO**; 46 g **CARB**; 18 g **SUGARS**; 1 g **FIBER**; 771 mg **SODIUM**

SHRIMP PITA
PIZZAS

Shrimp Pita Pizzas

MAKES 4 servings **PREP** 15 minutes
WARM at 350° for 10 minutes **COOK** 4 minutes

STAPLES

3 tbsp olive oil

¼ tsp freshly ground black pepper

⅛ tsp salt

INGREDIENTS

4 large pitas (6 to 7 inches across)

¼ cup plain Greek yogurt

3 tbsp red wine vinegar

1 lb cleaned shrimp (20–24 count)

4 cups loosely packed baby spinach, chopped

1 cup classic hummus

■ Wrap pitas in foil and warm in 350° oven while cooking shrimp.

■ Make a dressing: Combine yogurt, oil, vinegar, ⅛ tsp pepper and the salt in a small bowl. Whisk until smooth.

■ In a medium bowl, toss shrimp with 3 tbsp dressing. In a second bowl, toss spinach with ¼ cup dressing.

■ Heat a grill pan or large cast-iron skillet over medium-high. Add shrimp and cook 1 to 2 minutes. Flip and cook 1 to 2 minutes more, until cooked through. Remove to a clean bowl and toss with remaining dressing.

■ Spread hummus on warm pitas. Top with spinach and shrimp. Sprinkle with ⅛ tsp pepper.

PER SERVING 504 **CAL**; 18 g **FAT** (3 g **SAT**); 39 g **PRO**; 47 g **CARB**; 4 g **SUGARS**; 1 g **FIBER**; 801 mg **SODIUM**

When time is particularly short, these open-face pita sandwiches go together in less than 20 minutes.

SLOW COOKER BEEF STEW

Slow Cooker Beef Stew

MAKES 6 servings **PREP** 25 minutes **COOK** 9 minutes **SLOW COOK** on HIGH for 6 hours or LOW for 8½ hours

STAPLES

¼ cup all-purpose flour

1¼ tsp salt

½ tsp freshly ground black pepper

¼ cup canola oil

INGREDIENTS

2¼ lbs beef chuck stew meat, cut into 1- to 2-inch pieces

1 pkg (10 oz) white or brown mushrooms, trimmed and cut into wedges

1 cup red wine

1½ lbs russet potatoes, peeled and cut into 1-inch pieces

1 can (14.5 oz) diced tomatoes with garlic and onions

5 medium carrots, peeled and sliced into ½-inch rounds

■ In a large bowl, toss beef with flour, ½ tsp salt and the pepper. Heat 2 tbsp oil in a large stainless skillet over medium-high. Add half the beef and brown, 4 minutes. Remove to a 5-qt slow cooker. Repeat with remaining oil and beef and transfer second batch to slow cooker. Reduce heat under skillet to medium and add mushrooms and wine. Cook 1 minute, scraping up browned bits.

■ Stir skillet contents plus potatoes, tomatoes, carrots, ¾ tsp salt and 1 cup water into slow cooker. Cover and cook on HIGH for 6 hours or LOW for 8½ hours.

PER SERVING 599 **CAL**; 21 g **FAT** (5 g **SAT**); 61 g **PRO**; 37 g **CARB**; 8 g **SUGARS**; 4 g **FIBER**; 789 mg **SODIUM**

FOUR WAYS WITH LEEKS

Meet the onion's sweeter, mellower cousin.

LEEK TART

Leek Tart

MAKES 6 servings **PREP** 15 minutes
BAKE 30 minutes at 400°F

- 2 **leeks, white and light green parts only**
- 1 **tbsp unsalted butter**
- 1 **shallot, thinly sliced**
- 1 **box (2 sheets) frozen puff pastry, thawed**
- 1 **large egg, beaten**
- 4 **oz soft goat cheese**
- 4 **oz blue cheese**
- ½ **tsp fresh thyme leaves**
   Freshly ground black pepper

■ Heat oven to 400°. Line a baking sheet with parchment paper.

■ Split the leeks lengthwise, slice crosswise into 1-inch chunks and wash and dry well. Melt the butter in a medium skillet over medium-low. Add the leeks and shallot. Cook, stirring, until softened but not browned, about 7 minutes. Remove pan from heat.

■ Unfold both pieces of puff pastry. Brush ½ inch of the bottom edge of 1 sheet with a bit of beaten egg and place on parchment-lined baking sheet. Overlap the top ½ inch of the second sheet and press into 1 even sheet. Fold and press all edges inward to form 1-inch rim around pastry sheet. Brush rim and outside edges with beaten egg.

■ In a medium bowl, beat remaining egg with goat and blue cheeses. Spread cheese mixture inside pastry shell. Top with leek mixture and sprinkle with thyme and some freshly pepper.

■ Bake at 400° 30 minutes. Sprinkle with more fresh thyme.

PER SERVING 206 **CAL**; 15 g **FAT** (8 g **SAT**); 9 g **PRO** 11 g **CARB**; 3 g **SUGARS**; 1 g **FIBER**; 348 mg **SODIUM**

Leek and Cauliflower Soup

MAKES 4 servings   **PREP** 10 minutes
COOK 27 minutes

- **4 cups thinly sliced leeks, white and light green parts only (from about 3 medium leeks)**
- **2 tbsp unsalted butter**
- **2 tbsp olive oil**
- **1 head cauliflower, trimmed, halved and thinly sliced**
- **6 cups unsalted chicken stock**
- **1½ tsp finely chopped dill, plus sprigs for serving**
- **2 tsp salt**
- **1 tsp white wine vinegar**
- **¼ tsp ground black pepper**
- **Shredded cheddar, optional**

■ Wash and dry the leek slices well. Heat 1 tbsp each butter and oil in a medium pot over medium. Add the leeks, reduce heat to medium-low and cook, stirring frequently, until softened but not browned, 5 minutes. Transfer to a bowl.

■ To pot, add remaining 1 tbsp each butter and oil. Add cauliflower, increase heat to medium-high and cook, stirring occasionally, until browned, about 7 minutes. Add chicken stock, ½ tsp dill and cooked leeks. Cover and bring to a boil. Reduce heat to low and simmer, covered, 15 minutes. Remove pot from heat and let cool 3 minutes.

■ Blend with immersion blender (or transfer in batches to a blender and carefully pulse) until smooth. Stir in salt, vinegar, pepper and remaining 1 tsp dill. Serve garnished with shredded cheddar (if using) and fresh dill sprigs.

PER SERVING 220 **CAL**; 14 g **FAT** (5 g **SAT**); 13 g **PRO**; 11 g **CARB**; 4 g **SUGARS**; 1 g **FIBER**; 1,320 mg **SODIUM**

LEEK AND CAULIFLOWER SOUP

Use only the white and light green parts of the leek. To clean, slice in half lengthwise, leaving the root end intact. Submerge in water several times to wash away all dirt.

Roasted Chicken with Leek Vinaigrette

MAKES 4 servings **PREP** 20 minutes
ROAST 45 minutes at 450°F

- 1 **4-lb whole chicken**
- 2 **tbsp unsalted butter**
- 2 **tsp finely chopped fresh tarragon**
- ¾ **tsp plus ⅛ tsp ground black pepper**
- 1 **tsp plus pinch of salt**
- 6 **leeks, white and light green parts only**
- 1 **tbsp vegetable oil**
- ¼ **cup white wine vinegar**
- 1 **tsp Dijon mustard**
- 6 **tbsp extra-virgin olive oil**

■ Heat oven to 450°. Pat chicken dry.

■ Mix butter with 1 tsp tarragon, ⅛ tsp pepper and a pinch of salt. Rub the mixture under the skin of the breasts. Combine ¾ tsp salt with ½ tsp pepper and sprinkle all over bird, inside and out. Truss chicken legs.

■ Split leeks and wash and dry well. Reserve 1 leek half and toss others with vegetable oil and ⅛ tsp each salt and pepper in a 9x13-inch baking dish. Arrange, cut sides down, and place trussed chicken on top. Roast until chicken is cooked through, about 45 minutes.

■ Meanwhile, finely dice remaining leek half and mix with vinegar, mustard and ⅛ tsp each salt and pepper. Whisk in olive oil. Gently fold in remaining 1 tsp tarragon.

■ Transfer chicken and leeks to a platter and drizzle with dressing.

PER SERVING 603 **CAL**; 37 g **FAT** (9 g **SAT**); 49 g **PRO**; 19 g **CARB**; 5 g **SUGARS**; 31 g **FIBER**; 880 mg **SODIUM**

Mashed Celery Root and Frizzled Leeks

MAKES 4 servings **PREP** 15 minutes
COOK 25 minutes

- 2 **large celery roots, trimmed, peeled and cut into 1-inch chunks**
- 2 **cloves garlic, sliced**
- ¾ **cup unsalted chicken stock**
- 3 **tbsp unsalted butter**
- ¾ **tsp salt, plus more for sprinkling**
- ½ **tsp ground black pepper**
- 1 **leek, white and light green part only**
- 1 **cup vegetable oil**

■ Place celery roots and garlic in a medium pot of cool, lightly salted water. Bring to a boil, then reduce heat and simmer 25 minutes. Drain and return to pot. Mash with chicken stock, butter, salt and pepper until smooth.

■ Meanwhile, line a large baking sheet with paper towels. Trim the leek into 2-inch segments; then split and cut into matchsticks. Wash and dry very well.

■ Heat oil in a deep skillet over medium-high. Working in batches, add the leeks and fry until golden brown, about 2½ minutes. Transfer to the baking sheet and sprinkle with pinch of salt after each batch. Let cool.

■ Transfer celery root to a serving dish and top with frizzled leeks.

PER SERVING 235 **CAL**; 16 g **FAT** (5 g **SAT**); 5 g **PRO**; 22 g **CARB**; 4 g **SUGARS**; 4 g **FIBER**; 563 mg **SODIUM**

MASHED CELERY ROOT AND FRIZZLED LEEKS

ROASTED CHICKEN WITH LEEK VINAIGRETTE

BASICS DONE BETTER

Melissa Clark—mom, cookbook author and *New York Times* food columnist—takes your everyday (yawn) dinners to the next level with a few simple swaps.

CUMIN-CHICKEN
MEATBALLS WITH
GREEN CHILE SAUCE

Basic 1: Meatballs These relatively mild, cumin-flecked chicken meatballs are a gentle foil to the vibrant, fiery green chile sauce served with them. Chile pepper avoiders will happily eat the meatballs plain, while heat seekers can slather them in sauce. If you love garlicky, spicy, herbal flavors, keep this sauce recipe handy. It's excellent on pretty much everything, from roast chicken and fish to grilled steaks, to burgers, to plain rice, and will keep for a week in the refrigerator. It's also nice cooled down with a drizzle of plain yogurt, which makes it appealingly creamy. You can use either white- or dark-meat chicken to make the meatballs; the white meat will be milder, the dark meat more tender. Or substitute ground pork or turkey.

Cumin-Chicken Meatballs with Green Chile Sauce

MAKES 4 servings PREP 20 minutes COOK 2½ minutes BROIL 7 minutes

MEATBALLS

- 1 or 2 large slices white sandwich bread (or use ⅓ cup fluffy pulled-out center of any bread, such as a baguette or a country loaf)
- 2 tbsp milk, preferably whole
- ¾ tsp cumin seeds
- ¼ tsp red chile flakes
- ¼ tsp ground cumin
- 1 lb ground chicken
- 1 large egg, lightly beaten
- 2 cloves garlic, grated on a Microplane or minced
-   Finely grated zest of 1 lemon
- 2 tsp Worcestershire sauce
- 1¼ tsp kosher salt, plus more for sprinkling
- ½ tsp freshly ground black pepper
-   Extra-virgin olive oil, for drizzling
-   Rice or mashed potatoes, for serving

SAUCE

- 2 to 3 jalapeños, seeded
- ¼ cup fresh parsley leaves
- ¼ cup fresh cilantro or basil leaves
- 2 garlic cloves, grated on a Microplane or minced
- ¼ tsp kosher salt, plus more to taste
- 2 tbsp extra-virgin olive oil
- 1 tsp lemon juice, plus more to taste

■ Make the meatballs: Combine bread and milk in a large bowl and set aside for bread to soak while you toast cumin seeds.

■ In a small, dry skillet over medium, toast cumin seeds until fragrant, about 2 minutes.

■ Add chile flakes and toast 30 seconds. Stir in ground cumin and set aside.

■ To bowl containing bread and milk, add chicken, egg, garlic, lemon zest, Worcestershire, salt, pepper and toasted spices. Mix with your hands—mixture will be wet—until just combined and form into 1-inch balls. (At this point you can wrap meatballs well and refrigerate overnight before cooking.)

■ Heat broiler. Set rack at least 4 inches from heat source.

■ Arrange meatballs in a single layer, not touching, on 1 or 2 rimmed baking sheets. Drizzle with olive oil and broil, checking often and shaking baking sheet occasionally to help meatballs brown all over, 4 to 7 minutes.

■ While meatballs are cooking, make the sauce: In a blender, combine jalapeños, parsley leaves, cilantro, garlic, salt, olive oil and lemon juice with just enough water to make mixture move in the blender (about 1 to 2 tbsp). Blend until smooth and add more salt if needed (you might need up to another ¼ tsp). Serve sauce alongside meatballs. These work well served with either hot white rice or mashed potatoes.

PER SERVING 310 CAL; 21 g FAT (5 g SAT); 23 g PRO; 7 g CARB; 1 g SUGARS; 1 g FIBER; 892 mg SODIUM

Basic 2: Veggie Chili This version of vegetarian chili is simmered in a shallow skillet instead of a deep pot so that it comes together quickly enough for any weeknight (wider pan = quicker evaporation = dinner on the table faster). Serve with quick-pickled onions—red onions soaked in lime juice, salt and sugar—to add a tangy bite to the beans, contrasting with their starchy softness. There's also a lime crema in this recipe, which may feel like one step too many on a weeknight, in which case you can absolutely skip it. Or substitute a dollop of yogurt straight from the container to add a little creaminess. But do make the pickles; they're worth the extra 3 minutes it takes to throw them together.

Black Bean Skillet Dinner

MAKES 4 servings   **PREP** 10 minutes   **COOK** 34 minutes

CREMA

Finely grated zest of 1 lime

1 clove garlic, grated on a Microplane or minced

1 cup sour cream or Greek yogurt

Pinch of kosher salt

PICKLED ONIONS

Juice of 1 lime

1 small red onion, very thinly sliced

1 tsp sugar

¼ tsp kosher salt

BEANS

1½ tbsp extra-virgin olive oil

1 small yellow onion, diced

3 medium Cubanelle peppers, seeded and diced (about 1 cup)

1 small jalapeño, seeded and finely chopped

1 clove garlic, grated on a Microplane or minced

2 tsp dried oregano

1 tsp chili powder

3 cups canned black beans, drained and rinsed

1 can (15 oz) diced tomatoes, with their juices

1 tsp kosher salt

Diced avocado

Fresh cilantro leaves

■ Make the crema: In a small bowl, combine lime zest, garlic and sour cream. Season with salt.

■ Make the pickled onions: In another small bowl, combine lime juice, red onion, sugar and salt. Let stand while you prepare beans.

■ Cook the beans: Heat oil in a large skillet over medium-high. Add yellow onion, peppers and jalapeño. Cook, stirring frequently, until vegetables are softened and browned at edges, 10 to 12 minutes. Stir in garlic, oregano and chili powder and sauté until mixture smells garlicky, 1 to 2 minutes. Stir in beans, tomatoes and juices, ⅔ cup water and the salt. Reduce heat to medium and simmer until mixture has thickened, about 20 minutes. Taste and add more salt if needed.

■ Spoon beans into individual warmed bowls. Top with avocado, dollops of crema, pickled onions and cilantro.

PER SERVING 451 **CAL**; 22 g **FAT** (9 g **SAT**); 16 g **PRO**; 52 g **CARB**; 9 g **SUGARS**; 20 g **FIBER**; 1,164 mg **SODIUM**

BLACK BEAN
SKILLET DINNER

VIETNAMESE CARAMEL
SALMON

Basic 3: Salmon In Vietnam, thick bone-in catfish steaks are simmered in a dark and highly peppery caramel for upwards of an hour, until the fish practically falls apart in its bittersweet, pungent sauce. Here, catfish has been replaced with salmon. And by using brown sugar instead of making your own caramel, the process is speeded up that so the whole thing is ready in less than 30 minutes. The salmon still has time to absorb all the intense flavors of the caramel, but it doesn't overcook.

Vietnamese Caramel Salmon

MAKES 4 servings   **PREP** 15 minutes   **COOK** 6 minutes   **BROIL** 5 minutes

- **4** **skin-on salmon fillets, preferably center cut (6 to 8 oz each)**
- **1** **tbsp coconut or extra-virgin olive oil**
- **Fine sea salt to taste**
- ⅓ **cup packed light brown sugar**
- **3** **tbsp Asian fish sauce**
- **2** **tbsp soy sauce**
- **1** **tsp grated peeled fresh ginger**
- **Finely grated zest of 1 lime**
- **Juice of ½ lime**
- ½ **tsp freshly ground black pepper**
- **Sliced scallions (white and green parts), for garnish**
- **Thinly sliced jalapeño, for garnish**
- **Fresh cilantro leaves, for garnish**

■ Set an oven rack 6 inches from heat source (usually the second rack position, not the one closest to heat source) and turn on broiler.

■ Brush salmon all over with oil and season lightly with salt.

■ In a 12-inch oven-safe skillet set over medium-high, combine brown sugar, fish sauce, soy sauce, ginger, lime zest and juice, black pepper and 1 tbsp water. Bring to a simmer.

■ Place fish, skin sides up, in skillet. Reduce heat to low and simmer, without moving fillets, until fish is halfway cooked, 4 to 6 minutes.

■ Spoon pan juices over fish and transfer skillet to oven. Broil until fish is just cooked through and skin is caramelized in spots, 2 to 5 minutes for medium-rare, depending on thickness of fish.

■ Transfer fish to a plate and garnish with scallions, jalapeño and cilantro. Drizzle with pan sauce.

PER SERVING 393 **CAL**; 16 g **FAT** (5 g **SAT**); 41 g **PRO**; 19 g **CARB**; 18 g **SUGARS**; 0 g **FIBER**; 1,440 mg **SODIUM**

Basic 4: Turkey Breast If it's not Thanksgiving or Christmas, people tend to forget about turkey beyond a club sandwich or a substitute for ground beef in burgers and the like. Turkey parts, either legs or breast, make robust meals any time of the year. Here, a boneless whole turkey breast that's been rubbed down with a potent paste of anchovies, garlic, rosemary and lime zest is plopped right on top of a thicket of rosemary needles for roasting. The breast emerges moist and very fragrant, ready to be sliced and served hot. Leftovers are excellent in sandwiches.

Roasted Turkey Breast with Rosemary and Anchovies

MAKES 6 servings   **PREP** 20 minutes   **MARINATE** 30 minutes or up to 24 hours
ROAST at 400° for 25 minutes, then at 350° for 30 minutes   **REST** 10 minutes

- 1 **boneless turkey breast (about 2½ lbs)**
- 1 **bunch fresh rosemary (about 8 large sprigs)**
- 8 **to 12 oil-packed anchovies**
- 2 **large cloves garlic, finely chopped**
  Finely grated zest of 1 lime
- 1 **tsp kosher salt**
- 1 **tsp freshly ground black pepper**
- 2 **tbsp extra-virgin olive oil**

■ If turkey breast is pre tied, untie it. Pat dry with paper towels. Finely chop enough rosemary leaves to yield 1 tbsp; reserve remaining rosemary.

■ Using a mortar and pestle, or a bowl and the back of a wooden spoon, mash together anchovies, chopped rosemary, garlic, lime zest, salt and pepper. Stir in oil. Spread mixture all over turkey, place in a bowl and cover loosely with plastic wrap. Marinate at room temperature at least 30 minutes or refrigerate up to 24 hours.

■ Heat oven to 400°.

■ Place reserved rosemary sprigs on a small rimmed baking sheet. Roll turkey breast up into a nice, even roast and tie it with kitchen twine so it keeps its shape and doesn't unroll as it cooks. Put turkey, skin side up, on top of rosemary.

■ Roast turkey 25 minutes. Reduce heat to 350° and continue roasting until a thermometer inserted in thickest part of meat registers 160°, another 20 to 30 minutes. Allow meat to rest 10 minutes before untying and slicing.

PER SERVING 274 **CAL**; 8 g **FAT** (2 g **SAT**); 42 g **PRO**; 2 g **CARB**; 0 g **SUGARS**; 0 g **FIBER**; 732 mg **SODIUM**

ROASTED TURKEY
BREAST WITH
ROSEMARY
AND ANCHOVIES

SESAME CHICKEN WITH CASHEWS AND DATES

Basic 5: Stir-Fry In the classic Taiwanese dish—called Three Cups Chicken—a sauce of toasted sesame oil, dark soy sauce and honeyed rice wine gives pieces of chicken and scallions an extraordinary depth of flavor, while chiles and fresh ginger add verve. In this version, slivers of dates and roasted cashews are tossed in to add both a sugary depth and a substantial crunch. It makes a great dish ever so slightly more interesting, both texturally and flavorwise.

Sesame Chicken with Cashews and Dates

MAKES 4 to 6 servings   **PREP** 15 minutes   **COOK** 17 minutes

- **4 tbsp toasted sesame oil**
- **1 2-inch piece fresh ginger, peeled and sliced into 12 thin coins**
- **8 cloves garlic, smashed and peeled**
- **1 bunch (about 8) scallions (white and green parts), cut into 2-inch lengths**
- **3 to 4 dried red chiles or ½ tsp red chile flakes**
- **½ cup unsalted roasted cashews**
- **6 boneless chicken thighs (about 2 lbs; preferably with skin on, but off is okay), cut into 2-inch chunks**
- **⅓ cup rice wine or dry sherry**
- **3 tbsp dark soy sauce or tamari**
- **4 pitted dates, thinly sliced**
- **3 cups fresh basil or cilantro leaves or a combination**
- **Rice vinegar or fresh lime juice to taste, for serving**
- **Cooked rice, for serving**

■ Heat a 12-inch skillet or wok over high until very hot, at least 2 minutes. Add 2 tbsp sesame oil to wok and swirl it around; oil should thin on contact. When oil is hot, add ginger, garlic, scallions and chiles. Stir-fry until garlic is golden at edges, 2 to 3 minutes.

■ Add 2 tbsp sesame oil, the cashews and chicken; stir-fry until chicken starts to brown, 4 to 5 minutes (reduce heat if cashews are browning too quickly). Add rice wine, soy sauce and dates; simmer until sauce has reduced to a syrupy consistency and chicken is cooked through, 5 to 7 minutes.

■ Stir in basil, sprinkle with rice vinegar and serve over rice.

PER SERVING 515 **CAL**; 21 g **FAT** (4 g **SAT**); 38 g **PRO**; 43 g **CARB**; 5 g **SUGARS**; 2 g **FIBER**; 643 mg **SODIUM**

**VALENTINE'S CAKE
BALLS, PAGE 59**

FEBRUARY

45

48

53

SOUPER WOMAN

Soup practically runs in the veins of chef, mom and cookbook author Vivian Howard— it's one of her family's favorite go-to meals. With these recipes, it's about to become one of yours too!

SAUSAGE AND COLLARD
SOUP WITH BARLEY

Savory sausage and chewy pearled barley come together in this hearty meal-in-a-bowl. Collard greens—packed with calcium, iron and omega-3 fatty acids—give it a terrific nutritional boost. They're added the last 10 minutes of cooking time to keep them fresh-tasting and bright green in color.

Sausage and Collard Soup with Barley

MAKES 8 servings **PREP** 15 minutes **COOK** 1 hour, 21 minutes

- 1 lb country-style or breakfast sausage, casings removed if needed
- 2 tsp unsalted butter
- 1 large onion, diced
- 5 cloves garlic, smashed
- 3 tsp kosher salt
- 3 qts (12 cups) unsalted chicken stock
- 1 can (15 oz) diced tomatoes
- 1 cup pearled barley
- 4 sprigs thyme
- 3 sprigs rosemary
- ½ tsp red chile flakes
- 1½ lbs collard greens, tough stems removed and leaves chopped into bite-size pieces
- Cornbread croutons

■ In a large Dutch oven, brown sausage in butter over medium, 5 to 6 minutes. Remove sausage and, if needed, drain off all but 2 tbsp fat. Add onion, garlic and 1 tsp salt. Let vegetables sweat about 5 minutes, taking care that they don't brown.

■ Stir in stock, scraping up any browned bits on bottom of pot. Add tomatoes and barley. Tie thyme and rosemary together with twine and throw them in with the chile flakes, browned sausage and 2 tsp salt.

■ Cover and bring soup to a serious simmer. Cook over medium-low about 1 hour. Add greens and cook 10 minutes. Pluck out herb bundle. Serve with croutons.

PER SERVING 539 **CAL**; 28 g **FAT** (7 g **SAT**); 26 g **PRO**; 49 g **CARB**; 9 g **SUGARS**; 9 g **FIBER**; 1,489 mg **SODIUM**

When the world has you down, make a pot of this comforting chicken soup packed with kale, potatoes and lima beans. A rind of Parmigiano-Reggiano cheese simmered in the broth infuses it with amazing flavor.

My Favorite Chicken Soup

MAKES 10 servings   **PREP** 25 minutes   **COOK** 1 hour, 45 minutes   **COOL** 30 minutes

STOCK

- 1 **whole chicken (2½ to 3½ lbs)**
- 2 **cups dried lima beans**
- 2 **medium carrots, split**
- 2 **stalks celery**
- 1 **yellow onion, split and peeled**
- 10 **cloves garlic**
- 8 **sprigs thyme**
- 2 **tsp dried oregano**
- 3 **bay leaves**
- ½ **tsp red chile flakes**
- 3 **qts (12 cups) water**

SOUP

- 2 **tbsp olive oil**
- 2 **cups diced yellow onion (about 2 small onions)**
- 2 **tsp kosher salt**
- 2 **russet potatoes, peeled and cut into 1-inch dice**
- 1 **3-inch piece Parmigiano-Reggiano rind or a 1.5 oz chunk Parmesan**
- 1 **lb kale, stemmed**
- 2 **tbsp light brown sugar**
- ½ **tsp freshly ground black pepper**
- **Pesto (optional)**

■ **Stock** Place chicken, breast side up, in a large Dutch oven. Add remaining ingredients, cover and bring to a boil. Reduce to a simmer and cook 1 hour or until the chicken is falling apart.

■ Let chicken cool in broth 30 minutes. Transfer chicken to a rimmed plate. Pluck out thyme, bay leaves, celery, carrot and onion (but feel free to leave the garlic) and pour the beany broth into a bowl.

■ **Soup** Wipe Dutch oven dry, add oil and heat over medium. Add onion and 1 tsp salt and sweat 5 minutes. Add beany broth, potatoes and cheese rind to pot. Cover and bring to a boil. Reduce to a simmer and cook 20 minutes. Meanwhile, pick meat off chicken and roughly chop kale into spoon-friendly pieces.

■ After 20 minutes, add chicken, kale, sugar, pepper and 1 tsp salt. Cook 20 minutes more. The goal is for the beans and potatoes to break down and make the broth rich, almost creamy.

■ Remove cheese rind. Add salt to taste and serve with a dollop of pesto, if using.

PER SERVING 353 **CAL**; 7 g **FAT** (2 g **SAT**); 34 g **PRO**; 41 g **CARB**; 8 g **SUGARS**; 11 g **FIBER**; 522 mg **SODIUM**

TURKEY AND
WHITE YAM CHILI

Although the terms "yam" and "sweet potato" are used interchangeably, the tubers are actually not even related. A true yam is a starchy tropical vegetable that is a somewhat rare find here—and when you do, they are likely to have been imported from the Caribbean. Either a yam or a sweet potato gives this smoky, chipotle-infused chili a touch of sweetness.

Turkey and White Yam Chili

MAKES 6 servings   **PREP** 15 minutes   **COOK** 1 hour, 9 minutes

1	**lb ground turkey**
1	**tbsp olive oil**
1	**medium yellow onion, diced**
5	**cloves garlic, thinly sliced**
2½	**tsp kosher salt**
2	**tsp ground cumin**
1	**tsp ancho chile powder**
1	**tsp garlic powder**
1	**tsp smoked paprika**
½	**tsp dark chili powder**
¼	**tsp cayenne pepper**
¼	**tsp ground cinnamon**
⅛	**tsp ground nutmeg**
1	**tsp freshly ground black pepper**
1	**can (6 oz) tomato paste**
1	**large chipotle pepper in adobo, finely minced**
1	**can (15.5 oz) pinto beans, drained**
4	**cups unsalted chicken stock**
1	**tbsp light brown sugar**
1	**large white yam or sweet potato, cut into ½-inch dice**

■ In a large Dutch oven, brown turkey in oil over medium-high, about 5 minutes. Remove with a slotted spoon. Lower heat slightly; add onion, garlic and ½ tsp salt. Cook about 3 minutes. Add spices and toast, stirring, about 1 minute.

■ Stir in tomato paste and chipotle. Return turkey to pot and add beans, chicken stock, sugar and 2 tsp salt. Bring to a simmer and add diced yam.

■ Cover and cook at a brisk simmer about 1 hour. Check yams periodically: You want them to crush easily under pressure but not completely dissolve into the chili.

■ Serve warm.

PER SERVING 291 **CAL**; 9 g **FAT** (2 g **SAT**); 26 g **PRO**; 28 g **CARB**; 10 g **SUGARS**; 6 g **FIBER**; 1,123 mg **SODIUM**

You can use either seafood broth or water in this seafood stew—it will have a more delicate flavor when made with water. Although it's a little tricky to poach the eggs in the simmering soup, they make a rich and eye-catching finishing touch, especially when paired with crispy bacon.

Eastern Carolina–Style Shrimp Stew

MAKES 8 servings   **PREP** 15 minutes   **COOK** about 1 hour

- **8 oz sliced smoked bacon, cut into 1-inch pieces**
- **2 medium yellow onions, diced**
- **6 cloves garlic, sliced**
- **1 tbsp plus 1 tsp kosher salt**
- **1 head fennel, halved and thinly sliced (about 4 cups), fronds reserved for garnish**
- **3 tbsp tomato paste**
- **3 medium russet potatoes, peeled and sliced into ½-inch rounds**
- **1 lemon, zest removed with a vegetable peeler**
- **1 large sprig rosemary**
- **½ tsp red chile flakes**
- **2 quarts (8 cups) seafood stock or water**
- **2 lbs peeled and deveined medium shrimp**
- **1 tsp freshly ground black pepper**
- **8 large eggs (optional)**
- **Crusty bread**

- Brown bacon in a large Dutch oven or cast-iron pot over medium, about 8 minutes. When crisp, remove with a slotted spoon. Reduce heat to low and add onions, garlic and 1 tsp salt. Sweat about 3 minutes or until translucent. Add fennel and cook 3 minutes.

- Whisk in tomato paste and let brown slightly, about 2 minutes. Add potatoes, lemon zest, rosemary, chile flakes, 1 tsp salt and the stock. If stock doesn't cover potatoes by 2 inches, add water to do so.

- Over very low heat, bring stew to a boil (this may take up to 30 minutes). Reduce to a simmer and cook 7 to 10 minutes, until potatoes are just tender. Meanwhile, toss shrimp with 2 tsp salt and the pepper.

- Once potatoes are just tender, raise heat slightly and bring stew to a boil.

- If using, crack each egg into a small bowl and carefully drop into stew around perimeter of pot. Take care not to break yolks or stir eggs into stew; you want whole eggs to poach. After about 3 minutes, drop seasoned shrimp in center of pot and around eggs. Once shrimp are submerged, turn off heat and let the whole thing sit 3 minutes. Taste for seasoning and adjust with additional salt and perhaps some lemon juice.

- To serve, make sure each bowl gets an egg, some potatoes and plenty of shrimp. Sprinkle with bacon and fennel fronds. Serve with some bread for soaking up the broth.

PER SERVING 414 **CAL**; 18 g **FAT** (6 g **SAT**); 43 g **PRO**; 21 g **CARB**; 7 g **SUGARS**; 4 g **FIBER**; 1,493 mg **SODIUM**

RED CURRY,
BUTTERNUT SQUASH
AND LEEK STEW

This Thai-inspired soup is a little bit sweet, a little bit spicy and super-simple to make, thanks to a few spoonfuls of jarred red curry paste.

Red Curry, Butternut Squash and Leek Stew

MAKES 6 servings   **PREP** 20 minutes   **COOK** 24 minutes

- 2 tbsp vegetable oil
- 2 cups leeks, white and light green parts, sliced into ⅓-inch rounds
- 2 tbsp minced ginger
- 3 cloves garlic, thinly sliced
- 1 tsp kosher salt
- 3 tbsp red curry paste
- 1 large butternut squash, peeled and cubed (about 7 cups)
- 1 quart (4 cups) unsalted chicken broth
- 1 can (14 oz) coconut milk
- 2 tbsp lime juice
- ½ cup cilantro, chopped
- ¼ cup mint, chopped
- ½ cup salted roasted peanuts, chopped

■ In a medium Dutch oven, heat oil over medium. Add leeks, ginger, garlic and ½ tsp salt and sweat about 3 minutes. Stir in curry paste and cook 1 minute to develop flavor.

■ Add squash, broth and ½ tsp salt. Cover and bring to a gentle boil. Cook 20 minutes or until squash is tender. Check liquid level every now and again to make sure it's not drying out. Add water or stock if needed.

■ Once squash is done, use the back of a spoon to break up about half the squash—the soup should end up chunky. (Ideally, you'll have some smooth squash along with some chunks.)

■ Stir in coconut milk and lime juice. Taste and adjust salt and lime juice as needed. Serve very warm with cilantro, mint and peanuts sprinkled over the top.

PER SERVING 365 **CAL**; 25 g **FAT** (14 g **SAT**); 9 g **PRO**; 31 g **CARB**; 7 g **SUGARS**; 6 g **FIBER**; 974 mg **SODIUM**

TABLE FOR 2

Forget reservations! Valentine's dinner at home can be romantic when you make it together.

GREEN AND WHITE LASAGNA, PAGE 48

BEEF FILET WITH
BLUE CHEESE
BUTTER, PAGE 48

Green and White Lasagna

MAKES 2 servings **PREP** 15 minutes
COOK 7 minutes **BAKE** at 375° for 30 minutes
COOL 10 minutes

- 1 tbsp olive oil
- 1 pkg (8 oz) sliced mushrooms, chopped
- 4 cups packed fresh baby spinach, coarsely chopped
- ¾ cup jarred light Alfredo sauce
- ½ cup fresh basil leaves, chopped
- ½ tsp freshly ground black pepper
- ¾ cup part-skim ricotta or 1% cottage cheese
- 1 large egg yolk
- 4 tbsp grated Parmesan
- 5 no-boil lasagna noodles (about 8×4 inches each)
- 4 slices mozzarella (about 2½ oz)

  Green salad

■ Heat oven to 375°. Line an 8½×4½-inch loaf pan with foil. In a large stainless skillet, heat oil over medium-high. Add mushrooms and cook 4 minutes. Stir in spinach and cook 3 minutes. Remove from heat and add Alfredo sauce, ¼ cup basil and ¼ tsp pepper.

■ In a bowl, stir ricotta, egg yolk, 3 tbsp Parmesan and ¼ tsp pepper.

■ Spoon ¼ cup spinach sauce into bottom of foil-lined pan. Top with a noodle, a third of the spinach sauce and 2 slices mozzarella. Follow with a noodle, half the ricotta mixture and another noodle. Spread with a third of the sauce and top with a noodle. Continue layering with remaining ricotta mixture, noodle, spinach sauce, basil and mozzarella. Sprinkle with 1 tbsp Parmesan and cover with foil. Bake 20 minutes. Uncover and bake 10 minutes. Cool 10 minutes and serve with a green salad.

PER SERVING 592 **CAL**; 27 g **FAT** (11 g **SAT**); 37 g **PRO**; 48 g **CARB**; 8 g **SUGARS**; 4 g **FIBER**; 1,342 mg **SODIUM**

Beef Filet with Blue Cheese Butter

MAKES 2 servings **PREP** 10 minutes
GRILL 6 minutes **ROAST** at 425° for 25 minutes

- 2 filet mignon steaks (4 to 6 oz each)
- 2 tbsp unsalted butter, cut into small pieces
- 2 tbsp crumbled blue cheese
- ¾ lb small potatoes, quartered
- 1 tbsp olive oil
- 2 tsp fresh rosemary, chopped
- ¼ tsp plus ⅛ tsp each salt and freshly ground black pepper

  Green peas or other veggie

■ Heat oven to 425°. Remove steaks from refrigerator and let come to room temperature.

■ In a small bowl, combine butter and blue cheese. Stir slightly, then shape with your hands into a 2½-inch log. Wrap in plastic and refrigerate.

■ On a small rimmed sheet pan, toss potatoes with oil, rosemary and ¼ tsp each salt and pepper. Roast 25 minutes, shaking pan and flipping potatoes halfway.

■ Season steaks with ⅛ tsp each salt and pepper. Heat grill or grill pan to medium-high. Add steaks and cook 3 minutes. Flip and cook 3 minutes for medium-rare.

■ Thinly slice blue cheese butter and place 2 slices on each steak. (Save extra butter for another use.) Serve with roasted potatoes and peas.

PER SERVING 557 **CAL**; 31 g **FAT** (14 g **SAT**); 38 g **PRO**; 30 g **CARB**; 1 g **SUGARS**; 4 g **FIBER**; 607 mg **SODIUM**

Miso-Sugar Pork with Sesame Green Beans

MAKES 2 servings **PREP** 15 minutes
BROIL 18 minutes **COOK** 9 minutes

- 1 small pork tenderloin (about 1 lb)
- 2 tbsp red or white miso paste (see below)
- 2 tbsp packed dark brown sugar
- ¼ tsp freshly ground black pepper

  Pinch cayenne
- ½ lb green beans, trimmed
- 2 tsp sesame oil
- 1 tsp sesame seeds
- ⅛ tsp salt
- 1½ cups cooked rice

■ Heat broiler to HIGH. Arrange oven rack 5 to 6 inches from heat. Line a small baking sheet with foil and coat with nonstick spray. Bring a medium pot of lightly salted water to a boil.

■ Place pork on a cutting board and pat dry. In a small bowl, combine miso, sugar, ⅛ tsp pepper and the cayenne. Rub all over pork and place on foil-lined sheet. Broil 18 minutes, turning every 4 to 5 minutes to brown on all sides. Let rest 10 minutes.

■ Meanwhile, add green beans to boiling water and cook 5 minutes. Drain.

■ In a wok or medium nonstick skillet, heat oil over medium-high. Add green beans, sesame seeds and ⅛ tsp each salt and pepper; cook 4 minutes.

■ Slice pork and serve with green beans and rice.

Note Look for miso paste in the refrigerated section of health food stores or gourmet grocers.

PER SERVING 625 **CAL**; 13 g **FAT** (3 g **SAT**); 54 g **PRO**; 73 g **CARB**; 20 g **SUGARS**; 4 g **FIBER**; 790 mg **SODIUM**

MISO-SUGAR PORK WITH
SESAME GREEN BEANS

BALSAMIC TUNA WITH ITALIAN SLAW

RED VELVET CAKE FOR TWO

Want to make a special Valentine's cake but don't want tempting leftovers hanging around the house for days? This clever, perfectly scaled cake is made in a wedge that can be cut into just 4 servings.

Balsamic Tuna with Italian Slaw

MAKES 2 servings   **PREP** 15 minutes
COOK 5 minutes

- **2 fresh tuna steaks (about 6 oz each)**
- **5 tbsp balsamic vinegar**
- **1 cup each shredded Tuscan kale, radicchio and endive**
- **¼ cup shaved Parmesan**
- **3 tbsp extra-virgin olive oil**
- **¼ tsp plus ⅛ tsp salt and freshly ground black pepper**

■ Place tuna steaks in a large resealable plastic bag and add ¼ cup vinegar. Let marinate on the counter while you make slaw.

■ For slaw, in a bowl, combine kale, radicchio and endive with Parmesan, 2 tbsp oil and 1 tbsp vinegar; toss to combine. Season with ⅛ tsp each salt and pepper.

■ In a medium nonstick skillet, heat 1 tbsp oil over medium to medium-high. Remove tuna from marinade and season with ¼ tsp each salt and pepper. Sear 5 minutes, turning once. Serve with Italian Slaw.

PER SERVING 339 CAL; 12 g FAT (4 g SAT); 46 g PRO; 11 g CARB; 0 g SUGARS; 2 g FIBER; 743 mg SODIUM

Red Velvet Cake for Two

MAKES 4 servings   **PREP** 15 minutes   **BAKE** 20 minutes at 350°F

RED VELVET CAKE
- **¾ cup plus 2 tbsp all-purpose flour**
- **2 tsp cocoa powder**
- **¼ tsp baking powder**
- **⅛ tsp salt**
- **6 tbsp unsalted butter, softened**
- **½ cup packed light brown sugar**
- **1 large egg**
- **½ cup milk**
- **1 to 1½ tsp red food coloring**
- **¼ tsp vanilla extract**

CREAM CHEESE FROSTING
- **¼ cup (½ stick) unsalted butter**
- **2 oz (¼ cup) cream cheese, softened**
- **1½ cups confectioners' sugar**
- **¼ tsp vanilla extract**

■ **Red Velvet Cake** Coat a 9-inch round cake pan with nonstick spray. Cut 1 circle of parchment paper and place in pan. Spray paper.

■ In a medium bowl, whisk flour, cocoa powder, baking powder and salt.

■ In a large bowl, with an electric mixer, beat butter until smooth. Beat in light brown sugar until fluffy, 2 minutes. Beat in egg until incorporated. On low, beat in half the flour mixture, followed by milk, red food coloring and vanilla, then remaining flour mixture. Spread batter into prepared pan.

■ Bake 20 minutes or until set in center. Cool in pan 10 minutes, then turn out of pan, remove paper and turn back over. Cool completely. Once cake has cooled, place cake layer on a cake stand or platter. Top with ¾ cup Cream Cheese Frosting (canned or make your own). Cut cake in half crosswise and stack. Cut in half crosswise and stack again to create a 4-layer cake wedge.

■ **Cream Cheese Frosting** Beat butter and cream cheese until smooth. Gradually beat in confectioners' sugar and vanilla, adding more confectioners' sugar until frosting reaches a good spreading consistency.

PER SERVING 641 CAL; 32 g FAT (19 g SAT); 6 g PRO; 84 g CARB; 62 g SUGARS; 1 g FIBER; 180 mg SODIUM

HEALTHY FAMILY DINNERS

These tacos aren't just for Tuesdays—they're great any night of the week (including Super Bowl Sunday!).

SLOW COOKER
ROPA VIEJA

LAMB WITH
MINT CREMA

Slow Cooker Ropa Vieja

MAKES 8 servings **PREP** 20 minutes **COOK** 5 minutes **SLOW COOK** on HIGH for 6 hours or LOW for 8 hours

- 1 **can (14.5 oz) diced tomatoes**
- 1 **can (6 oz) tomato paste**
- 1 **bay leaf**
- 1 **tsp dried oregano**
- 1 **tsp ground cumin**
- ¼ **tsp whole black peppercorns**
- ¾ **tsp salt**
- ¾ **cup pimiento-stuffed Spanish olives, drained and halved**
- 2 **tbsp vegetable oil**
- 2 **lbs flank steak, trimmed**
- ¼ **tsp freshly ground black pepper**
- 1 **medium onion, halved and sliced**
- 1 **red bell pepper, seeded and sliced**
- 1 **green bell pepper, seeded and sliced**
- 1 **jalapeño, halved, seeded and thinly sliced**
- 10 **cloves garlic, chopped**
- 16 **corn tortillas, warmed**
- ⅓ **cup cilantro, chopped**
- 4 **radishes, sliced**
- 2 **limes, cut into wedges**

■ In a slow cooker, whisk first 6 ingredients. Stir in ½ tsp salt. Finely chop ¼ cup olives and stir into slow cooker.

■ In a large skillet, heat oil over medium-high. Meanwhile, pat steak dry and sprinkle all over with ¼ tsp each salt and black pepper. Cook until browned, about 5 minutes, turning halfway.

■ Add steak to slow cooker. Top with onion, red and green peppers, jalapeño and garlic.

■ Cook on HIGH for 6 hours or LOW for 8 hours. Remove steak and shred. Return shredded meat to slow cooker; add ½ cup olives and stir to combine.

■ Divide meat mixture evenly among warm tortillas; sprinkle with cilantro and top with radishes. Serve with lime wedges.

PER SERVING 363 **CAL**; 14 g **FAT** (4 g **SAT**); 28 g **PRO**; 29 g **CARB**; 6 g **SUGARS**; 5 g **FIBER**; 744 mg **SODIUM**

"Ropa vieja" is Spanish for "old clothes." The term refers to the long strands of meat in this classic dish of braised and shredded flank steak.

Lamb with Mint Crema

MAKES 4 servings **PREP** 15 minutes **COOK** 8 minutes

- 1 **tbsp vegetable oil**
- ½ **small onion, finely chopped**
- 1 **lb ground lamb**
- ¼ **tsp cumin**
- ¼ **tsp ginger**
- ¼ **tsp paprika**
- ¼ **tsp garlic powder**
- ¼ **tsp freshly ground black pepper**
- ⅛ **tsp cinnamon**
- ½ **tsp plus ⅛ tsp salt**
- 8 **corn tortillas, warmed**
  Mint Crema (recipe below)
- 2 **cups thinly sliced romaine hearts**
- 1 **tbsp finely chopped cilantro**
- 1 **tbsp finely chopped mint**
- 1 **tbsp lemon juice**

■ In a large nonstick skillet, heat oil over medium. Add onion and cook 2 minutes. Add next 7 ingredients and ½ tsp salt. Cook, stirring to break up lamb, about 6 minutes, until browned.

■ Spread each warm tortilla with 1 tbsp Mint Crema. Toss romaine with cilantro, mint, lemon juice and ⅛ tsp salt.

■ Using a slotted spoon, divide lamb evenly among tortillas and top with romaine mixture.

PER SERVING 391 **CAL**; 21 g **FAT** (9 g **SAT**); 22 g **PRO**; 26 g **CARB**; 4 g **SUGARS**; 4 g **FIBER**; 377 mg **SODIUM**

Mint Crema Stir ½ cup sour cream, 1 tbsp each finely chopped mint and cilantro, 1 tbsp lemon juice, 1 tsp lemon zest and ⅛ tsp salt.

Mushroom and Poblano

MAKES 4 servings **PREP** 5 minutes **COOK** 13 minutes

- **2 tbsp** vegetable oil
- **1 lb** sliced mixed mushrooms
- **1 medium** poblano, seeded, quartered and thinly sliced
- **½ cup** diced white onion
- **2 large** cloves garlic, grated
- **1½ tsp** ground cumin
- **¼ tsp** plus ⅛ tsp salt
- **¼ cup** dark beer (such as Negra Modelo)
- **2 tbsp** finely chopped cilantro
- **8** corn tortillas, warmed
  Pico de Gallo (recipe at right)
- **½ cup** crumbled queso fresco or feta

■ In a large nonstick pan, heat 1 tbsp oil over medium.

■ Add half the mushrooms, poblano, onion, garlic and cumin plus ⅛ tsp salt; cook 6 minutes, until browned all over. Transfer to a plate. Repeat with remaining oil, mushrooms, poblano, onion, garlic and cumin plus ⅛ tsp salt; cook 6 minutes and leave in pan.

■ Return first batch of veggies to pan. Add beer and cook, scraping up browned bits, 1 minute. Remove pan from heat and stir in cilantro and ⅛ tsp salt.

■ Divide veggies evenly among warm tortillas. Top with Pico de Gallo and queso fresco.

PER SERVING 291 **CAL**; 13 g **FAT** (3 g **SAT**); 10 g **PRO**; 37 g **CARB**; 10 g **SUGARS**; 7 g **FIBER**; 429 mg **SODIUM**

Pico de Gallo Core and dice 2 tomatoes; place in a fine-mesh strainer over a bowl. Add ½ cup finely diced white onion, ½ seeded and finely diced jalapeño and ⅛ tsp salt; toss to combine. Let drain 20 minutes. Transfer to a clean bowl; stir in 2 tbsp lime juice, 1 tbsp chopped fresh cilantro and ⅛ tsp salt.

Poblanos are the type of chile most often used in chiles rellenos, the cheese-stuffed and batter-fried dish so popular at Mexican restaurants. They are generally quite mild and have a rich, fruity flavor.

Spicy Chicken

MAKES 4 servings **PREP** 10 minutes **COOK** 10 minutes

- **1 tbsp** vegetable oil
- **1 lb** boneless, skinless chicken thighs
- **½ tsp** salt
- **¾ cup** no-pulp orange juice
- **2 large** cloves garlic, grated
- **1 tbsp** very finely chopped chipotle pepper in adobo
- **8** corn tortillas, warmed
  Chile-Lime Crema and Pickled Onions (recipes below)
- **1** avocado, sliced

■ In a large nonstick skillet, heat oil over medium-high. Pat chicken dry and sprinkle all over with ¼ tsp salt. Add to skillet and cook 6 to 8 minutes, turning halfway, until browned and cooked through. Transfer to a cutting board and let rest.

■ Add orange juice, garlic, chipotle and ¼ tsp salt to skillet. Cook, stirring, about 2 minutes, until thickened. Remove skillet from heat.

■ Thinly slice chicken and return to skillet, tossing to coat.

■ Spread each warm tortilla with 2 tsp Chile-Lime Crema. Divide chicken evenly among tortillas and top with Pickled Onions and avocado slices.

PER SERVING 448 **CAL**; 16 g **FAT** (5 g **SAT**); 24 g **PRO**; 47 g **CARB**; 19 g **SUGARS**; 6 g **FIBER**; 582 mg **SODIUM**

Chile-Lime Crema Stir ½ cup sour cream, 1 tbsp lime juice, 1 tsp lime zest, ¼ tsp cayenne and ⅛ tsp salt.

Pickled Onions In a bowl, combine ½ red onion, very thinly sliced; ¾ cup cider vinegar; 1½ tbsp sugar and ¼ tsp salt. Let stand at least 10 minutes.

SPICY
CHICKEN

MUSHROOM
AND POBLANO

SWORDFISH AND SLAW

These light and fresh fish tacos get a healthy dose of crunch from a quick purple-cabbage slaw flavored with scallions, cilantro and lime juice.

Swordfish and Slaw

MAKES 4 servings **PREP** 15 minutes **COOK** 5 minutes **BAKE** at 300° for 6 minutes

- ½ **tsp chili powder**
- ¼ **tsp salt**
- 1 **lb swordfish, skin removed**
- 1 **tbsp vegetable oil**
- 8 **corn tortillas, warmed**
- ⅓ **cup jarred salsa verde**
  Cabbage Slaw (recipe at right)

■ Heat oven to 300°. Combine chili powder and salt. Pat swordfish dry and sprinkle salt mixture evenly over both sides.

■ Meanwhile, heat oil in an oven-safe stainless-steel skillet over medium-high. Add fish and cook 2 to 3 minutes; flip and cook 1 to 2 minutes, until sides are nearly opaque. Transfer to oven and bake 6 minutes, until just cooked through.

■ Transfer fish to a cutting board and let rest 3 minutes. Slice thinly. Divide slices evenly among warm tortillas. Top each with 2 tsp salsa verde and some Cabbage Slaw.

PER SERVING 313 **CAL**; 12 g **FAT** (2 g **SAT**); 23 g **PRO**; 29 g **CARB**; 5 g **SUGARS**; 5 g **FIBER**; 448 mg **SODIUM**

Cabbage Slaw Toss 2 cups thinly sliced purple cabbage, 2 thinly sliced medium scallions, ⅔ cup roughly chopped cilantro, 2 tbsp lime juice and ⅛ tsp each salt and black pepper. Let stand at least 10 minutes.

ALL DRESSED UP

With just a few artful sprinkles, drizzles or dips, simple sweets suddenly get glam.

VALENTINE'S CAKE
BALLS

These fabulous treats may look like they were crafted by a master pastry chef, but they are incredibly easy to make with no-bake cake balls, a few simple ingredients and eye-catching but easy decorating techniques.

Valentine's Cake Balls

FOR THE CANDY COATING

- 1 (12-oz) package bright white candy melts
- 1 (12-oz) package cocoa candy melts
- 4 oz red candy melts
- 4 oz pink candy melts
- 4 tsp vegetable oil

FOR THE BASE

- No-Bake Cake Balls (see recipe at right)
- Pretzel rods
- Brownies, cut into 2- to 3-inch hearts

OPTIONS FOR DECORATING

- Glitter dust
- Jimmies
- Sparkling sugar
- Heart candies
- Nonpareils
- Confectioners' sugar
- Cocoa powder

■ **For the candy coating,** place candy melts in 4 separate bowls, one for each color. Add 1 tsp of the vegetable oil to each bowl. Microwave the white candy melts at 50% 1 minute. Stir and continue to melt at 50% in 30-second increments until a few lumps remain. Stir until smooth. Repeat with cocoa melts, red candy melts and pink candy melts.

■ **To dip cake balls,** using either a fork or a skewer, dip a cake ball in melted coating, then gently tap so excess drips off (see instructions at right for Decorating Techniques). Sprinkle with desired decorations, if using. Carefully push ball off skewer onto parchment and let dry at least an hour. To dip pretzels, dip each rod halfway into melted coating, letting excess drip off. Sprinkle with desired decorations and place on parchment paper-lined sheet or cooling rack. Let dry at least an hour. For brownies, sift confectioners' sugar and/or cocoa powder over cooled brownies. (If opting to use jimmies on brownies, sprinkle them over the batter before baking.)

No-Bake Cake Balls Finely crumble an 11.5-oz prepared chocolate loaf cake (such as Entenmann's) into a large bowl. Stir in ¼ cup canned chocolate or vanilla frosting, pressing crumbs together with a silicone spatula to make a dough. Between your palms, roll 1 tbsp dough into a ball. Place on a parchment paper-lined sheet pan and repeat until finished. Refrigerate 15 minutes before dipping.

Decorating Techniques

Marbling Drizzle contrasting coating colors over base coating color in bowl before dipping (go to familycircle .com/marbling) to see how it's done.

Stripes For contrasting stripes, let the base coating dry completely, then drizzle on the second color.

Sugars, Jimmies & Glitter These all need to be sprinkled on immediately after coating so they adhere. They look best on a single-color base.

DUTCH BABY,
PAGE 73

MARCH

64

81

82

HEALTHY FAMILY DINNERS

Trying to get the family to eat more vegetables? Take veggie noodles for a spin—they're trendy and tremendously healthy.

CHICKEN AND SHRIMP PHO WITH DAIKON NOODLES

Many stock and broth brands now offer recipe-ready broths for pho, miso soup and ramen. If you swap one in for the spiced chicken stock here, keep an eye on the sodium level—it can get high.

Chicken and Shrimp Pho with Daikon Noodles

MAKES 4 servings   **PREP** 15 minutes   **COOK** 20 minutes

- 1 **lb boneless, skinless chicken thighs**
- 8 **cups unsalted chicken stock**
- 1 **cinnamon stick**
- 1 **2-inch piece fresh ginger**
- 1 **tsp dark brown sugar**
- ½ **tsp fennel seeds**
- 1 **pod star anise**
- 2 **daikon radishes (about 1¼ lbs), peeled and cut into 4-inch pieces**
- ½ **lb cleaned large shrimp**
- ⅓ **cup each fresh basil, cilantro and mint, roughly chopped**
- 4 **scallions, thinly sliced**
- ½ **jalapeño, thinly sliced (optional)**
- 5 **tsp reduced-sodium soy sauce**
- 1 **tbsp lime juice**
- ¼ **tsp salt**
  Lime wedges, hoisin sauce and sriracha sauce (optional)

■ In a large pot over high, bring first 7 ingredients plus 2 cups water to a boil. Cover, reduce to a simmer and cook 10 minutes. Remove chicken and cool.

■ Continue simmering broth, covered, 10 more minutes.

■ While broth is simmering, spiralize daikon using smallest blade. Divide among 4 large bowls.

■ With a slotted spoon, remove cinnamon stick, ginger and star anise from broth; discard. Add shrimp, cover, remove from heat and let stand at least 3 minutes.

■ Sprinkle daikon noodles with herbs, scallions and jalapeño, if using. Thinly slice cooled chicken and divide among bowls.

■ Add soy sauce and lime juice to pot. Ladle broth into bowls, dividing shrimp evenly among them. Sprinkle each serving with a pinch of salt. Serve lime wedges and sauces on the side, if using.

PER SERVING 330 **CAL**; 7 g **FAT** (1 g **SAT**); 53 g **PRO**; 15 g **CARB**; 8 g **SUGARS**; 4 g **FIBER**; 784 mg **SODIUM**

Most supermarkets now stock ready-made veggie noodles from butternut squash, sweet potato, beet, carrot and zucchini. It you can't find butternut squash noodles, sweet potato noodles work just as well here.

Butternut Squash Spaghetti and Meatballs

MAKES 6 servings   **PREP** 25 minutes   **BAKE** at 400° for 10 minutes   **COOK** 15 minutes

1	**lb ground turkey**
½	**cup 1% cottage cheese**
½	**cup plain dry bread crumbs**
½	**cup basil leaves**
6	**tbsp shredded Parmesan**
5	**cloves garlic**
¾	**tsp freshly ground black pepper**
¼	**tsp plus ⅛ tsp salt**
1½	**lbs butternut squash noodles**
4	**tbsp extra-virgin olive oil**
1	**large shallot, diced**
1	**can (28 oz) crushed tomatoes**
2	**tbsp balsamic vinegar**
2	**tsp sugar**

■ Heat oven to 400°. In a bowl, combine first 3 ingredients. Finely chop ¼ cup basil and add to bowl with 4 tbsp Parmesan. Grate 2 cloves garlic into bowl and add ¼ tsp pepper and ⅛ tsp salt. Mix well and shape into 36 meatballs, using 1 scant tablespoonful turkey mixture for each. Place on a parchment-lined rimmed baking sheet.

■ On a second large rimmed baking sheet, toss squash noodles with 2 tbsp oil and ¼ tsp each salt and pepper.

■ In a large lidded pot, heat 2 tbsp oil over medium. Slice 3 cloves garlic and add to pot along with shallot. Cook, stirring, 3 to 5 minutes. Coarsely chop remaining basil. Add tomatoes, basil, vinegar, sugar and ¼ tsp pepper to pot. Partially cover and cook 5 minutes.

■ Place noodles and meatballs in oven. Bake noodles 10 minutes. Bake meatballs 5 minutes, then spoon into sauce. Cover and cook 5 more minutes.

■ Using tongs, transfer noodles to a platter. Top with meatballs and sauce and sprinkle with 2 tbsp Parmesan.

PER SERVING 294 **CAL**; 10 g **FAT** (2 g **SAT**); 11 g **PRO**; 43 g **CARB**; 12 g **SUGARS**; 8 g **FIBER**; 545 mg **SODIUM**

BUTTERNUT SQUASH
SPAGHETTI AND
MEATBALLS

ZUCCHINI NOODLES
WITH ASPARAGUS,
PEAS AND BACON

Veggie noodles are inherently light. For 6 more grams of protein—and to keep you full longer—top each serving with a poached or fried egg.

Zucchini Noodles with Asparagus, Peas and Bacon

MAKES 4 servings   **PREP** 15 minutes   **COOK** 17 minutes

- ½ **lb asparagus**
- 1 **yellow pepper, seeded**
- 8 **oz bacon, cut into 1-inch pieces**
- 2 **lbs spiralized zucchini**
- ½ **tsp salt**
- 2 **tbsp all-purpose flour**
- 1 **cup milk**
- 2 **large cloves garlic, grated**
- 1 **cup frozen peas, thawed**
- ¼ **cup basil, very thinly sliced**
- ½ **tsp freshly ground black pepper**

■ Trim woody ends from asparagus and peel bottom 2 inches if needed; slice on the bias into ¼-inch-thick pieces, leaving tips intact. Cut pepper lengthwise into 8 pieces, then slice crosswise into ¼-inch strips.

■ Heat a large stainless skillet over medium. Add bacon and cook until crispy, 8 to 9 minutes. Transfer to a paper towel-lined plate. Pour off bacon fat, then return 2 tbsp fat to skillet.

■ Meanwhile, heat a large nonstick skillet over medium and cook zucchini and ¼ tsp salt, covered, until crisp-tender, 5 to 6 minutes, stirring occasionally. Drain zucchini.

■ Add yellow pepper to bacon fat and cook 1 minute. Add asparagus; cook 1 minute more. Sprinkle vegetables with flour and cook 30 seconds, stirring well.

■ Stir in milk and garlic. Add peas and half each of the bacon and basil. Cook until sauce thickens, about 4 to 5 minutes. Remove from heat.

■ Add zucchini, ¼ tsp salt and the black pepper and toss to coat. Transfer to a serving dish and sprinkle with remaining basil and bacon. Serve immediately.

PER SERVING 244 **CAL**; 13 g **FAT** (5 g **SAT**); 12 g **PRO**; 22 g **CARB**; 9 g **SUGARS**; 5 g **FIBER**; 582 mg **SODIUM**

SESAME CARROT
SALAD OVER
TERIYAKI PORK

Sesame Carrot Salad over Teriyaki Pork

MAKES 4 servings   **PREP** 15 minutes   **COOK** 5 minutes

- ¼ **cup rice vinegar**
- 2 **tbsp low-sodium soy sauce**
- 1 **tbsp finely chopped ginger**
- 2 **cloves garlic, finely chopped**
- ½ **lb spiralized carrots (from about 2 very large carrots)**
- 1 **tbsp toasted sesame oil**
- 4 **tsp black or white sesame seeds (or a mix of both)**
- ¼ **tsp salt**
- ¼ **cup hoisin sauce**
- 1 **lb boneless pork chops**
- ¼ **tsp freshly ground black pepper**
- 1 **tbsp vegetable oil**
- 2 **cups cooked brown rice**

■ In a small bowl, whisk the first 4 ingredients. In a medium bowl, pour 2 tbsp vinegar mixture over carrot noodles. Add sesame oil, sesame seeds and ⅛ tsp salt. Toss until carrot noodles are coated with sauce.

■ Add hoisin sauce to remaining vinegar mixture and stir to combine.

■ Pat pork chops dry and sprinkle with pepper and ⅛ tsp salt.

■ In a medium stainless skillet, heat oil over medium. Add pork and cook 1½ minutes, until browned. Flip pork and add hoisin mixture to skillet. Cook 2½ minutes, until temperature reaches 140°. Remove pork and cook sauce about 1 minute, until thickened.

■ Divide rice among 4 bowls and top each serving with a pork chop. Spoon sauce over chops and pile carrot salad on top.

PER SERVING 475 **CAL**; 22 g **FAT** (6 g **SAT**); 29 g **PRO**; 40 g **CARB**; 7 g **SUGARS**; 4 g **FIBER**; 813 mg **SODIUM**

Golden Beets with Sausage

MAKES 4 servings   **PREP** 15 minutes   **COOK** 20 minutes

- 1½ **lbs golden beets, peeled and spiralized**
- 3 **tbsp canola oil**
- 3 **links mild fresh pork or chicken sausage, casings removed**
- 1 **medium onion, halved and thinly sliced**
- 10 **oz mushrooms, sliced**
- 5 **oz fresh baby spinach**
- ⅛ **tsp salt**

  Coarsely ground black pepper, to taste
- ¼ **cup shredded Asiago cheese**

■ Place beet noodles in a large bowl of cool water to cover.

■ In a large pot, heat 1 tbsp oil over medium-high. Crumble in sausage and brown, stirring, 4 minutes. Remove to a plate with a slotted spoon and reduce heat to medium. Add 1 tbsp oil, the onion and mushrooms. Cook 5 minutes, adding ¼ cup water to scrape up bits from bottom of pan.

■ Stir in spinach and cook 3 minutes, until wilted. Stir sausage back into pot and turn off heat.

■ Remove noodles from water and pat dry. In a large nonstick skillet, heat 1 tbsp oil over medium-high. Add noodles and cook 6 minutes, tossing with salt and pepper. Add sausage mixture to skillet and cook 2 minutes. Divide among 4 bowls and top each serving with 1 tbsp Asiago and more pepper to taste.

PER SERVING 334 **CAL**; 17 g **FAT** (8 g **SAT**); 21 g **PRO**; 26 g **CARB**; 5 g **SUGARS**; 4 g **FIBER**; 712 mg **SODIUM**

GOLDEN BEETS
WITH SAUSAGE

BREAKFAST WITHOUT BORDERS

Global politics are complicated—thankfully, breakfast isn't. Here's a look at how the rest of the world starts the day.

RICE AND VEGGIE
BOWL

Southeast Asia The finishing touch on this dish is sambal, a traditional condiment in Indonesia, Malaysia and Thailand. The most widely available variety in the U.S. is Indonesian-style sambal oelek. If you find it too spicy, tame the heat by adding roasted red pepper: Puree 1 large piece in a mini chopper and stir in a few teaspoons of sambal.

Rice and Veggie Bowl

MAKES 4 servings   **PREP** 15 minutes   **COOK** 15 minutes   **LET STAND** 10 minutes

- 1½ **cups light coconut milk**
- 1 **cup basmati rice**
- ¾ **tsp salt**
- 3 **tbsp vegetable oil**
- 1 **large sweet onion, sliced**
- 2 **small baby bok choy, sliced**
- 4 **large eggs**
- ½ **seedless cucumber, sliced**
  Sambal oelek (Indonesian hot chile paste)

■ Combine coconut milk, rice, ½ cup water and ¼ plus ⅛ tsp salt in a lidded pot. Bring to a boil, reduce heat to medium-low and simmer 15 minutes. Remove from heat and let stand 10 minutes.

■ Meanwhile, heat 1 tbsp oil in a large nonstick skillet over medium-high. Add onion and sauté 7 minutes, sprinkling with ⅛ tsp salt, until golden. Remove to a plate and keep warm. Add bok choy to skillet, sprinkle with ⅛ tsp salt and cook 3 minutes. Remove to a plate and keep warm. Add 2 tbsp oil to skillet and gently crack eggs into pan. Cook 3 minutes without flipping. Sprinkle with ⅛ tsp salt.

■ For each serving, spoon ¾ cup rice into a bowl. Surround with ¼ of the onion, ¼ of the bok choy, 1 fried egg, a few cucumber slices and some sambal oelek.

Time-Saver Tip Cook the coconut rice up to 4 days in advance. Slice the veggies the night before.

PER SERVING 450 **CAL**; 20 g **FAT** (6 g **SAT**); 13 g **PRO**; 55 g **CARB**; 9 g **SUGARS**; 2 g **FIBER**; 804 mg **SODIUM**

AVOCADO TOAST

Australia This easy meal started appearing on Australian cafe menus in the early '90s. It exploded onto the U.S. scene around 2013 and has become an Instagram darling.

Germany A Dutch baby (also referred to as German pancake) is a super-puffy baked treat. It's often served topped with fresh fruit or a fruit compote.

Avocado Toast

MAKES 4 servings **PREP** 10 minutes
COOK 4 minutes

- 1 **cup quartered cherry tomatoes**
- 1 **tsp olive oil**
- ¼ **tsp kosher salt, plus more to taste**
-    **Coarsely ground black pepper**
- 4 **slices sourdough bread**
- 2 **avocados, pitted and peeled**
- 1 **tbsp fresh lemon juice**
- 3 **tbsp unsalted butter**
- 4 **large eggs**

■ Toss tomatoes with oil and a pinch each of salt and pepper.

■ Toast bread. Meanwhile, mash avocados with lemon juice, ¼ tsp salt and pepper to taste.

■ In a large nonstick skillet, heat butter over medium and gently crack eggs into skillet. Cook 3 to 4 minutes without flipping, covering with a lid to set yolks.

■ Divide avocado among toasts. Top each with an egg, tomatoes and salt and pepper to taste.

Time-Saver Tip For a speedier breakfast, hard-boil eggs in advance, then peel, chop and sprinkle over toasts along with kosher salt and pepper.

PER SERVING 407 **CAL**; 29 g **FAT** (9 g **SAT**); 10 g **PRO**; 29 g **CARB**; 1 g **SUGARS**; 5 g **FIBER**; 522 mg **SODIUM**

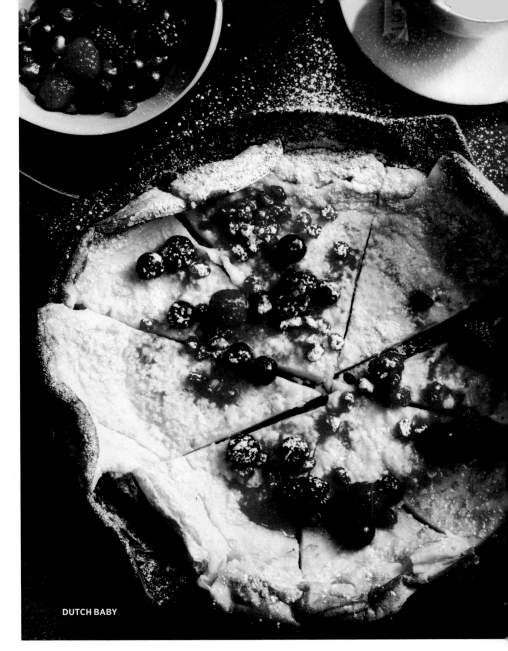

DUTCH BABY

Dutch Baby

MAKES 6 servings **PREP** 5 minutes **BAKE** at 400° for 20 minutes

- 2 **tbsp unsalted butter**
- 6 **large eggs**
- 1 **cup milk**
- 1 **cup all-purpose flour**
- ⅓ **cup granulated sugar**
- ½ **tsp salt**
- 1 **to 2 tbsp confectioners' sugar**

■ Heat oven to 400°. Add butter to a 12-inch cast-iron skillet and place in oven to melt.

■ Meanwhile, whisk eggs and next 4 ingredients in a large bowl. Carefully remove skillet from oven and swirl so butter coats bottom of pan. Pour in egg mixture and return pan to oven. Bake 18 to 20 minutes, until puffed and golden. Sprinkle with confectioners' sugar and serve.

PER SERVING 259 **CAL**; 10 g **FAT** (5 g **SAT**); 10 g **PRO**; 32 g **CARB**; 16 g **SUGARS**; 1 g **FIBER**; 186 mg **SODIUM**

Israel Thought to have originated in northern Africa, this dish then traveled to Israel with immigrants. Variations include eggs baked in a green or white sauce.

Shakshuka

MAKES 6 servings   **PREP** 15 minutes   **COOK** 27 minutes

- **2 tbsp olive oil**
- **½ large yellow onion, diced**
- **4 cloves garlic, sliced**
- **1 tsp smoked paprika**
- **1 tsp ground cumin**
- **¼ tsp ground cinnamon**
- **¼ tsp crushed red pepper**
- **1 can (28 oz) crushed tomatoes**
- **1 cup diced roasted red peppers**
- **¼ tsp salt**
- **¾ cup crumbled feta cheese**
- **⅓ cup fresh parsley, chopped, plus ¼ cup parsley leaves**
- **6 large eggs**
- **Crusty bread or cooked couscous (optional)**

■ In a medium deep skillet, heat oil over medium. Add onion and garlic and cook 5 minutes. Sprinkle with next 4 ingredients. Cook 2 minutes.

■ Stir in tomatoes, peppers and salt. Cover, reduce heat and simmer 10 minutes, stirring occasionally.

■ Stir in ½ cup feta and ⅓ cup chopped parsley. Crack an egg into a small bowl, make a small indentation in sauce and drop egg into indentation. Repeat with remaining eggs. Cook 5 minutes, then cover and cook 5 more minutes, until yolks are almost set. Remove from heat; let stand 2 minutes or until desired doneness. Sprinkle with ¼ cup each feta and parsley. Serve with bread or couscous, if desired.

Time-Saver Tip Follow first 2 steps of recipe and cool. Spoon into a lidded dish and refrigerate up to 1 week. Reheat in a skillet.

PER SERVING 222 **CAL**; 14 g **FAT** (5 g **SAT**); 12 g **PRO**; 15 g **CARB**; 8 g **SUGARS**; 3 g **FIBER**; 751 mg **SODIUM**

SHAKSHUKA

APPLE BLINI

Russia Traditionally, thin crepelike blini are served during Maslenitsa, which is the week before Lent begins. These milk- and egg-laden pancakes work well with a wide variety of sweet or savory fillings.

Apple Blini

MAKES 8 servings **PREP** 15 minutes **LET STAND** 20 minutes **COOK** 21 minutes

- 2 **cups whole milk**
- 3 **large eggs**
- 1 **cup all-purpose flour**
- 1 **cup buckwheat flour**
- 1 **tbsp granulated sugar**
- ¼ **tsp baking soda**
- ¼ **tsp plus ⅛ tsp salt**
- ½ **cup boiling water**
- 2 **tbsp vegetable oil**
- 1 **tbsp lemon juice**
- 4 **small Fuji apples, peeled and halved**
- 4 **tbsp unsalted butter**
- ¼ **cup packed dark brown sugar**
  Sweetened whipped cream

■ In a blender, combine milk and eggs; blend until mixed. In a medium bowl, whisk all-purpose flour and next 3 ingredients plus ¼ tsp salt. Add to milk mixture and blend until smooth, scraping down sides if any flour sticks. While blending, add boiling water, oil and lemon juice. Let stand 20 minutes.

■ Meanwhile, core apples and, on a mandoline or handheld slicer, cut apple halves into ⅛-inch-thick slices. In a large nonstick skillet, heat 3 tbsp butter over medium. Add apples, brown sugar and ⅛ tsp salt and cook 5 minutes, until softened.

■ For blini, melt ½ tbsp butter in a 10-inch skillet over medium to medium-high. Add a scant ¼ cup batter and swirl skillet so batter coats bottom. Cook 30 seconds, until top is dry, then run a silicone spatula under pancake and carefully flip (the first one may not come out well—just like

when making regular pancakes). Cook 30 more seconds and transfer to a plate, covering with a kitchen towel to keep warm. Repeat until you have 8 blini, then add ½ tbsp butter to pan and cook 8 more.

■ Place 1 blini on a plate and mound 1 tbsp apples on 1 quadrant. Fold in half and then in half again. Repeat with all blini and apples. Top each 2-blini serving with a few tablespoons of whipped cream.

Time-Saver Tip Prepare pancakes and stack them. Wrap well in plastic and refrigerate up to a week or freeze up to a month. If frozen, thaw overnight in the fridge. Gently reheat in the microwave while preparing apple filling.

PER SERVING 343 **CAL**; 15 g **FAT** (6 g **SAT**); 8 g **PRO**; 44 g **CARB**; 22 g **SUGARS**; 4 g **FIBER**; 205 mg **SODIUM**

STEPPED-UP SNACKS

Break out of your rut! You don't have to give up your standbys (hello, yogurt, peanut butter and cereal)—just make them better.

Yogurt: Yeah, yeah: PRObiotics, PROtein, all good stuff. But is yogurt exciting? Not so much. Which is why you need to try these two twists.

FROZEN SUNRISE POPS, PAGE 81

BANANA-PB
ROLL-UPS,
PAGE 81

Peanut Butter: It's filling and kind of a perfect food. Instead of eating it straight out of the jar (gasp, who does that?!), try these roll and dip tweaks.

Cereal: A bowlful works for breakfast, snack time or even dinner. But instead of pouring milk, consider these addictive savory and sweet treats.

SUSHI BAR SNACK

Frozen Sunrise Pops

Pictured on page 78.

MAKES about 14 pops   **PREP** 10 minutes
FREEZE 2 hours, 30 minutes

■ In a blender, whirl 2 cups plain Greek yogurt, 1 cup carrot or carrot-mango juice and ¼ cup agave nectar. Pour 2 tbsp carrot mixture into each ⅓-cup ice pop mold. Cover molds and freeze 30 minutes.

■ Add 1 cup frozen strawberries to remaining mixture and blend until combined; refrigerate mixture until ready to use. Fill each mold with about 2½ tbsp strawberry mixture. Push in 2 to 3 frozen raspberries.

■ Add sticks, cover molds and freeze at least 2 hours.

PER POP 77 **CAL**; 2 g **FAT** (1 g **SAT**); 4 g **PRO**; 12 g **CARB**; 9 g **SUGARS**; 2 g **FIBER**; 23 mg **SODIUM**

Parmesan Ranch Dip

MAKES 2 servings   **PREP** 5 minutes

■ Stir 1 cup plain yogurt, 1 tbsp freshly minced chives, 2 tsp grated Parmesan, 1 tsp each sugar and onion powder, ½ tsp garlic powder and ¼ tsp each salt and freshly ground black pepper. Serve with vegetables for dipping.

PER SERVING 98 **CAL**; 4 g **FAT** (3 g **SAT**); 5 g **PRO**; 10 g **CARB**; 8 g **SUGARS**; 0 g **FIBER**; 379 mg **SODIUM**

Five-Spice Peanut Dip

MAKES 4 servings   **PREP** 5 minutes

■ Stir 1 cup chunky peanut butter, 3 tbsp water, 2 tbsp reduced-sodium soy sauce, 1 tbsp lime juice, 1 tbsp agave nectar, ¾ tsp Chinese five-spice powder and ½ to ¾ tsp cayenne. Sprinkle with sliced scallion, if desired. Serve with vegetables for dipping.

PER SERVING 403 **CAL**; 32 g **FAT** (5 g **SAT**); 16 g **PRO**; 20 g **CARB**; 10 g **SUGARS**; 5 g **FIBER**; 529 mg **SODIUM**

Banana-PB Roll-Ups

Pictured on page 79.

MAKES 1 serving   **PREP** 5 minutes

■ Flatten 1 large slice sandwich bread with a rolling pin. Spread with creamy peanut butter and sprinkle with mini chocolate chips and sliced almonds. Place a small banana, trimmed to fit, at one end. Roll and slice.

PER SERVING 467 **CAL**; 23 g **FAT** (5 g **SAT**); 13 g **PRO**; 60 g **CARB**; 18 g **SUGARS**; 5 g **FIBER**; 434 mg **SODIUM**

Spiced Krispies Treat

MAKES 6 servings   **PREP** 5 minutes

■ Toss 1 cup mini marshmallows with ½ tsp ground cinnamon and ¼ tsp ground nutmeg until well coated. Stir in 2 cups Rice Krispies cereal and 1 cup cocoa-powder-dusted almonds.

PER SERVING 280 **CAL**; 16 g **FAT** (1 g **SAT**); 8 g **PRO**; 27 g **CARB**; 13 g **SUGARS**; 0 g **FIBER**; 105 mg **SODIUM**

Sushi Bar Snack

MAKES 6 servings   **PREP** 5 minutes

■ Stir 2 cups Rice Krispies cereal, 1 cup wasabi peas, 1 cup crumbled seaweed chips and 1 cup sweet pea crisps, broken into thirds. Sprinkle with a pinch of salt, if desired.

PER SERVING 304 **CAL**; 9 g **FAT** (2 g **SAT**); 9 g **PRO**; 47 g **CARB**; 8 g **SUGARS**; 2 g **FIBER**; 346 mg **SODIUM**

FOUR WAYS WITH PISTACHIOS

This little nut is coming out of its shell.

Pistachio-Bacon Bark

MAKES 12 servings **PREP** 5 minutes
REFRIGERATE 30 minutes

- **3 cups white chocolate chips**
- **6 slices cooked bacon, chopped**
- **½ tsp pistachio extract**
- **1 scant cup chopped, roasted salted pistachios**

■ Melt chocolate chips.

■ Stir in half of the chopped bacon and all of the pistachio extract.

■ Working quickly, spread mixture in an even layer over a parchment-lined baking sheet. Top with the pistachios and remaining bacon. Gently press into chocolate.

■ Refrigerate at least 30 minutes. Break apart to serve.

PER SERVING 220 **CAL**; 15 g **FAT** (6 g **SAT**); 5 g **PRO**; 19 g **CARB**; 17 g **SUGARS**; 1 g **FIBER**; 102 mg **SODIUM**

Pappardelle with Toasted Pistachios and Mint

MAKES 6 servings **PREP** 10 minutes

- **1 cup roughly chopped unsalted pistachios**
- **12 oz hot pappardelle**
- **¼ cup extra-virgin olive oil**
- **1 lemon, zested and juiced**
- **½ tsp salt**
- **½ tsp freshly ground black pepper**
- **8 oz Burrata cheese**
- **⅓ cup fresh mint leaves, hand-torn**

■ In a large pan over medium heat, toast the pistachios.

■ Add the pappardelle to the pan and remove from heat. Stir in the olive oil, lemon zest, lemon juice, salt and pepper. Break apart the Burrata and sprinkle on top, along with the hand-torn mint leaves.

PER SERVING 530 **CAL**; 28 g **FAT** (8 g **SAT**); 18 g **PRO**; 48 g **CARB**; 3 g **SUGARS**; 3 g **FIBER**; 300 mg **SODIUM**

Warm Rice Salad with Pistachios

MAKES 6 servings **PREP** 10 minutes

- **2 cups warm cooked basmati rice**
- **1 scant cup roughly chopped toasted unsalted pistachios**
- **1 cup thawed shelled edamame**
- **½ cup roughly chopped fresh dill**
- **½ cup golden raisins**
- **⅓ cup crumbled feta**
- **2 tbsp extra-virgin olive oil**
- **1 tbsp cider vinegar**
- **½ tsp salt**

■ In a large bowl, stir all of the ingredients. Serve warm or at room temperature. Makes 6 cups.

PER SERVING 391 **CAL**; 17 g **FAT** (3 g **SAT**); 12 g **PRO**; 49 g **CARB**; 12 g **SUGARS**; 4 g **FIBER**; 290 mg **SODIUM**

Persian Pesto with Pistachios

MAKES 8 servings **PREP** 5 minutes

- **1 cup packed parsley**
- **½ cup plus 2 tbsp toasted unsalted pistachios**
- **1 small clove garlic**
- **1 tsp lemon zest**
- **½ tsp ground coriander**
- **½ tsp red pepper flakes**
- **½ tsp salt**
- **¼ tsp ground cumin**
- **⅔ cup extra-virgin olive oil**
- **2 tbsp lemon juice**
- **1 lb cooked white-fleshed fish such as cod, sea bass or halibut**

■ In a food processor, pulse together the parsley, ½ cup of the pistachios, garlic, lemon zest and remaining spices.

■ With the food processor running, drizzle in olive oil and lemon.

■ Serve over cooked fish and garnish with remaining pistachios. Makes 1 cup.

PER SERVING 240 **CAL**; 26 g **FAT** (4 g **SAT**); 4 g **CARB**; 2 g **PRO**; 1 g **SUGARS**; 1 g **FIBER**; 151 mg **SODIUM**

Roll pistachios in a dish towel to remove their skins, which can muddy up the color of a recipe.

PISTACHIO-BACON BARK

PAPPARDELLE WITH TOASTED PISTACHIOS AND MINT

WARM RICE SALAD WITH PISTACHIOS

PERSIAN PESTO WITH PISTACHIOS

PINK LEMONADE
CAKE, PAGE 96

APRIL

90

99

101

HEALTHY FAMILY DINNERS

These fast and easy weeknight meals put your favorite spring foods—like asparagus, lamb, eggs and more—front and center.

GRILLED CHICKEN PASTA

Pappardelle is a wide, wonderfully chewy ribbonlike pasta. If you can't find it, you can substitute an equal amount of either linguine or fettuccine—just cook either type according to the package directions.

Grilled Chicken Pasta

MAKES 4 servings **PREP** 15 minutes **COOK** 9 minutes **GRILL** 10 minutes

- ½ **lb boneless, skinless chicken breasts**
- 2½ **tbsp olive oil**
- 1 **tsp salt**
- 1 **large lemon, zested and juiced**
- ½ **tbsp Dijon mustard**
- 1 **(8.8 oz) box pappardelle**
- ½ **lb asparagus, cut into 1-inch pieces**
- ½ **cup frozen peas**
- 4 **oz bocconcini (small mozzarella balls), quartered**
- ¼ **cup packed basil leaves, torn**
-    **Freshly ground black pepper**

■ Heat grill over medium-high. Pound chicken to even ½-inch thickness. Toss with ½ tbsp oil, ⅛ tsp salt and ½ tsp lemon zest. Whisk mustard, lemon juice, remaining lemon zest and ¼ tsp salt. Whisk in 1½ tbsp oil.

■ Grill chicken, covered, until cooked through, 4 to 5 minutes per side. Transfer to a cutting board to rest 5 minutes.

■ Meanwhile, bring a large nonstick pot of lightly salted water to a boil. Add pasta and cook to al dente, about 6 minutes. Slice chicken in half lengthwise, then thinly slice.

■ Drain pasta, reserving ⅓ cup pasta water. Return pot to heat. Add ½ tbsp oil and asparagus; cook 1 minute. Add peas and ⅛ tsp salt; cook 2 minutes. Remove from heat.

■ Add chicken, pasta, reserved pasta water, dressing, bocconcini, basil and ½ tsp salt to pot. Toss to coat. Top with freshly ground pepper.

PER SERVING 533 **CAL**; 22 g **FAT** (8 g **SAT**); 30 g **PRO**; 51 g **CARB**; 3 g **SUGARS**; 2 g **FIBER**; 701 mg **SODIUM**

Any oven-going skillet will work to make this dish, but cast iron is ideal. Searing the meat in cast iron gives the exterior a beautiful and delicious crust—and the way cast iron evenly conducts heat ensures that the interior of the meat will be juicy and tender throughout.

Apricot-Glazed Pork with Slaw

MAKES 4 servings   **PREP** 15 minutes   **COOK** 8 minutes   **ROAST** at 350° for 8 minutes   **BROIL** 3 minutes

- **1 lb pork tenderloin**
- **1 tsp salt**
- **½ tsp freshly ground black pepper**
- **2 tbsp vegetable oil**
- **¼ cup apricot jam**
- **2 cloves garlic, grated**
- **½ red cabbage, cored, halved lengthwise and thinly sliced**
- **2 medium carrots, grated**
- **¼ cup packed basil, thinly sliced**
- **3 scallions, thinly sliced on the bias**
- **3 tbsp red wine vinegar**
- **2 tbsp sliced almonds**
- **2 cups cooked brown rice**

■ Heat oven to 350°. Pat pork dry and sprinkle all over with ¼ tsp each salt and pepper.

■ In a medium oven-safe stainless skillet, heat oil over medium. Add pork and brown on all sides, about 2 minutes per side. Transfer skillet to oven and roast pork 8 minutes.

■ Meanwhile, in a small saucepan, heat jam, garlic, 2 tbsp water and ¼ tsp salt over medium until jam is melted, about 2 minutes. Toss cabbage with carrots, basil and ⅔ of scallions.

■ Remove pork from oven and pour apricot glaze over top. Broil 3 minutes, until temperature reaches 140°, for medium-rare. Rest on a cutting board 5 minutes (temp will rise to 145°).

■ To drippings in skillet, add vinegar, ½ tsp salt and ¼ tsp pepper; whisk to combine. Pour warm dressing over cabbage mixture and toss to coat well. Divide slaw among 4 plates. Slice pork and place on top of slaw; sprinkle with almonds and remaining scallions. Serve with rice.

PER SERVING 448 **CAL**; 13 g **FAT** (3 g **SAT**); 29 g **PRO**; 55 g **CARB**; 17 g **SUGARS**; 6 g **FIBER**; 705 mg **SODIUM**

APRICOT-GLAZED
PORK WITH SLAW

SPRING SALAD
WITH STEAK

Spring Salad with Steak

MAKES 4 servings   **PREP** 15 minutes   **COOK** 14 minutes

- **5**   **oz baby spinach**
- **2**   **oz watercress, long stems chopped**
- **2**   **Belgian endives, split and sliced into ½-inch pieces**
- **1**   **lb flank steak**
- **¼**   **tsp plus ⅛ tsp salt**
- **¼**   **tsp freshly ground black pepper**
- **2**   **tbsp vegetable oil**
- **2**   **tbsp light mayonnaise**
- **2**   **tbsp white wine vinegar**
- **1½** **tbsp prepared horseradish**
- **1**   **tsp sugar**
- **½**   **small red onion, thinly sliced**
- **4**   **medium radishes, thinly sliced**
- **2½** **oz blue cheese**
- **4**   **slices (1 oz each) focaccia**

■ In a large bowl, toss spinach, watercress and endive. Divide evenly among 4 bowls.

■ Pat steak dry and sprinkle all over with ¼ tsp salt and the pepper. In a large stainless skillet, heat ½ tbsp oil over medium. Cook steak 5 to 7 minutes per side, until temperature reaches 125°, for medium-rare. Transfer to a cutting board to rest 5 minutes (temp will rise to 135°).

■ Meanwhile, stir mayonnaise, vinegar, horseradish and sugar. Stir in ⅛ tsp salt and 1½ tbsp oil.

■ Top each salad with dressing, onion and radishes. Thinly slice steak against the grain, arrange over salads and crumble blue cheese on top. Serve with focaccia.

PER SERVING 408 **CAL**; 22 g **FAT** (7 g **SAT**); 34 g **PRO**; 18 g **CARB**; 2 g **SUGARS**; 4 g **FIBER**; 793 mg **SODIUM**

Potato Chip Spanish Tortilla

MAKES 4 servings   **PREP** 15 minutes
COOK 19 minutes   **BAKE** at 325° for 10 minutes

- **3**   **tbsp vegetable oil**
- **1**   **cup chopped yellow onion**
- **8**   **large eggs**
- **¾**   **tsp salt**
- **¼**   **tsp freshly ground black pepper**
- **3**   **cups 40%-less-fat kettle-cooked potato chips, crushed to about half their size**
- **2**   **cloves garlic, thinly sliced**
- **1**   **lb rainbow Swiss chard, tough ends trimmed, chopped into bite-size pieces**
- **½**   **cup parsley leaves**
- **2**   **tbsp chives, cut into 1-inch pieces**
- **½**   **tbsp red wine vinegar**

■ Heat oven to 325°. In a 10-inch oven-safe stainless skillet, heat 1 tbsp oil over medium. Add ⅔ cup onion and cook until softened, about 5 minutes. Cool slightly.

■ In a large bowl, beat eggs with ½ tsp salt and ⅛ tsp pepper. Add chips and cooled onion; stir.

■ Wipe out skillet, add 1 tbsp oil and heat over medium, swirling to coat sides of pan well. Add egg mixture; cook 5 minutes, until edges are set. Transfer skillet to oven and bake 8 to 10 minutes, until center is set and top starts to brown.

■ Meanwhile, heat ½ tbsp oil in a large nonstick skillet over medium. Add ⅓ cup onion and the garlic. Cook 3 minutes. Add half the chard; when slightly wilted, add remaining half. Cook, stirring often, until soft and tender, 5 to 6 minutes. Stir in ¼ tsp salt; keep warm.

■ Toss parsley and chives with vinegar and ½ tbsp oil. Mound herb salad in center of tortilla. Serve wedges with Swiss chard.

PER SERVING 257 **CAL**; 17 g **FAT** (4 g **SAT**); 11 g **PRO**; 17 g **CARB**; 3 g **SUGARS**; 3 g **FIBER**; 619 mg **SODIUM**

POTATO CHIP
SPANISH TORTILLA

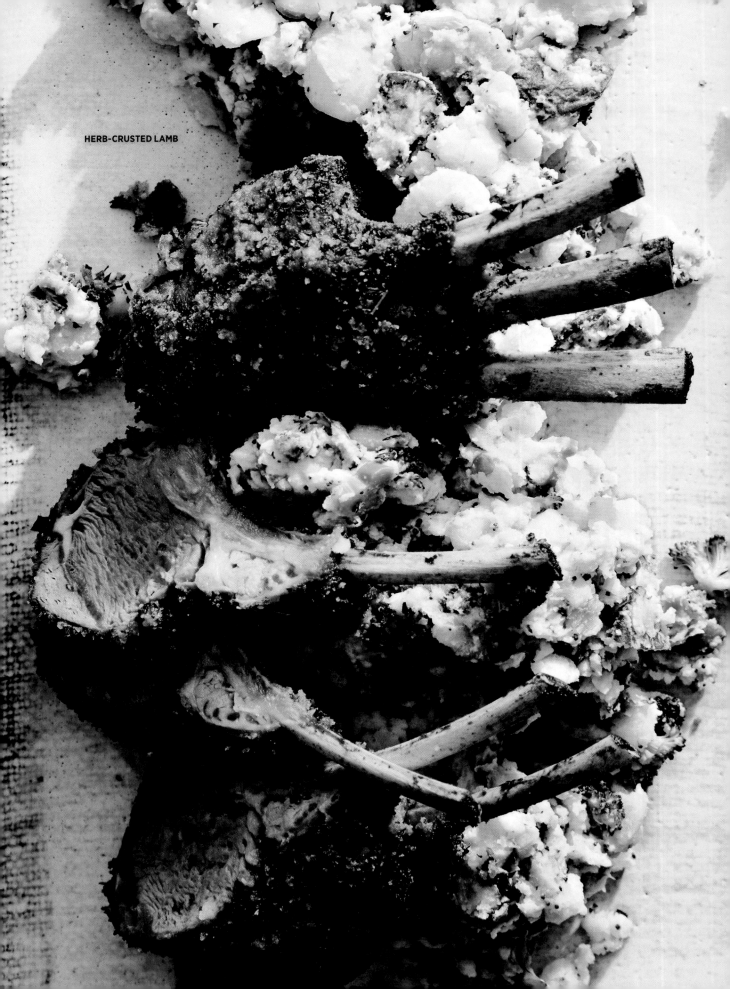

HERB-CRUSTED LAMB

This isn't a difficult or time-consuming dish to put together at all—in fact, it's perfectly doable on a busy weeknight. But it's elegant enough for company too!

Herb-Crusted Lamb

MAKES 4 servings **PREP** 15 minutes **COOK** 15 minutes **ROAST** at 400° for 25 minutes

- 1½ **tbsp plain bread crumbs**
- 2 **tbsp fresh parsley, finely chopped**
- 1 **tbsp fresh rosemary, finely chopped**
- 1 **tbsp fresh thyme, finely chopped**
- 1 **box (10 oz) frozen broccoli spears**
- 1 **lb red potatoes**
- ⅓ **cup light sour cream**
- ¼ **cup skim milk**
- 1 **tsp salt**
- ¼ **tsp plus ⅛ tsp freshly ground black pepper**
- 1 **small rack of lamb (8 ribs; about 1¼ lbs)**
- 1½ **tbsp vegetable oil**
- 1 **tbsp Dijon mustard**

■ Heat oven to 400°. In a small bowl, stir first 4 ingredients. Transfer to a plate and spread out in an even layer.

■ Finely chop frozen broccoli and place in a colander. In a medium saucepan, cover potatoes by 2 inches with cool water. Bring to a boil and cook 12 to 15 minutes, until tender when pierced with a knife. Drain over broccoli in colander and return veggies to pot. Smash potatoes and broccoli with sour cream, milk, ¾ plus ⅛ tsp salt and ¼ tsp pepper. Keep warm.

■ Meanwhile, pat lamb dry and sprinkle meaty side with ⅛ tsp each salt and pepper. In a medium oven-safe stainless skillet, heat oil over medium. Add lamb and brown on all sides, 2 to 3 minutes per side. Transfer to a cutting board.

■ Brush fatty side of rack with mustard. Press mustard into herb mixture on plate until well coated. Spritz coating with cooking spray.

■ Return lamb, crust side up, to skillet and place in oven. Roast 20 to 25 minutes, until temperature reaches 135°, for medium-rare. Rest on a cutting board 5 minutes (temp will rise to 145°). Slice ribs apart and serve over potato mixture.

PER SERVING 339 **CAL**; 15 g **FAT** (5 g **SAT**); 26 g **PRO**; 25 g **CARB**; 5 g **SUGARS**; 4 g **FIBER**; 802 mg **SODIUM**

BEYOND THE PALE

Gorgeous desserts for Easter, Passover or any spring meal.

MATZOH-BLUEBERRY ICEBOX CAKE

Perfect for Passover, this dessert is made with stacked layers of matzoh, sweetened cream cheese and frozen wild blueberries.

Matzoh-Blueberry Icebox Cake

MAKES 9 servings   **PREP** 20 minutes   **MICROWAVE** 1 minute   **REFRIGERATE** 4 hours or overnight

½   **cup plus 5 tbsp superfine sugar**

1   **pkg (8 oz) cream cheese, softened**

1¾   **cups heavy cream**

¾   **cup frozen wild Maine blueberries, thawed**

    6 matzohs

    Red and blue liquid food coloring

■ Line an 8×8-inch baking dish with plastic wrap, leaving overhang on 2 sides.

■ In a glass measuring cup, combine ¼ cup water and 2 tbsp sugar. Microwave 1 minute, then stir until sugar is dissolved to make a simple syrup.

■ Beat cream cheese in a medium bowl until smooth. Add 1 cup cream and ½ cup sugar. Beat until fluffy and smooth. Fold in blueberries.

■ Place 1 matzoh in prepared dish, generously brush with simple syrup and spread a generous ½ cup blueberry mixture over matzoh to edges. Repeat layering 4 times, top with remaining matzoh and brush liberally with simple syrup. Use overhanging plastic to cover stack and seal with another piece of plastic wrap. Refrigerate 4 hours or overnight.

■ Uncover stack and invert onto a plate. Remove and discard plastic. Beat ¾ cup cream with 3 tbsp sugar and a few drops each of red and blue food coloring to create a purple hue. Spread whipped cream on top and sides of cake and serve.

Lemon juice and zest team up in a sweet-tart combo—a showy ending to your Easter meal. If you wish, bake just 2 layers (instead of 4) in 8- or 9-inch round metal pans; add a few minutes of bake time for taller layers.

Pink Lemonade Cake

MAKES 16 servings   **PREP** 25 minutes   **BAKE** at 350° for 22 minutes

CAKE

- 2¾ **cups all-purpose flour**
- 2 **tsp baking powder**
- ½ **tsp salt**
- 1 **cup (2 sticks) unsalted butter, softened**
- 1¾ **cups granulated sugar**
- 3 **large eggs**
- 1 **cup milk plus 3 tbsp fresh lemon juice**
- 2 **tsp lemon zest**
- ½ **tsp lemon extract**
- **Pink and yellow gel food coloring**

FROSTING

- 1 **cup (2 sticks) unsalted butter, softened**
- 3 **cups confectioners' sugar**
- ½ **cup heavy cream**
- 1 **tsp lemon zest**
- ½ **tsp lemon extract**

■ **Cake** Heat oven to 350°. Coat four 8-inch round foil baking pans with nonstick spray. Line pan bottoms with parchment paper and coat with spray.

■ Whisk flour, baking powder and salt. In a large bowl, beat butter with sugar until light colored, about 2 minutes. Beat in eggs, one at a time, occasionally scraping down bowl. Beat in half the flour mixture, followed by all the milk mixture, lemon zest and lemon extract, then remaining flour mixture.

■ Measure a scant 1½ cups batter into each of 3 bowls (leave remaining batter in mixing bowl). Tint 1 bowl of batter with 4 to 5 drops pink food coloring. Tint 2nd bowl with 3 drops pink and 1 drop yellow food coloring. Tint 3rd bowl with 2 drops yellow and 1 drop pink food coloring. Tint last bowl with 1 drop yellow food coloring. Spread each bowl of batter into a separate prepared pan. Bake 20 to 22 minutes, until cakes spring back lightly when pressed. Cool 10 minutes in pans on wire racks, then invert onto racks and remove paper. Cool completely.

■ **Frosting** Have all ingredients at room temperature. Beat butter until smooth. Add confectioners' sugar and heavy cream; beat until fluffy and good spreading consistency. Beat in lemon zest and extract.

■ Place darkest pink layer on a cake stand and spread top with ½ cup frosting. Add next-lightest layer and spread top with ½ cup frosting. Stack remaining 2 layers with ½ cup frosting in between, then spread remaining frosting around side and top of cake. There won't be a lot of frosting; the idea is that the cake layers should be visible through the thin frosting.

Tip For easier slicing, refrigerate frosted cake 30 minutes to an hour before cutting with a serrated knife.

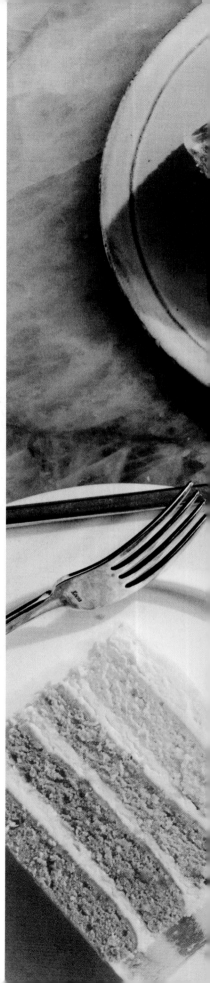

PINK LEMONADE CAKE

MERINGUES

These 6-ingredient treats make a spectacular centerpiece. Before baking, tint the whipped egg whites green or any color of the rainbow.

Meringues

MAKES about 60 cookies   **PREP** 15 minutes
BAKE at 200° for 2 hours

4	**large egg whites**
½	**tsp cream of tartar**
¼	**tsp salt**
1	**cup superfine sugar**
½	**tsp vanilla extract (clear, if possible)**
	Green liquid food coloring

■ Heat oven to 200°. Line 2 large baking sheets with parchment paper.

■ Combine egg whites, cream of tartar and salt in bowl of a stand mixer. Whip on medium speed until frothy. Increase to medium-high and gradually add sugar, a few tablespoons at a time, until glossy and very fluffy, about 3 minutes. Beat in vanilla.

■ Place 1⅓ cups meringue into each of 3 bowls (leave remaining meringue in mixer bowl). Tint each bowl of meringue a different shade with green food coloring.

■ Spoon 1 bowlful of meringue into a pastry bag fitted with a large star tip. Holding bag ½ inch above surface, pipe onto prepared baking sheets. Repeat with remaining bowls. Bake 2 hours. Cool completely on pans.

HOLIDAY CLASSICS

Looking for the perfect recipes to celebrate Easter or Passover? Look no further.

GLAZED HAM

For Easter, serve this looker with green beans and corn pudding—all ready in 2 (mostly unattended) hours.

Glazed Ham

MAKES 20 servings **PREP** 5 minutes
BAKE at 350° for 2 hours

- ½ **smoked bone-in butt or shank ham (7 to 9 lbs)**
- 1 **cup packed dark brown sugar**
- 1 **cup orange marmalade**
- ¼ **cup orange juice**
- ¼ **cup Dijon mustard**

■ Place oven rack in lower third. Heat oven to 350°.

■ If attached, remove rind from ham. Score fatty side of ham in 1-inch diamond pattern. Place in a shallow roasting pan; add 2 cups water and cover with foil. Bake 70 minutes. Meanwhile, for glaze, whisk remaining ingredients.

■ Remove foil and brush with ¾ cup brown sugar glaze. Continue to bake, uncovered, until ham is browned and temperature reaches 140°, about 50 minutes.

■ Transfer ham to a cutting board; let stand 15 minutes. Meanwhile, gently heat remaining glaze in a small saucepan. Serve with ham, along with Corn Pudding and Green Beans with Bacon.

Tip Carve like a Chef: Place ham on board so bone is vertical. Slice close to bone, ¾ of the way down. Cut across ham to bone in ¼-inch slices. Continue slicing until entire half is removed. Place ham on its side; finish cutting remaining sides starting at bone. Trim fat as desired.

Tip You can speed up the carving process by choosing a spiral-cut ham when shopping. Roast as directed, then just carve along the bone—the slices will be precut through the meat.

PER SERVING 267 **CAL**; 5 g **FAT** (1 g **SAT**); 35 g **PRO**; 23 g **CARB**; 21 g **SUGARS**; 0 g **FIBER**; 1,162 mg **SODIUM**

Green Beans with Bacon

MAKES 12 servings **PREP** 25 minutes
COOK 18 minutes

■ Bring a large pot of lightly salted water to a boil. Add 2 lbs trimmed fresh green beans and return to a boil. Cook 3 to 4 minutes and drain. Cook 8 slices bacon in a skillet until browned and crisp, about 5 minutes. Remove bacon to a paper towel-lined plate and pour off all but 2 tbsp drippings. Add 1 cup diced onion to skillet and sauté until softened, 5 minutes. Crumble bacon and add to skillet with ⅓ cup cider vinegar, 1 tbsp sugar and ½ tsp freshly ground black pepper. Cook until sugar is dissolved and mixture is bubbly, about 4 minutes. Add green beans; toss to coat and heat through.

PER SERVING 74 **CAL**; 3 g **FAT** (1 g **SAT**); 3 g **PRO**; 8 g **CARB**; 4 g **SUGARS**; 3 g **FIBER**; 73 mg **SODIUM**

Corn Pudding

MAKES 12 servings **PREP** 15 minutes
COOK 5 minutes **BAKE** at 350° for 50 minutes

■ Coat a 2-quart baking dish with cooking spray. Cook 6 slices bacon in a skillet until crisp, about 5 minutes. Transfer to a paper towel-lined plate, then crumble. In a large bowl, whisk 4 large eggs, ½ cup heavy cream, 3 tbsp cornstarch, 2 tbsp sugar, ½ tsp salt and ⅛ tsp cayenne. Stir in crumbled bacon, 4 trimmed and chopped scallions, 1 drained can (15.25 oz) whole corn kernels and 1 can (14.75 oz) creamed corn. Pour into prepared pan and top with ½ cup shredded sharp cheddar. Bake at 350° until golden and a knife inserted in top comes out clean, about 50 minutes.

■ Let stand 10 minutes.

PER SERVING 138 **CAL**; 9 g **FAT** (4 g **SAT**); 6 g **PRO**; 11 g **CARB**; 5 g **SUGARS**; 2 g **FIBER**; 411 mg **SODIUM**

For Passover, preorder the bird from a kosher butcher or, if shopping at your local market, check that the packaging says "kosher for Passover." Feeding a crowd? Grab a second bird and roast it alongside the first, adding a little extra time as needed.

Lemony Roast Chicken

MAKES 6 servings   **PREP** 15 minutes
ROAST at 425° for 25 minutes, then at 400° for 45 minutes

- 4   **tbsp kosher for Passover margarine, softened**
- 2   **cloves garlic, minced**
- 1½   **tbsp lemon zest**
- ½   **tsp dried oregano**
- ½   **tsp salt**
- ¼   **tsp freshly ground black pepper**
- 1   **large whole kosher for Passover chicken (about 4 lbs)**

■ Heat oven to 425°. In a small bowl, stir margarine, garlic, lemon zest, oregano, ¼ tsp salt and ⅛ tsp pepper.

■ With fingers, gently make a pocket between skin and meat on breast, thighs and legs. Rub margarine mixture under skin. Season chicken all over with remaining salt and pepper.

■ Place chicken on a rack in a roasting pan. Roast 25 minutes, then reduce heat to 400° and roast 45 minutes or until temperature reaches 165° in thigh. Carve and serve with Roasted Carrots and Potatoes and Apple-Spinach Salad.

PER SERVING 551 **CAL**; 42 g **FAT** (15 g **SAT**); 42 g **PRO**; 1 g **CARB**; 0 g **SUGARS**; 0 g **FIBER**; 775 mg **SODIUM**

Roasted Carrots and Potatoes

MAKES 6 servings   **PREP** 10 minutes
ROAST at 400° for 45 minutes

■ In a large bowl, toss 1¾ lbs halved small red potatoes and 1½ lbs 3-inch pieces of peeled carrots with 3 tbsp olive oil. Add 1 tbsp honey, 1 tsp lemon zest, ½ tsp each salt and dried oregano and ¼ tsp freshly ground black pepper. Toss to coat. Spread onto a large rimmed baking sheet and roast at 400° for 45 minutes or until tender, stirring occasionally.

PER SERVING 205 **CAL**; 7 g **FAT** (1 g **SAT**); 3 g **PRO**; 34 g **CARB**; 9 g **SUGARS**; 5 g **FIBER**; 384 mg **SODIUM**

Apple-Spinach Salad

MAKES 6 servings   **PREP** 15 minutes

■ In a medium bowl, whisk ¼ cup cider vinegar, 1 tbsp honey, ½ tsp salt and ¼ tsp freshly ground black pepper. While whisking, add ½ cup olive or walnut oil in a thin stream. In a large bowl, toss 10 oz baby spinach, 3 cored and thinly sliced apples (such as Gala, Fuji and/or Honeycrisp) and 12 sliced pitted dates with ¼ cup dressing. Top with ½ cup toasted chopped walnuts and serve with extra dressing on the side.

PER SERVING 301 **CAL**; 18 g **FAT** (2 g **SAT**); 3 g **PRO**; 33 g **CARB**; 25 g **SUGARS**; 5 g **FIBER**; 232 mg **SODIUM**

LEMONY ROAST CHICKEN
AND ROASTED CARROTS
AND POTATOES

PLUM TARTS AND
PLUM-COCONUT
MOCKTAIL,
PAGE 127

111

118

123

THE DINNER PLAN

Two busy moms have come up with a blueprint for making mealtime less stressful.

SHRIMP SUMMER
"ROLL" SALAD

Make-Ahead One family's favorite dish is Vietnamese summer rolls—rice paper sheets wrapped around shrimp, raw vegetables, rice noodles and herbs. The wrapping can be hard, though, so sometimes they skip that part. Over time, the rolls evolved into this salad. If you prefer the convenience of ready-to-eat shrimp, use them; you can also substitute shredded rotisserie chicken or cubed tofu. The salad is dressed with a thinned version of the typical peanut sauce served with summer rolls.

Shrimp Summer "Roll" Salad

MAKES 4 servings **PREP** 20 minutes **COOK** 3 minutes

- 8 oz thin rice noodles (also called rice vermicelli)
  Salt
- ¾ lb large unpeeled shrimp
- 2 large handfuls thinly sliced iceberg or other lettuce
- 2 carrots, peeled, halved lengthwise and thinly sliced
- 1 red bell pepper, cored and cubed
- ½ English cucumber, quartered and sliced
- 1 ripe avocado, pitted, peeled and diced
- 1 large handful fresh cilantro, roughly chopped (optional)
  Peanut Sauce (recipe right), thinned with a little warm water

■ Prepare noodles according to package instructions. While they soak, bring a medium saucepan of water to a boil over high. Once water is boiling, season with 2 large pinches of salt. Add shrimp and simmer until just cooked through, about 3 minutes. Drain and rinse under cold water until cool. Peel, devein and cut shrimp into thirds (or leave whole, if you prefer).

■ Divide noodles among 4 shallow bowls. Top with lettuce, carrots, pepper, cucumber, avocado, cooked shrimp and cilantro (if using). Drizzle with thinned Peanut Sauce and serve.

■ You can keep all prepped ingredients separate in the fridge and let people compose their own salads, or compose them in advance, cover tightly with plastic wrap and refrigerate up to 1 day. Either way, cut and add the avocado and dress the salad right before serving.

PER SERVING 513 CAL; 19 g FAT (3 g SAT); 26 g PRO; 65 g CARB; 9 g SUGARS; 6 g FIBER; 715 mg SODIUM

Peanut Sauce

MAKES about 1 cup

- ½ cup creamy peanut butter
- ¼ cup warm water
- 2 tbsp soy sauce
- 2 tbsp fresh lime juice
- ½ tbsp packed brown sugar
- 3 cloves garlic, minced
- 1 tbsp grated peeled fresh ginger
  Sriracha or hot sauce of your choice

■ In a small bowl, combine first 7 ingredients with sriracha to taste. Whisk, then check seasonings.

■ Keep, covered, in the fridge up to 1 week.

This creamy, full-flavor, all-purpose dipping sauce does double duty as a salad dressing when thinned with a little warm water until just pourable. You can make this in a food processor; put the garlic in whole and use about 1 inch of peeled ginger.

Extra-Fast There are two somewhat unconventional items that belong in every pantry: coconut milk and Thai curry paste. With these on hand, everyday ingredients such as pork and broccoli turn into familiar but still slightly exotic dinners. Red curry paste is spicier than green; use whichever you prefer. The moms like Maesri and Mae Ploy brands.

Pork and Broccoli Curry

MAKES 4 servings   **PREP** 15 minutes   **COOK** 9 minutes, 20 seconds

- 1 **tbsp vegetable oil**
- 2 **large shallots, thinly sliced**
- 1 **lb boneless pork chops, patted dry and cut against the grain into ¼-inch-thick slices**
- 2 **tbsp red or green Thai curry paste**
- 1 **can (13.5 oz) unsweetened regular or light coconut milk**
- 1 **tbsp fish sauce or 1 tsp anchovy paste**
- 1 **tbsp lightly packed brown sugar**
- 2 **cups small broccoli florets**
- 1 **lime, zested and halved**
  Salt
  Steamed rice
  Handful of fresh cilantro, roughly chopped (optional)

■ In a large skillet, heat oil over medium-high until it shimmers. Add shallots and cook, stirring often, until softened, 2 minutes. Add pork and cook, stirring often, until just browned, 2 minutes. (The meat should still be pink inside.) Add curry paste and cook, stirring, until fragrant, about 20 seconds.

■ Add next 3 ingredients and bring to a simmer. Add broccoli, reduce heat to medium-low and gently simmer, stirring occasionally, until crisp-tender, 5 minutes. Stir in lime zest and a generous squeeze of lime juice. Check seasonings, adding salt to taste. Serve with rice and, if using, cilantro.

PER SERVING 526 **CAL**; 22 g **FAT** (10 g **SAT**); 30 g **PRO**; 52 g **CARB**; 6 g **SUGARS**; 3 g **FIBER**; 838 mg **SODIUM**

PORK AND BROCCOLI
CURRY

One-Dish One mom grew up eating some version of this dish weekly. It was a snap for her mom to make, no one ever tired of it and there was only one pan to wash. Potatoes and lemon were constants, but sometimes her mom would throw in carrots, cherry tomatoes or even a green veg such as sliced asparagus or frozen peas (closer to the end of the cooking time). Sweet potatoes, parsnips and mushrooms are also good options. Feel free to substitute rosemary or thyme for the oregano; fresh herbs are wonderful here, too. Dark meat is more flavorful, but include a breast for any white-meat fans.

One-Pan Chicken with Lemon and Potatoes

MAKES 5 servings   **PREP** 15 minutes   **BAKE** at 450° for 35 minutes

Scant ¼ cup olive oil

¼ cup fresh lemon juice

½ tbsp dried oregano

1 tsp paprika

Salt and black pepper

1½ lbs unpeeled potatoes (small red- or white-skinned are nice here), cut into 1-inch pieces

1 small red or yellow onion, cut into 8 wedges

4 cloves garlic, smashed

5 large chicken thighs or 10 drumsticks or a combination (about 2½ lbs total), patted dry

1 small lemon, sliced (optional)

■ Heat oven to 450°, with a rack in middle position. In a 15×10-inch or larger baking dish, add oil, lemon juice, oregano and paprika; season very generously with salt and pepper, and stir. Add potatoes, onion, garlic and chicken. Using your hands, combine well, coating ingredients with as much oil mixture as possible.

■ Spread potatoes and onion across dish and top with chicken, skin sides up. Sprinkle a little more salt and pepper on chicken and top with lemon slices, if using. (It's a nice touch, but the dish will be fine without it.)

■ Bake until potatoes are tender and chicken is just cooked through, about 35 minutes. If chicken is cooked but potatoes aren't tender yet, transfer chicken to a platter and tent with foil to keep warm. Toss potatoes, return them to oven and cook until tender, 5 to 10 minutes more. Check seasonings, then serve topped with pan juices (spoon off any excess fat first, if needed).

PER SERVING 404 **CAL**; 18 g **FAT** (4 g **SAT**); 30 g **PRO**; 30 g **CARB**; 3 g **SUGARS**; 4 g **FIBER**; 588 mg **SODIUM**

Pantry The light flavors of chicken sausage go particularly well with the mushrooms, white beans and brothy-lemony sauce, but you can also use turkey or pork sausage. And if you don't like or have mushrooms—the only nonpantry ingredient in the dish—leave them out and cook the onion over medium heat instead.

Rigatoni with Sausage, White Beans and Mushrooms

MAKES 6 servings   **PREP** 10 minutes   **COOK** 16 minutes

Salt

1   lb rigatoni

2   tbsp olive oil

12   oz chicken sausage (without apple), turkey sausage, or sweet Italian sausage, crumbled

1   small yellow onion, chopped

8   oz button or mixed mushrooms, sliced (optional)

1½   cups low-sodium chicken broth

1   can (15.5 oz) cannellini beans, drained and rinsed

Leaves from 2 sprigs fresh thyme or a scant ½ tsp dried

Pinch of crushed red pepper flakes

Freshly ground black pepper

Fresh lemon juice

Freshly grated Pecorino Romano or Parmesan cheese

■ Bring a large pot of water to a boil over high. Once water is boiling, season generously with salt; it should taste like seawater. When water returns to a boil, add pasta, quickly stir to separate noodles, then cover pot. When water returns to a boil again, uncover and boil pasta until al dente, stirring occasionally.

■ Meanwhile, in a large high-sided sauté pan, heat 1 tbsp oil over high until it shimmers. Add crumbled sausage and cook, stirring until browned, about 5 minutes. Transfer to a plate and set aside.

■ Return pan to stove and heat 1 tbsp oil over medium-high. Add onion and mushrooms (if using) and cook, stirring often, until onion is softened and mushrooms are golden, about 6 minutes. Add broth, scraping up any caramelized bits on bottom of pan, and bring to a simmer. Add beans, thyme, pepper flakes and reserved sausage with any juices. Season with salt and pepper and simmer, stirring occasionally, until sausage is cooked through and mixture has thickened slightly, about 5 minutes.

■ When pasta is ready, drain it, reserving about 1 cup cooking water, then pour noodles over sausage mixture and add a big splash of lemon juice. Toss to combine over medium. If pasta looks dry, add some cooking water. Check seasonings and serve with grated cheese.

PER SERVING 509 **CAL**; 12 g **FAT** (3 g **SAT**); 27 g **PRO**; 72 g **CARB**; 6 g **SUGARS**; 4 g **FIBER**; 714 mg **SODIUM**

RIGATONI WITH SAUSAGE, WHITE BEANS AND MUSHROOMS

**VEGGIE ITALIAN
HEROES**

Staggered Although it's hard to turn down a classic Italian hero, you can feel a little regret after stuffing yourself with approximately half a pound of fatty cured meats (no offense, capicola). So the moms came up with this veggie alternative that's just as drippy and delectable. They left in the cheese because it's the ideal foil, although you can skip it if you'd like. You can also drizzle the sandwich with just olive oil and vinegar (red wine or balsamic is nice) instead of making the vinaigrette.

Veggie Italian Heroes

MAKES 6 servings   **PREP** 15 minutes   **ROAST** at 425° for 30 minutes

- 2 small zucchini, cut into ½-inch-thick slices
- 2 bell peppers (any color), seeded and cut lengthwise into thick slices
- 2 small red onions, halved lengthwise and cut into thick slices
- 1 small eggplant, peeled in alternating vertical strips and cut into ½-inch-thick slices
  Salt and black pepper
  Crushed red pepper flakes
  Olive oil
- 6 hoagie rolls (about 6 inches long)
- 8 oz fresh mozzarella, cut into 12 slices
- ¼ cup Italian Vinaigrette, plus more for serving (recipe right)

■ Heat oven to 425°, with racks in two middle positions. Line two 18×13-inch sheet pans with parchment paper or foil for easier cleanup, if you like. Arrange zucchini, bell peppers and onions in sections on one pan and put eggplant on the other. Season all veggies with salt and pepper and some pepper flakes, then drizzle with olive oil (use a bit more for eggplant because it's more absorbent). Toss each type of veggie with your hands and rub slices together to help distribute seasonings and oil, then spread them out in a single layer.

■ Roast veggies until lightly browned on bottom, about 15 minutes, then flip them over and alternate pan locations. Roast until tender and golden brown, about 10 minutes more for eggplant and 15 for zucchini, peppers and onions.

■ Meanwhile, cut rolls in half horizontally but not all the way through (you want a "hinge" to help keep the sandwich together). Layer each bottom half with one-sixth of the mozzarella, eggplant, zucchini, bell peppers and onions. (If you have more veggies than will fit on rolls, save for another use.) Drizzle with Italian Vinaigrette, then fold sandwiches closed. Offer additional vinaigrette on the side for drizzling.

PER SERVING 474 **CAL**; 27 g **FAT** (7 g **SAT**); 14 g **PRO**; 40 g **CARB**; 9 g **SUGARS**; 4 g **FIBER**; 838 mg **SODIUM**

Italian Vinaigrette

MAKES about ¾ cup

- ¼ cup olive oil
- ¼ cup grapeseed or vegetable oil
- ¼ cup red wine vinegar
- 1 small clove garlic, minced
  Large pinch of dried oregano
  Salt and black pepper

■ In a small bowl, whisk first 5 ingredients, then season with salt and pepper. (Or, in a 12 oz or larger jar with a lid, combine ingredients, cover, then shake vigorously.) Check seasonings. Quickly dip a piece of lettuce in dressing, shake off any excess and check seasonings again.

Leave veggies, cheese, rolls and vinaigrette, covered, on the counter up to 2 hours—everyone can assemble their own sandwich.

INSTANT GRATIFICATION

The Instant Pot craze has taken the "craze" out of cooking. Fast, satisfying one-pot dinners are coming right up!

INDIAN BUTTER
CHICKEN

The "multi" in multicooker is your friend. It's a pressure cooker, slow cooker, rice cooker, steamer, yogurt maker and warmer. Oh, and you can also sauté in it.

Indian Butter Chicken

MAKES 6 servings **PREP** 20 minutes
SAUTÉ 5½ minutes **TIME TO PRESSURE** 10 minutes
PRESSURE COOK 8 minutes

- **4 tbsp unsalted butter, cubed**
- **1 medium yellow onion, diced**
- **5 cloves garlic, minced**
- **1 2-inch piece ginger, minced**
- **1 tsp salt**
- **1 cinnamon stick**
- **1 tsp curry powder**
- **1 tsp garam masala**
- **1 tsp paprika**
- **½ tsp cumin seeds**
- **½ tsp coriander seeds (optional)**
- **¼ tsp freshly ground black pepper**
- **¼ tsp cayenne pepper**
- **1 can (14.5 oz) crushed tomatoes**
- **1½ to 2 lbs boneless, skinless chicken thighs, cut into bite-size pieces**
- **¼ cup heavy cream**
- **3 cups cooked brown rice**
- **Cilantro leaves**

■ Set multicooker to Sauté function and add 2 tbsp butter. When butter has melted, add onion and cook 3 minutes. Stir in garlic and ginger and cook 2 minutes.

■ Add salt and spices; cook, stirring well, 30 seconds, until fragrant. Stir in tomatoes, scraping the bottom well. Stir in chicken.

■ Seal and cook 8 minutes on Manual, then release manually.

■ Stir in heavy cream and 2 tbsp butter. Divide rice among 6 bowls. Top with butter chicken and sprinkle with cilantro.

PER SERVING 404 **CAL**; 19 g **FAT** (9 g **SAT**); 24 g **PRO**; 34 g **CARB**; 4 g **SUGARS**; 4 g **FIBER**; 608 mg **SODIUM**

Green Chile Mac and Cheese

MAKES 6 servings **PREP** 5 minutes
TIME TO PRESSURE 12 minutes
PRESSURE COOK 3 minutes
NATURAL RELEASE 3 minutes

- **4 cups water**
- **½ tsp salt**
- **1 lb medium pasta shells**
- **1 cup buttermilk**
- **8 oz pepper Jack cheese, shredded**
- **4 oz goat cheese**
- **1 can (4 oz) chopped mild green chiles**
- **¼ cup toasted panko**

■ Add first 3 ingredients to multicooker and stir to submerge pasta; seal and cook 3 minutes on Manual. Let cool 3 minutes via Natural release, then release manually. Drain, if needed.

■ Stir in buttermilk, cheeses and chiles until well combined and slightly thickened.

■ Divide mac and cheese among 6 bowls. Top with toasted panko.

PER SERVING 519 **CAL**; 19 g **FAT** (10 g **SAT**); 25 g **PRO**; 61 g **CARB**; 6 g **SUGARS**; 0 g **FIBER**; 638 mg **SODIUM**

Soy-Braised Short Ribs

MAKES 4 servings **PREP** 15 minutes
TIME TO PRESSURE 25 minutes
PRESSURE COOK 30 minutes
NATURAL RELEASE 10 minutes
SAUTÉ 10 minutes

- **4 lbs bone-in cross-cut (flanken) beef short ribs (¾ inch thick)**
- **½ tsp salt**
- **¼ tsp freshly ground black pepper**
- **1 Asian or Bosc pear, peeled, quartered and cored**
- **2 large cloves garlic**
- **1 2-inch piece fresh ginger**
- **6 scallions**
- **½ cup reduced-sodium soy sauce**
- **2 tbsp toasted sesame oil**
- **1 tbsp rice vinegar or mirin**
- **½ cup low-sodium beef broth**
- **1 tbsp cornstarch**
- **Toasted sesame seeds**
- **Warm cooked white rice, kimchi and gochujang (Korean hot chile paste)**

■ Pat ribs dry and sprinkle all over with salt and pepper.

■ Add pear, garlic, ginger and 4 scallions to food processor; pulse until finely chopped. Transfer to a large bowl. Whisk soy sauce, sesame oil and vinegar into pear mixture.

■ Add ribs and toss to coat. Divide between 2 resealable gallon-size bags. Massage each bag vigorously 5 minutes or marinate in refrigerator 2 hours.

■ Empty contents of both bags into multicooker. Add broth, seal and cook 30 minutes on Manual. Let cool 10 minutes via Natural release, then release manually.

■ Transfer ribs to a platter. Pour cooking liquid into a de-fatter and return skimmed liquid to pot. Combine cornstarch with 1 tbsp cool water. Stir into pot, set to Sauté and cook, whisking, 8 to 10 minutes, until thickened.

■ Spoon some sauce over ribs; sprinkle with sesame seeds. Thinly slice remaining scallions and sprinkle on top. Serve with rice, kimchi, gochujang and remaining sauce on the side.

PER SERVING 497 **CAL**; 29 g **FAT** (10 g **SAT**); 40 g **PRO**; 19 g **CARB**; 8 g **SUGARS**; 4 g **FIBER**; 1,321 mg **SODIUM**

Salmon and Potatoes

MAKES 4 servings   **PREP** 10 minutes
TIME TO PRESSURE 15 minutes
PRESSURE COOK 3 minutes   **SAUTÉ** 8 minutes

- 1 **lb center-cut salmon**
- ½ **tsp salt**
- ½ **cup dry white wine**
- 1 **lb baby tricolor potatoes, halved**
- 1 **small shallot, quartered**
- 4 **sprigs fresh tarragon**
- 5 **thin slices lemon**
- 2 **tbsp unsalted butter, cubed**
  Flaky sea salt

■ Pat salmon dry and sprinkle all over with ¼ tsp salt.

■ Add wine, ¼ tsp salt and ½ cup water to multicooker. Add potatoes and shallot; top with 2 tarragon sprigs and 3 lemon slices.

■ Place steaming rack over potatoes. Place salmon on rack; top with 2 lemon slices and 1 tarragon sprig. Seal and cook 3 minutes on Manual, then release manually. Meanwhile, finely chop leaves from remaining tarragon sprig.

■ Carefully remove salmon and steaming rack. With a slotted spoon, transfer potatoes and shallots to a bowl, discarding lemon and tarragon.

■ Switch multicooker to Sauté function and simmer sauce 8 minutes, until reduced by half. Turn off cooker and add butter and chopped tarragon; stir until butter melts.

■ Return potato mixture to pot, tossing to coat and warm potatoes. Use slotted spoon to transfer to 4 plates.

■ Divide fish among plates and drizzle with butter sauce. Sprinkle with sea salt to taste.

PER SERVING 321 **CAL**; 13 g **FAT** (5 g **SAT**); 24 g **PRO**; 21 g **CARB**; 3 g **SUGARS**; 4 g **FIBER**; 415 mg **SODIUM**

This Lime-Gingersnap Cheesecake cooks in half the time of traditional cheesecake. Steam created in your multicooker makes for awesomely moist desserts (see ya, messy water bath!). A 7-inch springform pan is common for pot-in-pot cooking. We like Norpro's version because of its nonstick coating and tight seal.

Lime-Gingersnap Cheesecake

MAKES 6 servings   **PREP** 15 minutes   **TIME TO PRESSURE** 10 minutes   **PRESSURE COOK** 25 minutes
COOL 30 minutes   **REFRIGERATE** 2 hours

CRUST
- 30 **gingersnap cookies**
- 1 **tbsp sugar**
- 4 **tbsp unsalted butter, melted**

FILLING
- 12 **oz cream cheese, at room temperature**
- 2 **tbsp lime yogurt**
- ½ **cup sugar**
- ¼ **tsp salt**
- 2 **large eggs, at room temperature**
- 2 **tsp cornstarch**
  Zest of 1 lime plus 1 tbsp juice
- 3 **thin slices of lime, halved**

■ Add 2 cups water to multicooker and insert steaming rack. (If your pot is nonstick, consider investing in a silicone rack.) Wrap outside of a 7-inch springform pan with aluminum foil. Grease pan lightly.

■ **Crust:** In a food processor, pulse cookies until very finely ground. Add sugar and butter and pulse until crumbs are evenly moistened. Press into bottom and about ½ inch up sides of greased pan.

■ **Filling:** In clean food processor bowl, process first 4 ingredients for 2 minutes, until smooth.

■ Add eggs one at a time, processing well after each. Add cornstarch and lime juice and process. Add lime zest and pulse just to incorporate. Transfer filling to pan; cover pan with foil.

■ Fold a 19-inch piece of aluminum foil in thirds to use as a sling. Place springform pan on foil sling and lower onto steaming rack, folding edges to fit inside pot. Seal multicooker and cook 25 minutes on Manual, then release manually.

■ Use sling to carefully lift cheesecake and remove to a cooling rack. Cool to room temperature, about 30 minutes. Cover with plastic wrap and refrigerate at least 2 hours.

■ Garnish with lime slices.

PER SERVING 521 **CAL**; 32 g **FAT** (18 g **SAT**); 8 g **PRO**; 52 g **CARB**; 29 g **SUGARS**; 0 g **FIBER**; 481 mg **SODIUM**

LIME-
GINGERSNAP
CHEESECAKE

Why You Need One

■ This pot is fast.

■ You have to wait for the device to reach pressure, but once cooking is under way, you'll see serious time savings. For example: White rice can be on the table in about 4 minutes.

■ It's easy.

■ You can play around with the manual settings, but the preset buttons deliver great results without much thought. Just hit "meat" or "stew" or "slow cook" and get on with your day.

■ Stop stirring.

■ This is the ultimate set-it-and-forget-it device. With most functions, you can't open the cooker, so there's no need to stand over it. It'll beep when done, so just keep an ear out.

■ It's a great way to cheat.

■ Steam russet potatoes faster than you can bake them and prepare homemade chicken stock without the hours of simmering.

How to Convert Slow Cooker Recipes to Instant Pot Recipes

■ Make sure that your original recipe contains at least 1 cup of liquid—if not, add enough to bring up the volume.

■ Add dairy and starch after pressure cooking. Dairy products can curdle, and starch can burn.

■ Cut the amount of wine in half and cook it down a bit via the Sauté function. You can use the original amount of beer, but let it cook off as well.

SWEET DREAMS

The contestants from *MasterChef Junior* were challenged to create desserts using alternative sweeteners. The results? Nothing childish about them.

BAKED DOUGHNUTS
WITH MATCHA OR
CHOCOLATE GLAZE

Remy B., 14
New York City

Go-to ingredient to cook with on the show? Matcha. I'm obsessed with it.
Top dish to cook for your family? Seafood. **Best thing about being on**
MasterChef Junior? The judges' feedback. **Favorite judge?** Christina Tosi.
Name of your future restaurant? Pop. When me, my sister and my best
friend grow up, our dream is to open a pop-up store called Pop that sells
cake pops. We really want to make a crème brûlée one, put marshmallows on
top and brûlée it.

Baked Doughnuts with Matcha or Chocolate Glaze

MAKES 9 doughnuts   **PREP** 5 minutes   **BAKE** at 350° for 14 minutes

- **2   cups all-purpose flour**
- **2   tsp baking powder**
- **1   tsp salt**
- **2   large eggs**
- **¾   cup heavy cream**
- **½   cup honey**
- **1   tbsp unsalted butter, melted**
- **1   vanilla bean, split and scraped**
- **Matcha or Chocolate Glaze (recipes right)**
- **Freeze-dried raspberries or toasted coconut flakes, for garnish**

■ Heat oven to 350°. In a large bowl, whisk flour, baking powder and salt. Set aside.

■ In a stand mixer, beat next 5 ingredients on medium speed. Slowly add flour mixture until incorporated.

■ Add batter to a pastry bag and pipe into a doughnut pan. Bake 14 minutes, until doughnuts are lightly golden and spring back when touched. Cool in pan on a rack 5 minutes.

■ Dip tops of cooled doughnuts in Matcha or Chocolate Glaze. Garnish with crumbled freeze-dried raspberries or toasted coconut flakes.

Matcha Glaze In a stand mixer, beat 4 oz softened cream cheese, 6 tbsp water, 1 tbsp honey and 1 tsp matcha powder until smooth.

Chocolate Glaze Heat ½ cup heavy cream in a small pot until simmering. Remove from heat and stir in 1 cup dark chocolate chips and 1 tsp honey until smooth.

Pierce C., 12,
Oak Park, IL

Best thing about being on *MasterChef Junior*? I got really close to all the kids, especially the ones from Chicago. **Top dishes to cook for your family?** Panna cotta and salmon. **Go-to ingredient to cook with on the show?** Lemon. **Favorite judge?** Joe Bastianich. **Name of your future restaurant?** Pierce's Perfect Food. It sounds a little childish, but maybe I'll come up with another name along the way.

Vanilla Panna Cotta with Guava-Raspberry Puree and Blood Orange Segments

MAKES 4 servings   **PREP** 5 minutes   **REFRIGERATE** 1 hour

1¾	**cups heavy cream**
2	**tbsp honey**
1	**vanilla bean, split and scraped**
½	**cup whole milk**
2	**tsp powdered gelatin**
	Guava-Raspberry Puree, for garnish (recipe right)
	Blood Orange Segments, for garnish (recipe right)

■ Add 4 cups ice cubes to a large bowl and fill with water to make an ice bath. Set aside.

■ In a medium pot over medium, bring heavy cream, honey and vanilla seeds to a simmer.

■ In a medium bowl, whisk milk and gelatin. While whisking milk mixture, add in ¼ of the hot cream mixture. Whisk tempered mixture back into pot. Cool pot in ice bath.

■ Once cool, pour panna cotta mixture into four 4-oz ramekins. Place on a tray and refrigerate until firm, about 1 hour. Garnish with Guava-Raspberry Puree and Blood Orange Segments.

Guava-Raspberry Puree In a small pot over medium-high, heat 1 peeled and cut-up guava, 1 cup raspberries, 1 tbsp honey and 1 tbsp water until simmering. Cook 5 minutes, until tender. Transfer to a blender with 1 tsp powdered gelatin; blend until smooth. Pass through a fine-mesh strainer, transfer to a squeeze bottle and refrigerate until ready to use.

Blood Orange Segments Place the segments of 2 blood oranges on a foil-lined baking sheet. Brush with 1 tsp honey. To caramelize, broil 3 to 4 minutes or use a kitchen torch. Let cool.

VANILLA PANNA COTTA WITH
GUAVA-RASPBERRY PUREE AND
BLOOD ORANGE SEGMENTS

PLUM TARTS AND
PLUM-COCONUT
MOCKTAIL

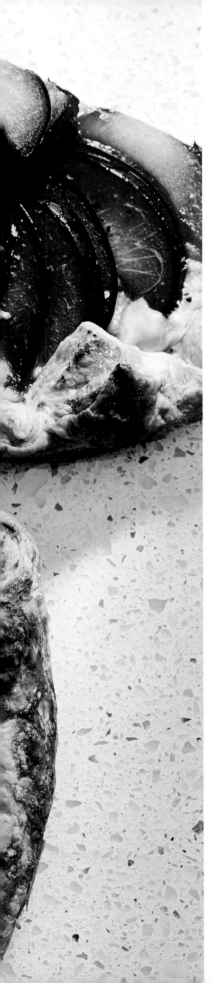

Maria D., 10,
Winnetka, CA

Favorite judge? Gordon Ramsey. He always kept me on my toes, and I have a bearded dragon named Gordon Ramsey. **Top dishes to cook for your family?** Spanakopita, mofongo, lamb chops, steak, cakes and bread. **Best thing about being on** *MasterChef Junior*? The cooking. Also talking to the chefs and what they said about my food. **Go-to ingredients to cook with on the show?** Agave, a whole bunch of spices, lobster and lamb. **Name of your future restaurant?** The Puerto Greekan. I want to open a food truck and a restaurant that sells Puerto Rican and Greek food and benefits kids with disabilities.

Plum Tarts and Plum-Coconut Mocktail

MAKES 2 tarts   **PREP** 10 minutes   **BAKE** at 425° for 18 minutes

- 1 **box frozen puff pastry, thawed**
- 2 **plums**
- 1 **tbsp agave**
  Freshly ground black pepper
- 2 **tbsp honey**
  Smoked Maldon sea salt

■ Heat oven to 425° with a rack in bottom position and another in center. Cut each puff pastry sheet into a 9×9-inch square. Place both on a parchment-lined baking sheet. With a fork, prick all over.

■ For each pastry square, fold in top right corner 1 inch. Fold top edge over folded corner, then fold in top left corner. Repeat on all sides. Bake on bottom rack 10 minutes, until puffed and very lightly golden.

■ Meanwhile, slice plums into ¼-inch-thick wedges. Arrange plums in center of each parbaked puff pastry in a circular pattern. Lightly brush both tarts all over with agave. Sprinkle with a pinch of pepper. Bake 8 minutes, until golden.

■ Drizzle with honey and sprinkle with salt. Let cool. Serve with Plum-Coconut Mocktail, if desired.

Plum-Coconut Mocktail In a small pot, bring 2 diced plums, ¼ cup agave, 2 tbsp water and 1 tsp lemon juice to a simmer. Cook 5 minutes, until tender. Stir in 1 tsp cornstarch and cook 1 minute. Transfer to a blender. Cut the top off 1 young coconut. Pour coconut water into blender with plum mixture; add a pinch of ground cinnamon. Blend until smooth. Serve in coconut with a straw.

BEST-ON-THE-BLOCK
BABY BACK RIBS
PAGE 139

JUNE

131

136

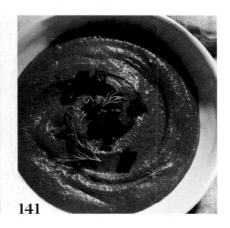

141

ROCK THE BLOCK

When Weber Grill Master Kevin Kolman hosts a block party, the whole neighborhood knows the food is going to be fantastic. You can follow his lead in your own backyard.

CHICAGO-STYLE
HOT DOGS

Aficionados of the Chicago-style hot dog insist on an all-beef frankfurter on a poppy seed bun topped with sport peppers, a dill pickle spear, diced onion, tomato slices, fluorescent-green sweet pickle relish, yellow mustard and a dusting of celery salt—no substitutions and no additions allowed. We heard about a guy who once tried adding ketchup. Let's just say he didn't suggest it again.

Chicago-Style Hot Dogs

MAKES 8 servings   **PREP** 10 minutes   **GRILL** 5 minutes

- 8 **slices tomato, each about ¼ inch thick**
- 8 **best-quality all-beef hot dogs with natural casings (slightly longer than the buns)**
- 8 **poppy seed hot dog buns, split**
- 16 **pickled sport peppers**
- 2 **dill pickles, each cut lengthwise into 4 spears**
- ½ **cup finely chopped white onion, rinsed in a fine-mesh strainer under cold water**
- ½ **cup super-green sweet pickle relish**

  Yellow mustard

  Celery salt

■ Prepare grill for direct cooking over medium heat (350° to 450°).

■ Cut each tomato slice in half to make half-moons. Cut a few well-spaced shallow diagonal slashes crosswise along one side of each hot dog.

■ Brush cooking grates clean. Grill hot dogs over direct medium heat, with lid closed, until lightly marked on the outside and hot all the way to the center, 4 to 5 minutes, turning occasionally. Remove from grill.

■ Place a hot dog in each bun and add 2 tomato half-moons, 2 peppers, 1 pickle spear, some onion and 1 tbsp relish. Add mustard to taste and finish with a pinch of celery salt. Serve warm.

Create two cooking zones: Spread coals under one side of the grate and leave the other side with no coals at all. This allows you to cook with both direct and indirect heat.

Santa Maria Tri-Tip Sandwiches

MAKES 6 servings **PREP** 20 minutes, plus 15 minutes for sauce
REFRIGERATE 3 to 24 hours
GRILL 25 to 35 minutes

- 1 tbsp freshly ground black pepper
- 2 tsp garlic salt
- 1 tsp mustard powder
- 1 tsp paprika
- ¼ tsp cayenne pepper
- 2 to 2½ lbs tri-tip roast, about 1½ inches thick
- 12 slices French bread
  Tri-Tip Barbecue Sauce (recipe right)

■ Combine first 5 ingredients and mix well. Rub mixture over roast, pressing it into meat. Cover with plastic wrap and refrigerate at least 3 hours or up to 24 hours.

■ Soak a handful of oak, mesquite or hickory chips in water at least 30 minutes.

■ Prepare grill for direct and indirect cooking over medium heat (350° to 450°).

■ Brush cooking grates clean. Drain chips and add to charcoal or to smoker box of a gas grill; close lid. When smoke appears, place tri-tip directly over fire, close lid and sear over direct medium heat on both sides, about 5 minutes total, turning once. Move to indirect heat, close lid and grill over indirect medium heat until internal temp reaches 140° for medium-rare, 20 to 30 minutes. Remove from grill; let rest 5 minutes. During last minute of grilling time, toast bread over direct heat. Remove from grill.

■ Cut meat on the diagonal across the grain into thin slices. For each sandwich, layer meat and a little sauce between 2 slices of bread. Serve warm or at room temp.

Tri-Tip Barbecue Sauce In a medium saucepan, heat 1 tbsp olive oil over medium-high. Add ½ cup finely diced red onion and 1 tsp minced garlic. Cook until soft, about 5 minutes, stirring occasionally. Add ½ cup each low-sodium chicken broth and steak sauce, ¼ cup ketchup, 1 tbsp finely chopped Italian parsley, 1 tbsp Worcestershire sauce, 1½ tsp ground coffee and ¼ tsp freshly ground black pepper; stir well and bring to a boil. Turn down heat to a simmer and cook until reduced to ½ cup, about 10 minutes, stirring occasionally. Remove from heat, let cool slightly and puree until smooth. Let cool, transfer to an airtight container and refrigerate until ready to use. Bring to room temp before serving.

Creamy Dilled Potato Salad

MAKES 12 servings **PREP** 20 minutes
COOK 20 minutes **REFRIGERATE** 4 hours or overnight

- 2½ lbs small red- and white-skinned potatoes (about 1-inch diameter), unpeeled
- 1 medium size onion, chopped
- 6 hard-cooked eggs, peeled and chopped
- 1 cup chopped dill pickles
- 1 cup light mayonnaise
- 3 tbsp brine from pickles
- 1 tsp garlic salt
- ¼ tsp black pepper
- 2 tbsp chopped fresh dill

■ Place potatoes in a large pot of lightly salted water. Boil 15 to 20 minutes or until tender. Drain well.

■ Cut the potatoes in half (cut larger potatoes in quarters so all pieces are about the same size). Place the potatoes, onion, eggs and pickles in a large bowl. Stir gently to combine.

■ In a small bowl, whisk together mayonnaise, brine, garlic salt, pepper and dill. Spoon mayo mixture into potato mixture and stir gently.

■ Cover and refrigerate 4 hours or overnight.

PER SERVING 176 CAL; 9 g FAT (2 g SAT); 113 mg CHOL; 424 mg SODIUM; 19 g CARB; 2 g FIBER; 5 g PRO

Macaroni Salad

MAKES 8 servings **PREP** 15 minutes
COOK 7 minutes

- 8 oz elbow macaroni, or other pasta shape
- ½ cup light mayonnaise
- 2 tbsp ketchup
- 1 tbsp sweet pickle relish
- ½ to 1 tsp hot pepper sauce
- ¼ tsp ground black pepper
- ⅛ tsp salt
- 1 cup grape tomatoes, halved
- 3 stalks celery, trimmed and sliced (1 cup)
- 2 large carrots, trimmed, peeled and grated (about 1 cup)
- 4 oz pepper Jack cheese, cut into ¼-inch pieces
- ½ green bell pepper, seeded and chopped

■ Heat a medium-size pot of lightly salted water to boiling. Add macaroni and cook 7 minutes or until desired tenderness. Drain and rinse with cool water to halt cooking.

■ Meanwhile, in a small bowl, whisk together mayonnaise, ketchup, pickle relish, hot sauce, pepper and salt.

■ Transfer drained pasta to a serving bowl. Add tomatoes, celery, carrots, cheese, green pepper and slightly more than half of the mayonnaise mixture. Stir gently to combine and coat all ingredients with dressing. Refrigerate until serving. Just before serving, stir in remaining dressing.

PER SERVING 234 CAL; 10 g FAT (4 g SAT); 20 mg CHOL; 345 mg SODIUM; 28 g CARB; 2 g FIBER; 8 g PRO

SANTA MARIA TRI-TIP
SANDWICHES

LEMON-DILL SHRIMP
WITH ORZO SALAD

Lemon-Dill Shrimp with Orzo Salad

PREP 15 minutes **MARINATE** 30 minutes
COOK about 10 minutes **GRILL** 2 to 4 minutes

- **16** extra-large cleaned shrimp (16–20 count), tails left on

  Vinaigrette (recipe below)

- **1** cup dried orzo pasta
- **⅓** cup plus 1 tbsp crumbled feta cheese (about 2 oz)
- **¾** cup finely diced red bell pepper
- **⅓** cup pitted Kalamata olives, cut into quarters
- **2** tbsp thinly sliced scallions
- **1½** tbsp finely chopped fresh oregano leaves

■ Have 4 metal or bamboo skewers ready. If using bamboo, soak in water at least 30 minutes.

■ Place shrimp in a medium bowl, add ¼ cup vinaigrette and toss to coat evenly. Cover and marinate in the fridge 30 minutes. Set aside bowl with remaining vinaigrette.

■ Prepare grill for direct cooking over high heat (450° to 550°).

■ On the stove, bring a medium saucepan three-fourths full of salted water to a boil. Add pasta and cook according to package directions for al dente. Drain pasta and add to vinaigrette in serving bowl. Add feta, bell pepper, olives, scallions and oregano and toss to combine. Set aside.

■ Thread 4 shrimp onto each skewer, bending each shrimp so skewer passes through it twice, near the head and near the tail. Brush cooking grates clean. Grill shrimp over direct high heat, with lid closed, until firm to the touch and just turning opaque in center, 2 to 4 minutes, turning once. Remove from grill and serve right away with pasta.

Vinaigrette In a large serving bowl, whisk ½ cup extra-virgin olive oil, 1 tsp grated lemon zest, ¼ cup fresh lemon juice, 1 tbsp finely chopped fresh dill, 1 tsp minced garlic, ½ tsp kosher salt and ¼ tsp freshly ground black pepper.

PEACH AND BLUE CHEESE BRUSCHETTA DRIZZLED WITH HONEY

Peach and Blue Cheese Bruschetta Drizzled with Honey

MAKES 4 servings **PREP** 10 minutes **GRILL** 8 minutes

- **4** oz cream cheese, softened
- **2** tbsp sugar
- **1** tbsp fresh thyme leaves
- **4** firm but ripe peaches
- **8** slices Italian or French bread, about ½ inch thick

  Extra-virgin olive oil

- **4** oz blue cheese, crumbled (scant 1 cup)
- **4** tbsp honey

■ Prepare grill for direct cooking over medium-low heat (350°).

■ Stir cream cheese, sugar and thyme until blended. Set aside. Cut each peach in half through stem end and discard pit. Lightly brush peach halves and bread on both sides with oil.

■ Brush grill grates clean. Grill peaches over direct medium-low heat, with lid closed, until lightly charred and beginning to soften, about 8 minutes, turning once. During last minute of grilling time, toast bread over direct heat, turning once. Remove peaches and bread from grill.

■ Spread each bread slice with an equal amount of cream cheese mixture. Cut peach halves into ¼-inch-thick slices. Divide slices evenly among bread slices, overlapping them slightly. Top with blue cheese and drizzle with honey. Serve right away.

Corn on the Cob with Basil-Parmesan Butter

PREP 10 minutes **GRILL** 10 to 15 minutes

- ¼ cup (½ stick) unsalted butter, softened
- ¼ cup freshly grated Parmigiano-Reggiano cheese (scant 1 oz)
- 2 tbsp finely chopped fresh basil leaves
- ½ tsp kosher salt
- ¼ tsp freshly ground black pepper
- ¼ tsp garlic powder
- 4 ears corn, husked

■ Prepare grill for direct cooking over medium heat (350° to 450°). In a small bowl, mash together first 6 ingredients with the back of a fork, then stir to distribute seasonings evenly throughout butter.

■ Brush cooking grates clean. Spread 1 tbsp seasoned butter all over each ear of corn. Grill corn over direct medium heat, with lid closed, until browned in spots and tender, 10 to 15 minutes, turning occasionally. Remove from grill and spread remaining butter on corn.

Triple-Play Barbecued Chicken

MAKES 4 to 8 servings   **PREP** 30 minutes   **COOK** 25 minutes   **GRILL** 45 minutes

SAUCE

- 2 tbsp extra-virgin olive oil
- ½ cup finely chopped yellow onion
- 2 tsp minced garlic
- 1 cup ketchup
- ½ cup lemon-lime soda (not diet)
- ¼ cup fresh lemon juice
- ¼ cup packed light brown sugar
- 2 tbsp whole-grain mustard

RUB

- 2 tsp smoked paprika
- 2 tsp kosher salt
  Finely grated zest of 1 lemon
- ½ tsp garlic powder
- ½ tsp freshly ground black pepper
- 4 whole chicken legs (10 to 12 oz each), trimmed of excess fat and skin and cut into thighs and drumsticks

■ In a saucepan, heat oil over medium. Add onion and garlic and cook until golden, about 10 minutes, stirring often. Stir in remaining sauce ingredients and bring to a simmer. Reduce heat to low and cook until sauce is slightly thickened, 10 to 15 minutes, stirring often.

■ Soak 2 large handfuls of hickory chips in water at least 30 minutes. Prepare grill for direct and indirect cooking over medium heat (350° to 450°).

■ Combine first 5 rub ingredients and mix well. Season chicken all over with rub. Brush cooking grates clean. Grill chicken, skin sides down, over direct medium heat, with lid closed, until golden, 8 to 10 minutes, turning occasionally.

■ Move chicken over indirect medium heat. Drain chips, add to charcoal or to smoker box of a gas grill and continue grilling, with lid closed, about 20 minutes. Brush chicken with a thin layer of sauce and continue grilling, with lid closed, until juices run clear and meat is no longer pink at the bone, about 15 minutes, turning and brushing occasionally with sauce. Remove chicken from grill and let rest 3 to 5 minutes. Serve warm with remaining sauce on the side.

TRIPLE-PLAY
BARBEQUED CHICKEN

CORN ON THE COB
WITH BASIL-
PARMESAN BUTTER

BEST-ON-THE-BLOCK
BABY BACK RIBS

Best-on-the-Block Baby Back Ribs

MAKES 8 to 10 servings **PREP** 30 minutes **COOK** 20 minutes **LET STAND** 30 minutes to 1 hour **GRILL** about 3 hours

RUB

- **2 tbsp kosher salt**
- **1 tbsp smoked paprika**
- **1 tbsp garlic powder**
- **1 tbsp pure chile powder**
- **2 tsp mustard powder**
- **2 tsp dried thyme**
- **1 tsp ground cumin**
- **1 tsp celery seeds**
- **1 tsp freshly ground black pepper**
- **4 racks baby back ribs (2½ to 3 lbs each)**

SAUCE

- **4 slices bacon**
- **1 cup ketchup**
- **½ cup unsweetened apple juice**
- **¼ cup cider vinegar**
- **1 tbsp unsulfured molasses (not blackstrap)**
- **2 tsp Worcestershire sauce**
- **½ tsp smoked paprika**
- **½ tsp ground cumin**
- **¼ tsp kosher salt**
- **¼ tsp freshly ground black pepper**
- **Hot pepper sauce (optional)**

MOP

- **½ cup unsweetened apple juice**
- **1 tbsp cider vinegar**

■ Have a rib rack ready. In a small bowl, combine salt with spices and mix well. Slide the tip of a dull dinner knife under membrane covering back of each rack of ribs. Lift and loosen until membrane breaks, then grab a corner of it with a paper towel and pull it off. Season ribs evenly with rub, pressing it into meat. Arrange ribs in rack so that all are standing and facing in the same direction. Let stand at room temperature 30 minutes to 1 hour before grilling.

■ Soak 4 large handfuls of hickory chips in water at least 30 minutes. Prepare grill for indirect cooking over low heat (300° to 350°).

■ Brush cooking grates clean. Drain 2 handfuls of chips and add to charcoal or to smoker box of a gas grill and close lid. When smoke appears, place rack with ribs over indirect low heat and cook, with lid closed, for 1 hour. Maintain temperature of grill between 300° and 350°.

■ While ribs are cooking, make sauce. On the stove, fry bacon in a medium skillet over low until crisp, 10 to 15 minutes, turning occasionally. Drain on paper towels. Let drippings in skillet cool to room temp. Eat bacon or save for another use. In a medium saucepan over low heat, combine remaining ingredients except hot sauce. Add 3 tbsp reserved bacon fat and whisk until smooth. Cook 5 minutes, stirring occasionally. If you prefer a spicy sauce, season with hot sauce. Remove from heat.

■ Combine mop ingredients in a small spray bottle. After first hour of cooking, drain remaining wood chips and add them to charcoal or smoker box. Lightly spray ribs with mop, particularly any areas that are looking a little dry. Close lid and cook 1 more hour. Maintain temperature of grill between 300° and 350°.

■ Lightly spray ribs with mop. If any ribs are cooking faster than others or look much darker, swap their positions for even cooking. Close lid; cook 30 minutes.

■ At this point, meat will have shrunk back from most bones by ¼ inch or more. If it has not, continue to cook until it does and remove ribs from grill. Close lid to maintain heat. Remove ribs from rack and lightly brush on both sides with sauce.

■ Return ribs to grill over indirect low heat. At this point you can pile all ribs on top of one another or stack them 2 racks to a pile. Continue to cook over indirect low heat, with lid closed, until tender and succulent, 15 to 30 minutes. To test if racks are done, one at a time, lift them bone side up at one end with tongs; if a rack bends so much in the middle that meat tears easily, it's ready. If meat does not tear easily, continue to cook until it does. When racks are ready, transfer to a platter and let rest 5 to 10 minutes.

■ Just before serving, lightly brush with sauce again. Cut racks into individual ribs and serve.

To qualify as best on the block, the seasoned "bark" (crust) and natural flavors of these pork ribs must complement both the hickory smoke and the sweet-tart sauce. We use some potent spices to accomplish this, but if you prefer milder ribs, add about half the recommended amount of chile powder to the rub and leave out the hot pepper sauce.

MODERN PICNIC MIX + MATCH

It's time to rethink what a picnic can be. There's not a traditional sandwich or salad to be found in this Mediterranean-style mix.

BASIC HUMMUS

BEET HUMMUS

QUINOA TABBOULEH

CARROT HUMMUS

Make them all or just a few—the beauty of these recipes is that they're great when eaten together, but each tastes just as good on its own.

Basic Hummus

MAKES 1¾ cups **PREP** 5 minutes

- 1 can (15.5 oz) chickpeas, drained and rinsed
- 2 tbsp fresh lemon juice
- 2 tbsp tahini
- 1 small clove garlic
- ¾ tsp salt
- 3 tbsp extra-virgin olive oil, plus more for drizzling

  Freshly ground black pepper

■ In food processor or blender, combine first 5 ingredients. Blend, scraping as needed, until well combined. With machine running, pour in oil and 1 tbsp water and blend until smooth.

■ Transfer to a bowl; drizzle with oil and top with pepper.

PER SERVING 128 **CAL**; 9 g **FAT** (1 g **SAT**); 3 g **PRO**; 10 g **CARB**; 2 g **SUGARS**; 3 g **FIBER**; 328 mg **SODIUM**

Beet Hummus

MAKES 2 cups **PREP** 5 minutes

- 1 recipe Basic Hummus or 1¾ cups store-bought hummus
- 1 pkg (8.8 oz) cooked beets (such as Love Beets)
- ¼ cup fresh dill
- ¼ tsp ground cumin (optional)

■ Prepare Basic Hummus or put purchased hummus in food processor or blender. Finely dice ¼ cup of the beets and reserve. Coarsely chop remaining beets and add to hummus along with dill and cumin (if using). Puree until smooth.

■ Transfer hummus to a bowl. Scatter finely diced beets on top of hummus with a little extra dill.

PER SERVING 126 **CAL**; 8 g **FAT** (1 g **SAT**); 3 g **PRO**; 12 g **CARB**; 4 g **SUGARS**; 3 g **FIBER**; 311 mg **SODIUM**

Carrot Hummus

MAKES 2½ cups **PREP** 5 minutes **COOK** 5 minutes

- 2 tbsp extra-virgin olive oil
- ½ tsp ground coriander
- ½ tsp ground cumin
- 6 medium carrots, finely shredded (about 2 cups)
- ½ tsp plus pinch of salt
- ½ cup carrot juice
- 1 recipe Basic Hummus or 1¾ cups prepared hummus
- 2 tbsp jarred harissa
- 1 tbsp toasted pine nuts

■ Heat 1 tbsp oil in a medium stainless-steel skillet over medium-high. Add the coriander and cumin and cook, stirring, until fragrant, about 30 seconds. Reserve ¼ cup of the carrots; add remaining carrots, salt and carrot juice to pan and stir well. Cook, covered, until softened, about 5 minutes. Cool slightly.

■ Add cooked carrots to Basic Hummus in food processor or blender and process until smooth. Transfer to a resealable container.

■ Stir together reserved carrots, harissa and a pinch of salt. Top hummus with harissa mixture, sprinkle with pine nuts and drizzle with remaining oil.

PER SERVING 144 **CAL**; 10 g **FAT** (1 g **SAT**); 3 g **PRO**; 12 g **CARB**; 5 g **SUGARS**; 3 g **FIBER**; 377 mg **SODIUM**

Quinoa Tabbouleh

MAKES 6 cups **PREP** 10 minutes

- 1½ cups cooked quinoa, cooled
- 2 cups heirloom cherry tomatoes, chopped
- 1 English cucumber, seeded and chopped
- 1 cup parsley leaves, roughly chopped
- ⅓ cup mint leaves, roughly chopped
- ¼ cup freshly squeezed lemon juice
- 2 tbsp extra-virgin olive oil
- ¾ tsp salt
- ⅛ tsp freshly ground black pepper

■ Combine first 5 ingredients in a large bowl. In a small bowl, whisk together lemon juice, olive oil, salt and pepper. Drizzle over quinoa mixture and toss together.

PER SERVING 117 **CAL**; 6 g **FAT** (1 g **SAT**); 4 g **PRO**; 14 g **CARB**; 2 g **SUGARS**; 3 g **FIBER**; 303 mg **SODIUM**

Plate it. Bowl it. Wrap it. The choice is yours! Or, well, theirs. These can be served any of three ways.

Shredded Chicken Salad

MAKES 6 cups **PREP** 15 minutes

- **3 cups shredded rotisserie chicken**
- **12 oz quartered marinated artichokes, halved, plus ¼ cup liquid from the jar**
- **1 cup jumbo pimiento-stuffed olives, roughly chopped**
- **4 ribs celery, chopped**
- **½ cup parsley, roughly chopped**
- **Zest of 1 lemon**
- **1 tbsp lemon juice**
- **¼ tsp salt**

■ Combine all ingredients in a large bowl. Serve chilled or at room temperature.

PER SERVING 195 **CAL**; 12 g **FAT** (3 g **SAT**); 16 g **PRO**; 6 g **CARB**; 0 g **SUGARS**; 4 g **FIBER**; 930 mg **SODIUM**

Marinated Mushrooms

MAKES 2 cups **PREP** 12 minutes **COOK** 6 minutes

- **3 tbsp olive oil**
- **1 lb cremini mushrooms, trimmed and thinly sliced**
- **½ tsp salt**
- **2 tbsp red wine vinegar**
- **2 small cloves garlic, chopped**
- **½ tsp chopped fresh oregano**
- **1 bay leaf**
- **⅛ tsp crushed red pepper**

■ Heat 2 tbsp oil in a medium skillet over medium. Add the mushrooms and ¼ tsp salt and cook, stirring occasionally, until softened, 5 to 6 minutes. Remove from heat. Stir in vinegar, garlic, oregano, bay leaf, crushed red pepper, ¼ tsp salt and 1 tbsp oil. Cool slightly.

■ Transfer to a quart-size jar and seal. Refrigerate up to 5 days. Serve at room temperature. Makes 2 cups.

PER SERVING 59 **CAL**; 5 g **FAT** (1 g **SAT**); 1 g **PRO**; 3 g **CARB**; 1 g **SUGARS**; 0 g **FIBER**; 149 mg **SODIUM**

Baklava Shortbread

MAKES 64 cookies **PREP** 20 minutes **CHILL** 2 hours or overnight **BAKE** 15 minutes at 325°F

- **2 cups all-purpose flour**
- **¾ cup pistachios, finely chopped**
- **½ tsp salt**
- **½ tsp ground cinnamon**
- **¾ cup (1½ sticks) unsalted butter, softened**
- **½ cup sugar**
- **4 tbsp honey**
- **2 large egg yolks**

■ In a small bowl, whisk together flour, 2 tbsp of the pistachios, salt and cinnamon. In a medium bowl, beat butter until creamy, 1 minute. Beat in sugar and 3 tbsp honey until fluffy, 2 minutes. Beat in egg yolks. Stir in flour mixture until dough comes together. Divide into quarters on a lightly floured surface.

■ With your hands, roll each quarter of dough into 6-inch log, 1 inch thick. Whisk remaining 1 tbsp honey with 2 tsp water. On cutting board, spread remaining pistachios in rectangle, about 7×5 inches. Brush logs with honey-water mixture and then roll in pistachios to evenly coat edge. Wrap each log in plastic; refrigerate 2 hours or overnight.

■ Heat oven to 325°. Unwrap logs. Cut each in 16 slices, about ¼ inch thick. Transfer to 2 large ungreased baking sheets.

■ Bake 15 minutes or until just golden around edges. Remove cookies to wire rack; cool completely. Store in airtight container up to 2 weeks.

PER COOKIE 47 **CAL**; 3 g **FAT** (1 g **SAT**); 1 g **PRO**; 5 g **CARB**; 5 g **SUGARS**; 0 g **FIBER**; 23 mg **SODIUM**

MARINATED MUSHROOMS

SHREDDED CHICKEN SALAD

BAKLAVA SHORTBREAD

WAFFLE ICE CREAM
SANDWICHES, PAGE 163

JULY

151

156

163

A BROOKLYN-STYLE COOKOUT

On the menu: irresistible Korean-style BBQ.

CHARRED SUMMER SQUASH AND ZUCCHINI SALAD

When chef Sohui Kim isn't in the kitchen at one of the Brooklyn restaurants she co-owns with her husband, she can't help herself—she cooks anyway.

Sohui lived the first decade of her life in Korea, a picky eater surrounded by delicious food that she still remembers. When her family moved to America, she and her brother went crazy over pizza and hamburgers (each gaining 10 pounds their first year here) while her dad opened a produce market with some fellow Korean immigrants. Working by his side, Sohui learned all about fruits and veggies she'd never seen before. Her hardworking father had hoped she'd go to law school after college, but Sohui followed her heart to cooking school, then various restaurant kitchens, where she perfected her skills and refined the homey, comforting food she describes as "influenced by everything" she's ever known, tasted and liked. Her Brooklyn backyard, a frequent gathering spot for friends, is the perfect place for the mom of two to infuse traditional Korean flavors into classic American cookout fare: chicken and ribs.

Charred Summer Squash and Zucchini Salad

MAKES 8 servings **PREP** 10 minutes **GRILL** 14 minutes **COOL** 5 minutes

1	**lb yellow summer squash**
1	**lb zucchini**
2	**tbsp vegetable oil**
2	**tbsp sesame oil**
2	**tbsp toasted sesame seeds**
2	**tbsp rice vinegar**
2	**to 3 tbsp gochujang (red chile paste)**
1	**tbsp honey**
1½	**tsp gochugaru (ground red chile flakes)**
1	**tsp minced garlic**
1	**tsp minced ginger**
½	**cup chopped scallions**
	Salt

■ Heat grill to medium-high. Cut squash and zucchini into ½-inch-thick rounds. Toss with vegetable oil and grill until slightly tender, 5 to 7 minutes per side. Transfer to a colander to drain. Let cool about 5 minutes. In a large mixing bowl, stir sesame oil and next 7 ingredients. Add grilled vegetables and scallions and toss until well coated. Season with salt to taste.

PER SERVING 121 CAL; 9 g FAT (1 g SAT); 2 g PRO; 9 g CARB; 5 g SUGARS; 1 g FIBER; 169 mg SODIUM

GRILLED EGGPLANT AND PEPPERS WITH SOY AND SESAME

Instead of defaulting to the usual cool, crisp green salad, try grilled veggies with bold dressings. Briefly grilling lettuce varies its texture and adds flavor for a more interesting side dish.

Grilled Romaine with Korean Dressing

MAKES 6 servings   **PREP** 10 minutes   **GRILL** 5 minutes

- ¼ **cup olive oil**
- 2 **bunches scallions, trimmed**
- 2 **large heads romaine or other hearty green, cut into quarters**
  Large pinch of kosher salt
- ¼ **cup sesame oil**
- 2 **tbsp rice wine vinegar**
- 2 **tsp honey**
- 2 **tsp minced garlic**
- 2 **tsp gochugaru (see tip page 151)**
- 5 **tsp fish sauce**
  Coarsely ground black pepper to taste

■ Heat grill to medium. Brush olive oil over scallions and cut sides of romaine. Season lightly with salt. Grill until charred on all sides, about 5 minutes for scallions, flipping halfway through, and 45 seconds to 1 minute per side for romaine. In a large bowl, combine remaining ingredients to make dressing. Add romaine and scallions and toss to coat well.

■ Arrange on a platter and serve immediately.

PER SERVING 218 **CAL**; 18 g **FAT** (3 g **SAT**); 4 g **PRO**; 13 g **CARB**; 6 g **SUGARS**; 6 g **FIBER**; 466 mg **SODIUM**

Grilled Eggplant and Peppers with Soy and Sesame

MAKES 6 servings   **PREP** 10 minutes   **GRILL** 7 minutes   **COOL** 5 minutes

- 1 **lb Japanese eggplant, halved lengthwise**
- 2 **red, orange or yellow bell peppers, cut into 1-inch strips**
- 1 **tbsp vegetable oil**
- 2 **scallions, halved lengthwise and thinly sliced**
- 1 **tbsp soy sauce**
- 1 **tbsp seeded and thinly sliced Holland chile (thin red chile)**
- 2 **tsp minced garlic**
- 2 **tsp toasted sesame seeds**
- 2 **tsp sesame oil**
  Salt

■ Heat grill to medium-high.

■ Toss eggplant and peppers with vegetable oil. Grill, cut sides down, until charred, 4 to 5 minutes. Flip and grill until browned and just tender, 2 minutes. Transfer to a mixing bowl and let cool 5 minutes.

■ Tear eggplant into strips. Add remaining ingredients and combine well. Season with salt to taste.

PER SERVING 80 **CAL**; 4 g **FAT** (1 g **SAT**); 2 g **PRO**; 8 g **CARB**; 5 g **SUGARS**; 3 g **FIBER**; 277 mg **SODIUM**

GRILLED ROMAINE
WITH KOREAN
DRESSING

SPICY CHICKEN STEW

Spicy Chicken Stew

MAKES 6 servings **PREP** 15 minutes
GRILL 8 minutes **COOK** 40 minutes

- 4½ **lbs chicken pieces**
- 1 **onion, peeled and quartered**
- 1 **tbsp olive oil**
- 8 **cloves garlic, minced**
- 2 **tbsp minced ginger**
- ¼ **cup reduced-sodium soy sauce**
- ¼ **cup gochujang***
- 3 **tbsp gochugaru***
- 1 **tbsp sugar**
- 1 **tsp fish sauce**
- 2 **Korean green chiles, seeded and thinly sliced**
- 1 **bunch scallions, thinly sliced**

- Heat grill to medium-high. Reduce heat to medium.

- Toss chicken and onion with oil to lightly coat; grill until well marked, 6 to 8 minutes.

- In a large pot, stir garlic, next 6 ingredients and 2 cups water. Add chicken and onion.

- Cook, covered, on grill 30 minutes. Stir in chiles and scallions; cook, uncovered, 5 to 10 minutes to cook chicken through and thicken sauce.

*Tip Two Korean must-haves: gochugaru (ground red chile flakes) and gochujang (red chile paste). Both products give finished dishes a fiery yet slightly sweet punch.

PER SERVING 512 **CAL**; 30 g **FAT** (8 g **SAT**); 43 g **PRO**; 17 g **CARB**; 7 g **SUGARS**; 3 g **FIBER**; 886 mg **SODIUM**

Sohui taste-tests new dishes for her restaurants and cookbooks on her kids—they guide her as to how far she can go.

GOCHUJANG-GLAZED SPARE RIBS

Gochujang-Glazed Spare Ribs

MAKES 8 servings **PREP** 15 minutes **GRILL** 1 hour, 12 minutes **REST** 15 minutes

- 1 **rack spare ribs (about 3½ lbs)**
- 2 **to 3 tsp kosher salt**
- 2 **tsp sugar**
- 5 **cloves garlic, minced**
- 2 **tbsp minced ginger**
- ¼ **cup low-sodium soy sauce**
- ¼ **cup gochujang (see tip left)**
- 3 **tbsp gochugaru (see tip left)**
- 2 **tbsp honey**
- 2 **tbsp rice wine vinegar**

- Heat grill to medium.

- Cut rack in half. Combine salt and sugar. Sprinkle over ribs.

- Whisk remaining ingredients.

- Using 4 sheets of heavy-duty aluminum foil, double-wrap each rack in its own packet.

- Place ribs on grill over direct heat and cook 1 hour with lid closed, occasionally turning packets without piercing foil.

- Remove from grill; rest 10 minutes. Carefully open packets, remove ribs and discard rendered fat and foil.

- Grill ribs over direct heat, with lid closed as much as possible, turning and basting with sauce until nicely charred, 10 to 12 minutes. Remove from grill; rest about 5 minutes. Cut into individual ribs and serve with any remaining sauce.

PER SERVING 366 **CAL**; 24 g **FAT** (9 g **SAT**); 25 g **PRO**; 12 g **CARB**; 7 g **SUGARS**; 1 g **FIBER**; 1,314 mg **SODIUM**

Doughnutlike pancakes with gooey brown sugar filling are a great spin on hand pies.

Hotteok: Korean Dessert Pancakes

MAKES 10 servings **PREP** 30 minutes **LET RISE** 1 hour, 30 minutes **COOK** 5 minutes per batch **COOL** 5 minutes

- **1 tbsp instant yeast**
- **2 cups warm water**
- **½ cup packed light brown sugar**
- **3 tbsp sesame seeds**
- **2 tbsp crushed or finely chopped almonds or walnuts**
- **4½ cups all-purpose flour, plus more for dusting**
- **2 tbsp granulated sugar**
- **2 tsp kosher salt**
- **2 tsp olive oil, plus more for cooking**

■ In a small bowl, combine yeast and warm water; stir well. Let sit 5 minutes in a warm place.

■ In another bowl, combine brown sugar, sesame seeds and nuts. In a large bowl, stir flour, granulated sugar and salt, then add oil and yeast mixture. Stir until dough comes together.

■ Dust clean work surface with flour. Turn dough out onto flour; knead until smooth. Form into a ball and place in a clean, lightly greased bowl.

■ Cover bowl with a kitchen towel; let rise in a warm spot until it has doubled in size, about 1 hour. Knead risen dough on floured surface until smooth, then form into a ball, cover and let rise 30 minutes.

■ Divide dough into 10 pieces; form each into a flattened ball and place on floured surface. Make a dent in center of each ball and fill with 1 tbsp brown sugar mix. Pinch balls shut.

■ In a nonstick pan, heat 1 tbsp oil over medium. Working in batches and adding ½ tbsp oil as needed, place 2 balls in pan. Cook until bottoms are browned, 2½ minutes, then flip and press down gently with a spatula to form flat pancakes 3 to 4 inches wide. Cook 2 to 2½ minutes, until browned. (It's OK if some filling oozes out.)

■ Let hotteok cool about 5 minutes before serving. Filling will be hot!

PER SERVING 289 **CAL**; 6 g **FAT** (1 g **SAT**); 7 g **PRO**; 52 g **CARB**; 9 g **SUGARS**; 2 g **FIBER**; 389 mg **SODIUM**

HOTTEOK: KOREAN
DESSERT PANCAKES

START SNACKING RIGHT

You've heard it before: Eat more veggies, eat more protein. Thanks to these satisfying, stuffed no-cook bites, it's done and done.

"EVERYTHING"
DEVILED EGGS,
PAGE 156

GREEK CHERRY
TOMATOES,
PAGE 156

"Everything" Deviled Eggs

MAKES 16 servings **PREP** 15 minutes

- 2 tbsp toasted sesame seeds
- 1 tbsp poppy seeds
- 1 tbsp dried minced garlic
- 1 tbsp dried minced onion
- 1 tsp coarsely ground sea salt
- 8 hard-cooked eggs
- ¼ cup mayonnaise
- 2 tsp water
- 1 tsp yellow mustard
- ⅛ tsp salt
- ⅛ tsp black pepper

■ Mix first 5 ingredients in a small bowl. Peel and halve eggs. Mash yolks in a bowl with mayonnaise, water, mustard, salt and pepper until smooth (or combine ingredients in a mini chopper and whirl until smooth). Return yolk mixture to centers of egg whites and sprinkle with 1 tsp "everything" seasoning mixture. Can be made up to 3 days in advance; add seasoning mixture just before serving.

PER SERVING 75 **CAL**; 6 g **FAT** (1 g **SAT**.); 4 g **PRO**; 1 g **CARB**; 0 g **SUGARS**; 0 g **FIBER**; 197 mg **SODIUM**

Greek Cherry Tomatoes

MAKES 30 servings **PREP** 25 minutes

- 15 large heirloom cherry tomatoes
- ¼ cup finely crumbled feta cheese
- 1 tbsp finely chopped fresh parsley
- 1 tsp fresh lemon zest
- 1 can (15 oz) cannellini beans
- 2 tbsp olive oil
- 2 tbsp fresh lemon juice
- 2 tsp jarred minced roasted garlic
- ¼ tsp salt
- ¼ tsp freshly ground black pepper

■ Slice tomatoes in half and scoop out seeds. Turn upside down onto paper towels and drain 5 minutes. Meanwhile, in a small bowl, toss feta, parsley and lemon zest. Drain and rinse cannellini beans. Add to food processor along with olive oil and lemon juice, garlic, salt and black pepper. Puree until smooth. Divide ¾ cup bean spread among tomatoes (you'll have some left over); sprinkle feta mixture on top. Keep refrigerated. Will keep up to 2 days filled or 4 days unfilled.

PER SERVING 25 **CAL**; 1 g **FAT** (0 g **SAT**); 1 g **PRO**; 3 g **CARB**; 0 g **SUGARS**; 1 g **FIBER**; 70 mg **SODIUM**

Salmon Cucumber Bites

MAKES 20 pieces **PREP** 20 minutes
ASSEMBLY 20 minutes

- 1½ seedless cucumbers
- 4 oz smoked salmon slices
  - Whipped cream cheese
  - Fresh chives

■ Cut cucumbers into ¾-inch rounds (you will need 20). Scoop out centers (opening should be 1 inch across and ½ inch deep). Separate salmon slices and place on a cutting board. Spread a very thin layer of whipped cream cheese on each slice and roll up tightly. Slice into ½-inch pinwheels, then fit one into each piece of cucumber, flattening slightly. Sprinkle with snipped fresh chives. Makes 20 pieces. Filled bites will keep up to 2 days in the fridge.

PER SERVING 22 **CAL**; 1 g **FAT** (1 g **SAT**); 2 g **PRO**; 1 g **CARB**; 0 g **SUGARS**; 0 g **FIBER**; 57 mg **SODIUM**

SALMON
CUCUMBER
BITES

OF BIRDS & BREWS

Three clever spins on classic beer-can chicken.

**MASTER BEER-CAN
CHICKEN RECIPE**

Start with room-temp beer, cider or soda—it will give the bird flavor more quickly. To impart a smoky kick, add soaked wood chips to the fire. Pair hickory chips with root beer, apple chips with cider and pecan chips with ginger beer. Tuck wing tips behind body to keep them from overcooking.

Master Beer-Can Chicken Recipe

MAKES 4 servings **PREP** 15 minutes **GRILL** 1 hour **REST** 10 minutes

1 **3½-lb whole chicken**
   Salt and black pepper
1 **can beer**

■ Prepare grill for indirect grilling. (Heat one side to medium-high and leave other side off.) Pat dry a whole 3½-lb chicken, place on a cutting board and season with salt and pepper. Pour (or drink!) ½ cup liquid from a can of beer and fit chicken over it, with legs pointing down and tips of drumsticks resting on cutting board. Transfer chicken, standing upright, to an aluminum pie plate or a baking pan lined with foil. Place over indirect heat and grill 25 minutes, then cover loosely with aluminum foil. Grill 25 to 35 minutes, until thighs reach 165°. Rest 10 minutes, carefully remove from can and slice.

Root Beer Enhancing root beer's inherent sweetness is easy with a combo of molasses, Chinese five-spice powder and salt.

SEASONING
Brush with 1 tbsp molasses, then rub with 2 tbsp five-spice powder + 1½ tsp kosher salt

BEER ALTERNATIVE
1 can (12 oz) root beer (such as Dr. Brown's)

Hard Cider Citrusy aromas in the rub mixture work with the fragrant cider to flavor the bird both inside and out.

SEASONING
Rub with 1 tbsp lemon zest + 1½ tsp kosher salt + ½ tsp ground coriander + ½ tsp cracked black pepper

BEER ALTERNATIVE
1 can (12 oz) hard cider (such as Angry Orchard Crisp Apple)

Ginger Beer Make it Jamaican: Add 2 tsp curry powder to the brown sugar and ginger before rubbing onto chicken.

SEASONING
Rub with 1 tbsp packed light brown sugar + 2 tsp ground ginger + 1½ tsp kosher salt

BEER ALTERNATIVE
1 can (12 oz) ginger beer (such as Gosling's)

COLD PLAY

Mom and entrepreneur Jeni Britton Bauer is the brains behind the crazy-delicious Jeni's Splendid Ice Creams, and her unique pints inspired these five frozen desserts.

LAYERED ICE CREAM POPS

DIPPED UNICORN CONES

"Flavor is everything," says Jeni Britton Bauer, founder of Jeni's Splendid Ice Creams. The Columbus, Ohio-based company is known for its unexpected taste combinations, like Ricotta Toast with Red Berry Geranium Jam and Salted Honey Pie.

While Jeni didn't start out dreaming of being an ice cream creator, she has always been fascinated by scents and flavors. At first Jeni wanted to be a pastry chef, then a perfumer, and then the two blended together. While her flavors are innovative, the ice cream itself is back-to-basics: dairy from grass-pastured cows with no artificial dyes, emulsifiers or anything synthetic.

Jeni honed her craft by infusing store-bought ice cream with essential oils, sort of like training wheels for her future experiments. Now, 22 years later, she has 1,000 employees, 34 stores in seven states and packaged pints in supermarkets nationwide. (They can also be ordered from jenis.com.) "We look for quality and true partners in what we do," she says.

Jeni has some true partners at home, too. Her husband, Charly, is the Head of Stewardship and spends his days helping to build community outreach. Their kids, Greta, 10, and Dashiell, 9, are always ready and eager to taste.

Jeni doesn't limit herself to ice cream when it comes to flavorful matchmaking. In the summer, she loves topping a tart fruit pie with her Lemon Buttermilk Frozen Yogurt. "Sometimes ice cream is the actual dessert," she says. "But sometimes it can be the wingman to another dessert." And that's how Jeni inspired us to come up with our own playful takes.

Layered Ice Cream Pops

Don't worry about spreading the ice cream too much—we learned the swirls can be quite forgiving!

MAKES 16 servings   **PREP** 15 minutes
FREEZE 30 minutes, then overnight

- **1** **prepared all-butter loaf cake (such as Entenmann's)**
- **2** **pints Jeni's Brambleberry Crisp ice cream**

■ Coat an 8½x4½x2½-inch loaf pan with nonstick spray. Line with plastic wrap, leaving a 2-inch overhang on all sides. Smooth wrinkles and set aside.

■ Using a serrated knife, split cake horizontally in half. Cut bottom half horizontally in half again. Reserve uncut top half.

■ Evenly spread 1 pint ice cream over bottom of pan. Top with a layer of cut cake, using reserved top half to fill in pan where needed. Freeze 30 minutes.

■ Top with another pint of ice cream and remaining cut layer of cake. Use reserved top half to fill in again, where needed. Save remaining cake for another use. Freeze loaf pan overnight.

■ In pan, slice cake in half lengthwise, then cut each half into eighths. Place an ice pop stick in center of each piece.

■ Serve immediately or freeze.

Dipped Unicorn Cones

To make the perfect drying stand for dipped cones, invert an egg carton and pop holes into the bottom of each egg holder. The holes should be big enough to hold cones upright.

MAKES 12 servings
MICROWAVE 1 minute, 15 seconds

- **½** **cup pink melting candy**
- **½** **cup blue melting candy**
- **½** **cup dark blue melting candy**
- **6** **tsp vegetable oil**
- **12** **sugar cones**
- **1** **pint Jeni's Supermoon ice cream**

■ Place each color of melting candy in a separate small microwave-safe bowl. Add 2 tsp oil to each. Microwave all bowls at 100% for 45 seconds. Stir, then repeat in 30-second increments until candy is melted and the same consistency.

■ Add 2 tbsp of each color of melted candy to a small bowl; place colors side by side so that each covers about a third of the bowl. (If they overlap, you will achieve a marbling effect.)

■ Dip top of each sugar cone into melted candy, then turn cone upright. To achieve a dripping effect, slowly rub cone back and forth between your hands. Let dry before adding ice cream.

WAFFLE ICE CREAM
SANDWICHES

Waffle Ice Cream Sandwiches

MAKES 3 waffle sandwiches **PREP** 10 minutes

1   pint Jeni's Strawberry Buttermilk or Darkest Chocolate ice cream

6   frozen waffles, toasted

½   cup topping, such as sprinkles, mini chocolate chips or ground almonds (optional)

1   cup white or regular chocolate chips, melted (optional)

■ Place a 3½-inch ring mold on a chilled plate. Add 2 large scoops ice cream to mold and, using the back of a spoon, smooth into an even layer. Using a spatula, transfer mold with ice cream to a waffle; remove mold. Top ice cream with another waffle and press down lightly. Repeat with remaining ice cream and waffles.

■ If adding topping but not dipping into chocolate, roll sandwiches in topping. Serve immediately or freeze.

■ If dipping into chocolate, freeze sandwiches 1 hour. Then, if desired, cut in half or into quarters. Dip one side of cut sandwiches into melted chocolate and let excess drip off. Sprinkle with topping, if using. Serve immediately or wrap individually and freeze.

Sorbet Cocktail

MAKES 4 servings **PREP** 5 minutes

8   small scoops Jeni's Frosé sorbet

4   oz gin

3½   oz St. Germain (elderflower liqueur)

½   oz freshly squeezed lemon juice

Lemon slices, for garnish

■ Add 2 small scoops sorbet to each of 4 cups or glasses. Place in freezer to avoid melting.

■ Combine gin, liqueur and lemon juice in a cocktail shaker with ice. Shake, then divide evenly among cups. Garnish each with a lemon slice.

Fudge Brownie Ice Cream Cake

MAKES 12 servings **PREP** 10 minutes
BAKE at 350° for 65 minutes
FREEZE 20 minutes, then 2 hours or overnight

1   box fudge brownie mix (such as Duncan Hines)

2   pints Jeni's Green Mint Chip ice cream

Ganache (right) (optional)

3   Andes mints, peeled lengthwise with a vegetable peeler

■ Heat oven to 350°. Grease a 7-inch springform pan and wrap outside in foil. Prepare brownie mix according to package directions for fudgy brownies. Bake 65 minutes, until edges start to pull away from pan. Cool to room temperature, then place in freezer 10 to 20 minutes to firm up and cool completely.

■ Run a thin knife between brownie and pan, then release ring. Using a serrated knife, carefully split brownie horizontally into 2 layers.

■ Replace ring around bottom brownie layer. Top with 1 pint ice cream and, using the back of a spoon, smooth into an even layer. Repeat with remaining brownie layer and ice cream. Freeze at least 2 hours or, preferably, overnight.

■ When ready to serve, run the thin knife between cake and pan, then release ring. Transfer to a cake stand or serving plate.

■ Pour ganache, if using, over center of top layer and allow to drip down the sides. Sprinkle with shaved mints. Serve immediately or return to freezer. Make the brownie up to 2 days in advance and store it in the fridge.

Ganache In a small pot, heat ¼ cup heavy cream until just boiling. Pour over 2 oz chopped semisweet chocolate. Stir until completely melted, smooth and shiny. Cool at least 5 minutes before pouring onto ice cream cake.

For optimal results, let ice cream sit at room temperature about 5 minutes before scooping. You're looking for the sweet spot when it's easy to scoop and spread but before it becomes liquid.

SORBET COCKTAIL, PAGE 163

FUDGE BROWNIE
ICE CREAM CAKE,
PAGE 163

BERRIES & CREAM

Heavy cream and cream cheese give the filling for this summery tart topped with peak-season blueberries rich flavor and a silky texture.

Although skyr is found next to the yogurt in the dairy section of most supermarkets, it is technically not yogurt but rather a type of Icelandic cheese. It is a little thicker than yogurt and full of protein. If you can't find it, yogurt makes a fine substitute in this tart.

Creamy Blueberry Tart

MAKES 12 servings **PREP** 10 minutes **COOK** 5 minutes **BAKE** at 350° for 20 minutes **CHILL** 2 hours

- ⅔ **cup heavy cream**
- ¼ **cup sugar**
- ½ **vanilla bean, split**
- 1 **tsp unflavored gelatin**
- 1 **8-oz pkg cream cheese, room temperature**
- 1 **5.3-oz container vanilla skyr or yogurt**
- 1 **9-inch graham cracker crust (tart or pie)**
- 1 **to 1½ cups blueberries**

■ In a saucepan, whisk heavy cream, sugar, seeds from vanilla bean and gelatin. Cook over medium, stirring, 3 minutes, until mixture is smooth.

■ Beat cream cheese until smooth. Blend in vanilla skyr. While beating, add cream mixture.

■ Pour into graham cracker crust. Smooth filling and top with 1 to 1½ cups blueberries. Chill 2 hours or until set.

CHEESEBURGER PIZZA,
PAGE 182

AUGUST

172

176

184

SCHOOLED ON FISH

Too smelly, too expensive, too, well, fishy? If these are a few of the reasons you're not serving seafood at home, these five recipes will conquer your family's fears.

**THAI-STYLE MUSSELS,
PAGE 175**

MANGO CRAB
CAKE SLIDERS,
PAGE 175

GRILLED SWORDFISH WITH PINEAPPLE-AVOCADO SALSA

Arctic Char with Chermoula

MAKES 4 servings   **PREP** 10 minutes
BROIL 6 minutes

- ½   **cup packed parsley leaves**
- 2   **tbsp packed cilantro leaves**
- 2   **cloves garlic**
- ⅓   **cup pitted Kalamata olives**
- 1   **tbsp fresh lemon juice**
- ½   **tsp ras el hanout (Moroccan spice blend)**
- ¼   **tsp crushed red pepper**
- ⅛   **tsp cumin**
- ¼   **tsp lemon zest**
- ¼   **tsp salt**
- ⅓   **cup plus 1 tbsp olive oil**
- 1   **lb arctic char, cut into 4 pieces**

■ Heat broiler. In a mini chopper, pulse to roughly chop parsley, cilantro and garlic. Transfer to a small bowl. Pulse olives to chop. Add to the small bowl with next 5 ingredients, ⅛ tsp salt and ⅓ cup oil. Stir.

■ Place fish on a foil-lined sheet and season with ⅛ tsp salt. Brush with 1 tbsp oil. Broil 4 inches from heat 6 minutes, until cooked through. Serve with a spoonful of chermoula on top of each piece.

PER SERVING 357 **CAL**; 28 g **FAT** (4 g **SAT**); 24 g **PRO**; 3 g **CARB**; 0 g **SUGARS**; 0 g **FIBER**; 291 mg **SODIUM**

Grilled Swordfish with Pineapple-Avocado Salsa

MAKES 4 servings   **PREP** 10 minutes   **GRILL** 9 minutes

- 1   **cup diced ripe pineapple (¼-inch dice)**
- ½   **small red onion, diced**
- 2   **tbsp cilantro, chopped**
- ½   **jalapeño, finely diced**
     Zest of 1 lime
- 1   **tbsp freshly squeezed lime juice**
- 2   **avocados, diced**
- ¾   **tsp salt**
- 4   **swordfish steaks (6 oz each)**
- ⅛   **tsp freshly ground black pepper**
- 1   **tbsp olive oil**
     Corn chips, for serving (optional)

■ Make the salsa: In a small bowl, combine first 6 ingredients. Fold in avocado and ¼ plus ⅛ tsp salt.

■ Season fish on all sides with ¼ plus ⅛ tsp salt and the pepper. Brush with oil. Heat a grill or grill pan over medium-high. Grill fish 5 minutes, until marked. Flip, reduce heat to medium and grill 3 to 4 minutes, until temperature reaches 145°.

■ Transfer to a plate. Serve with salsa and corn chips, if using.

PER SERVING 412 **CAL**; 26 g **FAT** (5 g **SAT**); 34 g **PRO**; 13 g **CARB**; 5 g **SUGARS**; 5 g **FIBER**; 645 mg **SODIUM**

ARCTIC CHAR WITH
CHERMOULA

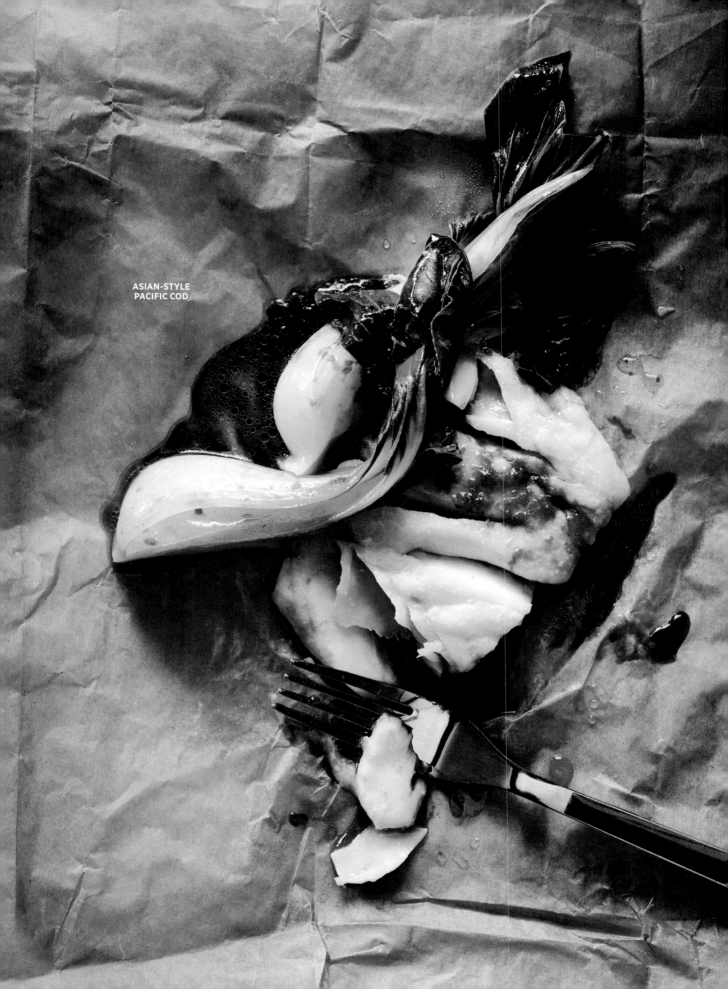

ASIAN-STYLE
PACIFIC COD

Asian-Style Pacific Cod

MAKES 4 servings **PREP** 15 minutes
BAKE at 450° for 10 minutes

- 4 **baby bok choy, quartered**
- 1 **large red bell pepper, sliced into ¼-inch strips (optional)**
- 2 **tsp reduced-sodium soy sauce**
- 2 **tsp vegetable oil**
- 1 **1-inch piece ginger, grated**
- 1 **clove garlic, grated**
- 4 **frozen cod fillets (5 oz each), thawed**
- 1 **tbsp honey**
- ½ **tsp salt**
  Cooked soba noodles, lightly tossed with Asian sesame dressing (optional)

■ Heat oven to 450°. Bring a large pot of water to a boil.

■ In a medium bowl, combine first 6 ingredients. Divide veggies evenly among 4 pre-cut folded parchment baking sheets, placing in the center, to right of center fold. Top each mound with a fillet, brush with honey and sprinkle with ⅛ tsp salt.

■ Seal parchment packets with narrow folds and twist the ends. Place on 2 baking sheets; bake about 10 minutes. Transfer to plates. Serve with soba noodles tossed with dressing, if desired.

PER SERVING 160 **CAL**; 3 g **FAT** (1 g **SAT**); 24 g **PRO**; 9 g **CARB**; 7 g **SUGARS**; 2 g **FIBER**; 891 mg **SODIUM**

Thai-Style Mussels

MAKES 6 servings **PREP** 15 minutes
COOK 25 minutes

- 2 **tsp vegetable oil**
- 1 **sweet onion, sliced**
- 1 **to 2 Thai chiles or ½ jalapeño, seeded and sliced**
- 1 **clove garlic, finely chopped**
- ½ **tsp plus ⅛ tsp salt**
- 2 **medium yellow potatoes, cut into ½-inch pieces**
- 2 **tbsp fresh lime juice**
- 2 **cans (15 oz each) coconut milk**
- 3 **tbsp green curry paste**
- 1 **pkg (¾ oz) fresh Thai basil**
- 12 **oz green beans, in 1-inch pieces**
- 2 **lbs mussels, cleaned**
- 2 **cups cooked basmati rice**

■ In a large, lidded nonstick skillet, heat oil over medium. Add onion, chile, garlic and ⅛ tsp salt. Cook 5 minutes, until softened. Add potatoes and ⅛ tsp salt; cook 2 minutes.

■ Add 1 tbsp lime juice, scraping up brown bits from bottom of pan. Add coconut milk, curry paste and 6 basil leaves. Increase heat to medium-high and bring to a boil. Reduce heat and simmer 10 minutes.

■ Stir in green beans, ¼ tsp salt and mussels. Cover and cook 8 minutes, until all mussels open. (Discard any that don't.) Stir in 1 tbsp lime juice and ⅛ tsp salt.

■ Tear remaining basil and sprinkle on top. Serve over rice.

PER SERVING 584 **CAL**; 36 g **FAT** (28 g **SAT**); 25 g **PRO**; 46 g **CARB**; 4 g **SUGARS**; 4 g **FIBER**; 1,076 mg **SODIUM**

Mango Crab Cake Sliders

MAKES 5 servings **PREP** 15 minutes
REFRIGERATE 10 minutes **COOK** 20 minutes

- 8 **oz lump crab meat**
- 1 **mango, diced small and tossed with 1 tsp sugar**
- 1 **cup panko**
- ¼ **cup mayonnaise**
- ½ **shallot, diced small**
- 1 **egg, lightly beaten**
- 1 **tbsp plus 1 tsp fresh lemon juice**
- ¼ **tsp smoked paprika**
- ¼ **tsp chili powder**
- ¼ **tsp salt**
- ⅛ **tsp cayenne pepper**
- ¼ **cup vegetable oil**
- 10 **Hawaiian sweet rolls**
- 2 **cups mixed salad greens**

■ Pick through crab and add to a large bowl along with half the mango mixture, ½ cup panko, mayonnaise, shallot, egg, 1 tbsp lemon juice and next 4 ingredients. Form into scant ¼-cup cakes and place on a parchment-lined baking sheet.

■ Dredge both sides of crab cakes in ½ cup panko. Refrigerate at least 10 minutes.

■ Add remaining mango mixture and ½ cup water to a small saucepan. Bring to a boil, stirring often and smashing. Reduce until almost all water evaporates, about 15 minutes. Remove from heat and stir in 1 tsp lemon juice.

■ While mango relish is cooking, heat oil in a large nonstick skillet over medium. Carefully add 5 crab cakes; cook 5 minutes per side. Transfer to a paper towel-lined plate to keep warm. Repeat with remaining crab cakes.

■ Slice sweet rolls in half and build each slider with 1 tbsp salad greens, a crab cake and mango relish. Serve warm.

PER SERVING 254 **CAL**; 13 g **FAT** (3 g **SAT**); 9 g **PRO**; 28 g **CARB**; 11 g **SUGARS**; 1 g **FIBER**; 211 mg **SODIUM**

POP ART

These ice pops are delicious and decidedly grown-up.
And they come in all shapes and sizes.

Dark Cherry Yogurt Pops

MAKES 10 pops   **PREP** 5 minutes
COOK 13 minutes   **FREEZE** 4 hours

- 1 **12-oz pkg frozen dark sweet cherries**
- ¼ **cup water**
- 1 **tbsp sugar**
- ½ **tsp gelatin**
- ¼ **cup heavy cream**
- 1 **16-oz full-fat vanilla yogurt**

■ In a medium pot over medium-high, heat frozen dark sweet cherries with water until thawed, about 3 minutes. Add sugar and cook, stirring occasionally and smashing, until slightly thickened, about 10 minutes. Let cool, then carefully puree with a hand blender.

■ Meanwhile, in a small pot over medium-low, whisk gelatin into heavy cream until just simmering. Remove from heat and blend into yogurt. Spoon 1 tbsp yogurt mixture into each mold followed by ½ tbsp puree. Repeat so there are a total of 4 yogurt layers and 3 puree layers. If desired, use a skewer to create more swirls. Insert included sticks or freeze 1 hour and place an ice pop stick in center of each. Freeze at least 4 hours.

PER POP 87 **CAL**; 3 g **FAT** (2 g **SAT**); 3 g **PRO**; 13 g **CARB**; 10 g **SUGARS**; 1 g **FIBER**; 27 mg **SODIUM**

Sangria Pops

MAKES 6 pops   **PREP** 5 minutes   **FREEZE** 4 hours

- 1 **cup red wine (such as a red blend, pinot noir or merlot)**
- ⅓ **cup cranberry juice cocktail**
- 3 **tbsp sugar**
- 1 **tsp lime juice**
- 2 **cups mixed frozen fruit (such as strawberry, mango and peach)**

■ Add red wine, cranberry juice cocktail, sugar and lime juice to a large measuring cup; stir to dissolve sugar.

■ Finely chop mixed frozen fruit. Spoon about 3 tbsp fruit into each of 6 ice pop pouches, then fill with wine mixture. Seal and freeze at least 4 hours.

PER POP 80 **CAL**; 0 g **FAT** (0 g **SAT**); 0 g **PRO**; 13 g **CARB**; 11 g **SUGARS**; 1 g **FIBER**; 2 mg **SODIUM**

ICED TEA/ LEMONADE POPS

Iced Tea/Lemonade Pops

MAKES 3 pops   **PREP** 5 minutes
FREEZE 12 minutes

- **3**   **very thin lemon slices**
- ⅓   **cup sweetened iced tea**
- ¼   **cup lemonade (such as Natalie's)**

■ Remove quick-freezing ice pop maker from freezer. Press 1 lemon slice up against wall of each of 3 molds and insert included sticks.

■ Divide sweetened iced tea evenly among molds. Freeze 4 minutes, until solid. Remove from freezer and divide lemonade evenly among molds. Freeze until solid, at least 8 minutes more.

Spike It Add 2 tsp vodka to the iced tea and 1 tbsp vodka to the lemonade before pouring into molds. Freeze a few extra minutes.

PER POP 18 **CAL**; 0 g **FAT** (0 g **SAT**); 0 g **PRO**; 5 g **CARB**; 5 g **SUGARS**; 0 g **FIBER**; 6 mg **SODIUM**

Pineapple Kiwi Pops

MAKES 12 pops   **PREP** 5 minutes
COOK 13 minutes   **FREEZE** 4 hours

- **12**   **thin peeled kiwi slices**
- **2**   **cups coconut water**
- **1**   **cup pineapple juice**

■ Fill a 12-cup muffin tin with foil baking liners. Place 1 slice peeled kiwi on bottom of each cup. In a large measuring cup, combine 2 cups coconut water with 1 cup pineapple juice. Divide evenly among baking cups.

■ Freeze 1 hour, then place an ice pop stick in center of each. Freeze at least 3 hours. Thaw slightly before removing from tin.

PER POP 24 **CAL**; 0 g **FAT** (0 g **SAT**); 0 g **PRO**; 6 g **CARB**; 5 g **SUGARS**; 0 g **FIBER**; 19 mg **SODIUM**

Help your sticks stand up: Cover the muffin tin tightly with foil and poke sticks through foil into the center of each mold.

PINEAPPLE KIWI POPS

GRILLED YESTERDAY, DINNER TONIGHT

Have leftover chicken, steak or veggies from a cookout? Turn it into a whole new meal.

SHRIMP SALAD ROLLS

Toss the shrimp, avocado, tomato and scallions together a few hours ahead, then add dressing and fill rolls just before serving.

Shrimp Salad Rolls

MAKES 4 servings   **PREP** 15 minutes

- 8 **oz leftover grilled shrimp, coarsely chopped (1½ cups)**
- 1 **firm-ripe avocado, pitted, peeled and diced**
- 1 **cup heirloom cherry tomatoes, quartered**
- 2 **scallions, trimmed and sliced**
- 2 **tbsp olive oil**
- 1 **tsp freshly grated lemon peel plus 2 tbsp fresh lemon juice**
- ¼ **tsp each salt and freshly ground black pepper**
- 8 **hot dog buns (top- or side-sliced)**
- 2 **cups prepared coleslaw**

■ In a large bowl, gently stir shrimp, avocado, tomatoes and scallions.

■ In a small bowl, whisk oil, lemon peel and juice, salt and pepper. Drizzle over shrimp mixture and stir to blend. Divide shrimp salad evenly among buns (about ⅓ cup in each); serve with coleslaw.

PER SERVING (2 rolls) 489 **CAL**; 22 g **FAT** (4 g **SAT**); 21 g **PRO**; 53 g **CARB**; 15 g **SUGARS**; 5 g **FIBER**; 693 mg **SODIUM**

GRILLED VEGGIE SLAB QUICHE

Grilled Veggie Slab Quiche

MAKES 8 servings   **PREP** 15 minutes   **BAKE** at 450° for 8 minutes, then at 375° for 35 minutes

- 1 **pkg refrigerated pie crusts (15 oz)**
- 1 **cup leftover grilled asparagus, chopped**
- ½ **cup leftover grilled red pepper strips**
- ½ **cup leftover grilled sweet onion, diced**
- 7 **large eggs**
- 1 **cup 1% milk**
- ¾ **tsp salt**
- ½ **tsp freshly ground black pepper**
- 1 **cup grated or crumbled cheese (whatever you have on hand!)**

■ Heat oven to 450°. Coat a 15×10×1-inch baking pan with nonstick spray. On floured surface, stack pie crusts and roll out to a 17×12-inch rectangle. Fit into pan and fold over pastry to form a stand-up edge. Line crust with foil and bake 8 minutes.

■ Remove crust from oven and lower temp to 375°. Remove foil. Scatter veggies evenly over crust. Whisk eggs, milk, salt and pepper. Pour into crust and scatter cheese on top. Bake 35 minutes, until puffed and set.

PER SERVING 347 **CAL**; 21 g **FAT** (9 g **SAT**); 13 g **PRO**; 30 g **CARB**; 4 g **SUGARS**; 2 g **FIBER**; 655 mg **SODIUM**

Especially if you're a kid, does it get any better than a combination of your two favorite foods—cheeseburgers and pizza? If peppery arugula is a bit much for younger ones, substitute shredded romaine instead.

Cheeseburger Pizza

MAKES 6 servings   **PREP** 15 minutes   **BAKE** at 450° for 22 minutes

1	**ball (16 oz) pizza dough (thawed, if frozen), at room temp**
½	**cup ketchup**
3	**tbsp yellow mustard**
2	**leftover hamburger patties (4 oz each), crumbled**
2	**cups shredded cheddar**
3	**cups arugula**
1	**tbsp red wine vinegar**
6	**large hamburger pickle chips, chopped (¼ cup)**
1	**medium tomato, diced**

■ Heat oven to 450°. On floured surface, roll dough to a 16-inch circle. Transfer to a greased round pizza pan. Whisk ketchup with mustard and spread over crust. Top with meat and cheese.

■ Bake on lowest oven rack 18 to 22 minutes, until crust is brown and cheese is melted. Meanwhile, toss arugula with vinegar. Remove pizza from oven and top with chopped pickles, arugula and diced tomato.

PER SERVING 452 **CAL**; 21 g **FAT** (9 g **SAT**); 25 g **PRO**; 42 g **CARB**; 8 g **SUGARS**; 0 g **FIBER**; 810 mg **SODIUM**

CHEESEBURGER
PIZZA

BBQ CHICKEN PASTA SALAD

You might think that apple, chicken, pasta and blue cheese make for a strange dish, but we loved the contrast of sweet, salty and spicy flavors.

Steak-and-Mushroom Lettuce Leaf Tacos

MAKES 4 servings **PREP** 15 minutes **COOK** 5 minutes

- 1 tbsp olive oil
- 8 oz cremini mushrooms, chopped
- 8 oz leftover grilled medium-rare flank steak, chopped into small pieces
- 1 tsp chili powder
- ½ tsp ground cumin
- ½ tsp salt
  Juice of 1 medium lime
- 1 large head green leaf lettuce, leaves separated and cleaned
- ½ cup sour cream
  Fresh cilantro leaves
  Bottled hot sauce (optional)
  Cooked rice and red beans, heated

■ In a large nonstick skillet, heat oil over medium-high. Add mushrooms and cook 3 minutes. Add steak, chili powder, cumin and salt and cook 2 minutes. Remove from heat and stir in lime juice.

■ Let everyone assemble their own tacos using lettuce leaves, seasoned steak, sour cream, cilantro and hot sauce (if using). Serve with rice and beans.

PER SERVING 418 **CAL**; 13 g **FAT** (6 g **SAT**); 25 g **PRO**; 48 g **CARB**; 4 g **SUGARS**; 7 g **FIBER**; 777 mg **SODIUM**

BBQ Chicken Pasta Salad

MAKES 4 servings **PREP** 10 minutes **COOK** 12 minutes

- 8 oz rigatoni
- 2 leftover barbecued chicken breasts (12 oz total)
- 3 cups baby spinach leaves
- 1 Gala apple, cored and diced
- ⅓ cup bottled barbecue sauce
- ¼ cup blue cheese dressing
- ½ cup crumbled blue cheese

■ Bring a large pot of lightly salted water to a boil. Add rigatoni and cook to al dente, about 12 minutes. Drain and transfer to a large serving bowl. Cool completely.

■ Meanwhile, cut chicken into bite-sized pieces. Once pasta is cool, add chicken, spinach and apple to bowl. Combine barbecue sauce with blue cheese dressing. Toss pasta salad with dressing and top with crumbled blue cheese.

PER SERVING 585 **CAL**; 16 g **FAT** (5 g **SAT**); 38 g **PRO**; 70 g **CARB**; 24 g **SUGARS**; 2 g **FIBER**; 838 mg **SODIUM**

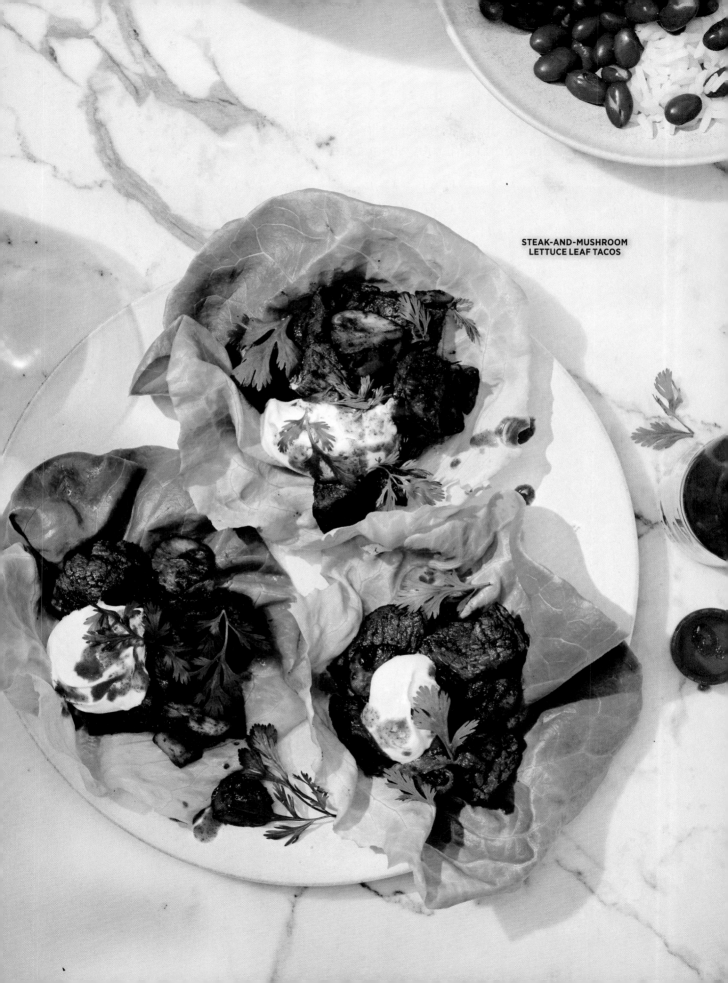

STEAK-AND-MUSHROOM
LETTUCE LEAF TACOS

DYNAMIC DUO

Many vegetables are at peak deliciousness at the end of the summer—but somehow corn and tomatoes always steal the show.

ROASTED
TOMATO
STRATA

The tomato is a fruit, so why not treat it like one? Play up its sweetness in a jam that's perfect with biscuits. Or go traditional and savory: This strata is loaded with tomato-friendly Gruyère, rosemary and thyme.

Roasted Tomato Strata

MAKES 6 servings   **PREP** 15 minutes   **BAKE** at 400° for 1 hour and at 350° for 25 minutes   **LET STAND** 10 minutes

Unsalted butter

6   large roma tomatoes, cored and quartered lengthwise

1   tbsp vegetable oil

1   tsp salt

½   tsp freshly ground black pepper

1   loaf (8 oz) Italian bread

2   tbsp chopped parsley

1   tsp chopped rosemary

1   tsp chopped thyme

2   cups half-and-half

5   large eggs

1   cup grated Gruyère cheese

1   tbsp tomato paste

■ Heat oven to 400°. Coat a 13×9-inch baking dish with unsalted butter.

■ On a foil-covered rimmed baking sheet, toss tomatoes with oil and ¼ tsp each salt and pepper. Roast 1 hour, turning halfway through.

■ Cut bread into 1-inch cubes. Spread in an even layer on another rimmed baking sheet. Bake 10 minutes, then cool to room temperature.

■ Meanwhile, combine herbs. In a large bowl, whisk half-and-half, eggs, Gruyère, tomato paste, 2 tbsp herb mixture, ¾ tsp salt and ¼ tsp pepper.

■ Transfer cooled bread to egg mixture and let soak about 30 minutes or until tomatoes are done, stirring occasionally. When tomatoes are done, lower oven temp to 350°.

■ Stir half the tomatoes into bread mixture; pour into prepared baking dish. Press remaining tomatoes on top.

■ Bake 25 minutes. Let stand 10 minutes, sprinkle with remaining herb mixture and serve warm.

PER SERVING 378 **CAL**; 23 g **FAT** (10 g **SAT**); 17 g **PRO**; 25 g **CARB**; 6 g **SUGARS**; 1 g **FIBER**; 836 mg **SODIUM**

TOMATO-GINGER JAM

Ripe tomatoes are tender, not soft. If yours seem super-soft, opt for roasting or simmer in sauces or soups.

Tomato-Ginger Jam

MAKES 2½ cups   **PREP** 5 minutes   **COOK** 56 minutes   **COOL** 15 minutes

- **3   lbs beefsteak tomatoes**
- **1   3-inch piece peeled ginger**
- **2   cups sugar**
- **¼   tsp salt**
- **1   tsp lemon juice**

■ Bring a large nonstick pot of water to a boil. Fill a large bowl with ice water.

■ Core tomatoes and cut a small X into bottom of each. Place in boiling water until skins begin to crack, 30 seconds to 1 minute.

■ Transfer tomatoes to ice bath. When cool enough to handle, peel tomatoes. Pour out boiling water and set aside pot.

■ Quarter peeled tomatoes and roughly chop ginger. Add both to a food processor and pulse until broken down but still chunky.

■ Pour tomato mixture into pot. Add sugar and salt; cook over medium until almost all water is evaporated, 45 to 55 minutes. Stir occasionally at first and frequently toward end of cooking, skimming and discarding foam as needed.

■ Remove from heat; stir in lemon juice. Pour jam into a resealable jar and cool 15 minutes. Store in the fridge up to 3 months.

PER 2-TBSP SERVING 59 **CAL**; 0 g **FAT** (0 g **SAT**); 1 g **PRO**; 17 g **CARB**; 16 g **SUGARS**; 1 g **FIBER**; 32 mg **SODIUM**

Toasted sesame oil and ponzu—a Japanese sauce made with lemon juice or rice vinegar, soy sauce, rice wine, kombu (seaweed) and dried bonito flakes—give the traditional American-style corn relish an Asian twist.

Grilled Chicken with Sesame-Ponzu Corn Relish

MAKES 4 servings   **PREP** 15 minutes   **SOAK** 30 minutes   **GRILL** 25 minutes   **REST** 5 minutes

1½	**lbs unshucked sweet corn (about 4 ears)**
6	**tbsp ponzu sauce**
2	**tbsp sesame oil**
4	**whole chicken legs (about 2½ lbs)**
1	**tbsp vegetable oil**
¾	**tsp salt**
¾	**tsp freshly ground black pepper**
6	**scallions, thinly sliced**
2	**tbsp thinly sliced fresh red chile**

■ Soak corn in husks in enough water to cover 30 minutes.

■ Heat grill over medium.

■ In a large bowl, whisk ponzu and sesame oil. Set aside 2 tbsp ponzu mixture in a small bowl.

■ Toss chicken with vegetable oil and sprinkle with ¼ tsp each salt and pepper.

■ Place chicken and corn on grill. Cook corn about 20 minutes, covered, turning halfway through. Cook chicken, covered, until temperature reaches 165°, 20 to 25 minutes, turning halfway through. Toward end of cooking, brush all over with reserved 2 tbsp ponzu mixture. Transfer to a cutting board and rest about 5 minutes.

■ Shuck cooled corn, remove silk and cut kernels from cobs. In a large bowl, combine corn with remaining ponzu mixture. Stir in scallions, chile and ½ tsp each salt and pepper.

■ Spoon corn relish over chicken and serve warm.

PER SERVING 646 **CAL**; 45 g **FAT** (11 g **SAT**); 38 g **PRO**; 25 g **CARB**; 5 g **SUGARS**; 3 g **FIBER**; 1,127 mg **SODIUM**

GRILLED CHICKEN
WITH SESAME-PONZU
CORN RELISH

If you prefer larger chunks of corn, slice down close to cob, then do the opposite side to get two wide slabs. Cut down remaining sides for thinner rows. Crumble larger pieces over tomatoes.

Corn and Tomato Salad

MAKES 6 servings   **PREP** 10 minutes

- 2½ **lbs heirloom tomatoes**
- ¼ **tsp salt**
- 3 **ears cold grilled corn**
- 3 **tbsp fresh lime juice**
- 2 **tbsp avocado or olive oil**
- 2 **tsp agave or light honey**
    Flaky sea salt, crumbled queso fresco or feta and torn cilantro

■ Slice tomatoes about ¼ inch thick. (Do not use top or bottom slices.) Place on a paper towel-lined baking sheet; sprinkle with salt. Cut corn from cobs.

■ Arrange tomato slices on a platter and sprinkle with corn.

■ Whisk lime juice, oil and agave. Drizzle over salad. Top with sea salt, cheese and cilantro.

PER SERVING 92 **CAL**; 6 g **FAT** (1 g **SAT**); 2 g **PRO**; 10 g **CARB**; 7 g **SUGARS**; 2 g **FIBER**; 318 mg **SODIUM**

CORN AND TOMATO SALAD

SWEET CORN ICE CREAM
WITH RASPBERRY SWIRL

Think cone instead of cob: Corn and raspberries come together for an ode-to-summer ice cream. The corn and the four egg yolks give the cooked custard a beautiful yellow hue.

Sweet Corn Ice Cream with Raspberry Swirl

MAKES 8 servings   **PREP** 20 minutes   **STEEP** 1 hour   **REFRIGERATE** 2 hours or overnight   **PROCESS** about 30 minutes   **FREEZE** 6 hours or overnight

- 1   **can (14 oz) sweetened condensed milk**
  Pinch of salt
- 1½   **cups heavy cream**
- 2   **ears fresh sweet corn**
- 4   **large egg yolks**
- ⅓   **cup seedless raspberry jam**

■ In a medium saucepan, stir condensed milk, salt and ¾ cup cream. Cut kernels from cobs; break cobs in half. Place kernels and cobs in saucepan. Bring to a simmer over medium, stirring. Remove from heat; steep, covered, 1 hour.

■ Discard cobs. Using an immersion or standing blender, puree corn mixture until smooth.

■ Pass mixture through a strainer into a clean medium saucepan. Place ¾ cup cream in a large bowl inside an ice bath.

■ Whisk egg yolks in a large bowl. Warm corn mixture over medium-low. Whisking constantly, add ¼ cup warm corn mixture at a time to yolks until yolks are just warmed (you'll use about half the corn mixture). Stir yolk mixture back into pot.

■ Cook custard over medium-low, stirring frequently to avoid curdling, until thick enough to coat spoon, 3 to 4 minutes.

■ Pour custard through a strainer into reserved cream. Stir to combine. Refrigerate at least 2 hours or overnight.

■ Pour custard into an ice cream maker and churn according to manufacturer's directions.

■ Transfer half the ice cream to a loaf pan. Spoon jam over ice cream, smoothing as much as possible, and top with remaining ice cream. Freeze at least 6 hours or overnight.

PER SERVING 392 **CAL**; 23 g **FAT** (14 g **SAT**); 7 g **PRO**; 42 g **CARB**; 40 g **SUGARS**; 0 g **FIBER**; 116 mg **SODIUM**

CHEDDAR-ZUCCHINI
QUICK BREAD, PAGE 216

SEPTEMBER

198

205

219

LUNCHTIME IN THE BAG

We love a sandwich as much as the next gal, but sometimes you need to mix things up. Try building a batch of bowls—all based on shredded chicken and brown rice—that do double duty for you and the kids.

Quick Chicken and Rice Bowls

FOR THE BASE:
- **Cooked brown rice**
- **Shredded chicken**

FOR MEXICAN STYLE, ADD:
- **Corn**
- **Cheese**
- **Salsa**
- **Lime**

FOR ASIAN STYLE, ADD:
- **Cooked shelled edamame**
- **Shredded carrot**
- **Torn fresh basil**
- **Miso Vinaigrette (recipe right)**

FOR SPICY MOROCCAN STYLE, ADD:
- **Roasted cubed sweet potato**
- **Crumbled feta cheese**
- **Chopped parsley**
- **Harissa Vinaigrette (recipe right)**

Start from scratch

- Make enough rice for the whole week.
- Broil the corn for a little char.
- Bake your chicken while you roast your sweet potato.

Get a little help

- **Fast:** Shred rotisserie chicken.
- **Faster:** Slice breasts purchased from the deli section.
- **Fastest:** Look for diced chicken on the salad bar.

Miso Vinaigrette: For each rice bowl, whisk 1 tbsp miso paste with 2 tbsp rice vinegar, 1 tsp honey, ½ tsp toasted sesame oil and ¼ tsp ground ginger. Whisk in 2 tbsp vegetable oil.

Harissa Vinaigrette: For each rice bowl, whisk together 1 tbsp harissa paste with 2 tbsp red wine vinegar and 2 tsp honey. Whisk in 2 tbsp vegetable oil.

Quick tip: Swap the brown rice for cauliflower rice or salad greens.

25 MEALS UNDER 25 MINUTES

A month's worth of recipes that will take the stress out of deciding what's for dinner.

THAI-GLAZED SALMON

Here's a weeknight meal-plan strategy: Peruse all 25 of these recipes and pick out 5 that look the best to you. Shop all at once for those recipes and you'll have everything you need to cook the minute you get home, with no stopping at the store.

Thai-Glazed Salmon

MAKES 4 servings

- ½ cup sweet chili sauce
- 2 tbsp light soy sauce
- 3 scallions, sliced
- 4 5-oz salmon fillets
- 1 pkg (12 oz) broccoli slaw
- 1 tbsp vegetable oil
- ¼ tsp salt
- ½ cup basil leaves, thinly sliced

■ Line a rimmed sheet pan with foil. Whisk sweet chili sauce with soy sauce and 1 of the scallions. Place salmon on pan and drizzle with ¼ cup sauce mixture. Bake at 450° for 12 minutes, then broil 2 minutes. Meanwhile, in a large nonstick skillet over medium-high cook broccoli slaw with remaining scallions and 1 tbsp vegetable oil 3 minutes. Season with salt. Remove from heat and stir in basil leaves. Serve salmon over slaw; drizzle with remaining sauce.

PER SERVING 376 **CAL**; 14 g **FAT** (2 g **SAT**); 832 mg **SODIUM**; 19 g **CARB**; 1 g **FIBER**; 14 g **SUGAR**; 35 g **PRO**

Shrimp over Fried Rice

MAKES 4 servings

- ⅓ cup light soy sauce
- 2 tbsp vegetable oil
- 2 tsp sesame oil
- 2 tbsp soy mixture
- 1¼ lbs medium peeled cleaned shrimp, thawed if frozen
- 1 pkg (10.8 oz) frozen mixed vegetables
- 2 pkg (8.8 oz each) fully cooked rice, heated
- 3 eggs, beaten

■ Heat broiler. Set top rack at least 4 inches from heat source. Whisk soy sauce, 1 tbsp of the vegetable oil and sesame oil in a medium bowl. Toss 2 tbsp soy mixture with shrimp and thread onto 4 skewers. Meanwhile, heat remaining 1 tbsp vegetable oil in a large nonstick skillet over medium. Add frozen mixed vegetables (we used a broccoli, snap pea, carrot and water chestnut mix) and ¼ cup water. Cover and cook 4 minutes. Uncover and add rice and remaining soy mixture. Push to one side of skillet and add eggs; cook, scrambling, 2 minutes. Stir eggs into rice, cover and keep warm. Broil shrimp 6 minutes, turning once.

PER SERVING 538 **CAL**; 21 g **FAT** (3 g **SAT**); 983 mg **SODIUM**; 45 g **CARB**; 1 g **FIBER**; 6 g **SUGAR**; 41 g **PRO**

Zoodles with Meat Sauce

MAKES 4 servings

- 6 cups zucchini noodles
  Salt for sprinkling, plus ½ tsp
- 1 tbsp vegetable oil
- 1 lb ground chuck
- ½ tsp salt
- ½ tsp black pepper
- 1 28-oz can crushed tomatoes
- 2 tbsp tomato paste
- 1 tbsp sugar
- ⅓ cup grated Parmesan
- 2 tsp fresh oregano, minced

■ Place zucchini noodles in a colander; sprinkle with salt. Let stand 5 minutes. Meanwhile, heat oil in a large pot over medium-high. Add ground chuck; brown 4 minutes. Stir in ½ tsp each salt and pepper, crushed tomatoes, tomato paste and sugar. Simmer 10 minutes, stirring often. Rinse and pat dry. Add to sauce with grated Parmesan and oregano; simmer 3 minutes.

PER SERVING 379 **CAL**; 19 g **FAT** (7 g **SAT**); 922 mg **SODIUM**; 24 g **CARB**; 6 g **FIBER**; 16 g **SUGAR**; 30 g **PRO**

We get it. Your teen is trying to be a vegetarian (because, Mom, the animals!!), but her definition involves eating only pizza and cheese puffs. Since she still needs protein, quinoa checks all the boxes. For your meat lovers, add ground beef or turkey to these stuffed peppers.

Quinoa-Stuffed Peppers

MAKES 4 servings

4	sweet bell peppers (any color), halved and seeded
3	tbsp extra-virgin olive oil
2	medium shallots
2½	cups baby kale
3	cups cooked quinoa (such as Minute or Ancient Harvest)
½	tsp salt
½	tsp black pepper
1	cup crumbled feta
2	tbsp fresh lemon juice

■ Fill a large pot with an inch of water, add steamer insert, bring water to a boil and add peppers. Cover and steam 5 minutes. Remove to a rimmed baking sheet. Meanwhile, heat 2 tbsp extra-virgin olive oil in a large nonstick skillet over medium. Add shallots and cook 3 minutes. Stir in kale and cook 3 minutes. Add quinoa, salt and black pepper. Remove from heat. Stir in ¾ cup of feta, lemon juice and remaining 1 tbsp extra-virgin olive oil. Divide among peppers and sprinkle with remaining ¼ cup feta. Broil 3 minutes.

PER SERVING 414 **CAL**; 21 g **FAT** (7 g **SAT**); 664 mg **SODIUM**; 43 g **CARB**; 8 g **FIBER**; 9 g **SUGAR**; 14 g **PRO**

Manhattan Clam Chowder

MAKES 5 servings

2	tbsp vegetable oil
¾	cup carrot, diced
¾	cup celery, diced
¾	cup onion, diced
1	lb russet potatoes, peeled and finely diced
1	(32 oz) bottle Clamato juice
6½	oz chopped clams in juice

■ Heat oil in a large stockpot over medium-high. Add carrot, celery and onion; sauté 7 minutes. Add potatoes to pot; cook 3 minutes. Stir in Clamato juice and 1 cup water. Bring to a boil, reduce heat to medium and simmer 15 minutes. Add clams with their juice. Heat through.

PER SERVING 218 **CAL**; 6 g **FAT** (0 g **SAT**); 1,153 mg **SODIUM**; 34 g **CARB**; 2 g **FIBER**; 12 g **SUGAR**; 7 g **PRO**

Pork and Peanut Noodles

MAKES 6 servings

1	lb linguine
1	lb ground pork
1	tbsp vegetable oil
6	scallions, chopped
⅔	cup frozen peas, thawed
½	tsp salt
¾	cup bottled peanut sauce
⅓	cup chopped salted peanuts

■ Bring a large pot of lightly salted water to a boil. Add linguine; cook 9 minutes. Drain. Meanwhile, brown pork in oil over medium-high 5 minutes. Add 4 of the scallions and peas; cook 3 minutes. Sprinkle with salt and add linguine. Remove from heat and toss with peanut sauce. Top with peanuts and remaining scallions.

PER SERVING 594 **CAL**; 22 g **FAT** (5 g **SAT**); 969 mg **SODIUM**; 71 g **CARB**; 2 g **FIBER**; 12 g **SUGAR**; 29 g **PRO**

QUINOA-STUFFED
PEPPERS

PORK AND
GREEN BEAN
STIR-FRY

While these super-quick recipes rely on a few convenience products here and there—such as bottled stir-fry sauce, curry paste and salad dressing—we really made an effort to choose only those products that are not highly processed or that do not contain a lot of less-than-healthy ingredients.

Pork and Green Bean Stir-Fry

MAKES 6 servings

- 2 **tbsp vegetable oil**
- 1¼ **lb pork tenderloin, in ¼-inch slices**
  Salt and black pepper
- 1 **pkg (5 oz) shiitake mushrooms, sliced**
- 4 **cloves garlic, sliced**
- ¾ **lb haricots verts or green beans**
- ½ **cup stir-fry sauce**
  Steamed white rice

■ Heat oil in a large wok over medium-high. Season pork with salt and pepper and brown in hot oil in 3 batches, 3 minutes per batch. Transfer to a plate. Add mushrooms and garlic to wok; sauté 2 minutes. Stir in haricots verts. Cover and cook 3 to 5 minutes, stirring occasionally. Stir in stir-fry sauce and pork. Heat through. Serve with rice on the side.

PER SERVING 300 **CAL**; 8 g **FAT** (1 g **SAT**); 948 mg **SODIUM**; 32 g **CARB**; 3 g **FIBER**; 6 g **SUGAR**; 25 g **PRO**

Chicken Cordon Bleu

MAKES 5 servings

- 5 **thin-sliced chicken breast cutlets**
- 5 **slices provolone cheese**
- 5 **slices thinly sliced ham**
  Salt and black pepper, for sprinkling
- 5 **tsp Dijon mustard**
- 10 **tsp seasoned panko bread crumbs**

■ Line a large baking sheet with foil; coat with nonstick spray. Spread chicken cutlets on foil. Fold provolone cheese into quarters. Wrap each piece of cheese in 1 piece of ham to enclose. Place each ham packet on half of a chicken cutlet. Fold other half over ham to enclose; sprinkle with salt and pepper. Spread each with 1 tsp Dijon mustard and top each with 2 tsp bread crumbs. Bake at 450° for 15 minutes, then broil 1 to 2 minutes until lightly browned on top. Serve with green salad on the side.

PER SERVING 301 **CAL**; 9 g **FAT** (5 g **SAT**); 795 mg **SODIUM**; 10 g **CARB**; 3 g **FIBER**; 2 g **SUGAR**; 42 g **PRO**

Sautéed Pork and Apples

MAKES 4 servings

- 2 **tbsp butter**
- 4 **boneless pork chops (1¾ lbs total)**
- ½ **tsp salt plus more for seasoning pork**
  Black pepper
- 3 **Golden Delicious apples, cored and cut into wedges**
- 1 **cup apple cider**
- 2 **tbsp cider vinegar**
- 1 **tbsp country-style Dijon mustard**
- 2 **tsp cornstarch**

■ Heat butter in a large stainless skillet over high. Season pork chops with salt and pepper. Add to skillet; cook 8 minutes, turning once. Transfer pork to a baking sheet; bake at 350° for 5 to 7 minutes. Meanwhile, add apples to skillet. Sauté 5 minutes on medium-high. While apples cook, whisk cider, vinegar, mustard and cornstarch. Add to skillet along with ½ tsp salt. Bring to a boil; cook 2 minutes. Place pork on a platter and top with apples and sauce. Serve with mashed cauliflower, if desired.

PER SERVING 527 **CAL**; 28 g **FAT** (11 g **SAT**); 803 mg **SODIUM**; 26 g **CARB**; 3 g **FIBER**; 19 g **SUGAR**; 43 g **PRO**

All you need is a rippin'-hot cast-iron skillet to make these fajitas. Swap in a nonstick one if it means that the kids will clean up (we're not beneath bribery).

Steak Fajitas

MAKES 4 servings

- 1 lb flank steak, thinly sliced
- 4 tsp plus 2 tbsp fajita seasoning (from a 1.25-oz pkg)
- 2 tbsp vegetable oil
- 2 bell peppers (any color), cored and thinly sliced
- 1 large onion, halved and sliced

  Warm flour tortillas

  Spicy guacamole, for serving

■ Toss flank steak with 4 tsp of fajita seasoning. Heat oil in a large cast-iron skillet over high. Add steak and cook, stirring, 3 minutes. Remove to a plate. Add peppers and onion; cook 5 minutes. Whisk ¼ to ⅓ cup water with 2 tbsp fajita seasoning; add to pan. Cook 3 to 5 minutes, until thickened. Add steak and heat through. Serve on tortillas with spicy guac on the side.

PER SERVING 405 **CAL**; 28 g **FAT** (15 g **SAT**); 570 mg **SODIUM**; 4 g **CARB**; 1 g **FIBER**; 2 g **SUGAR**; 33 g **PRO**

Skillet Chicken with Fresh Tomato Sauce

MAKES 4 servings

- 2 tbsp butter
- 4 small chicken breasts
- ¼ tsp salt plus more for sprinkling

  Black pepper
- 4 Roma tomatoes, coarsely chopped
- 2 cloves garlic, sliced
- ½ cup basil leaves, thinly sliced
- ½ cup fresh mozzarella pearls

■ Heat butter in a large stainless skillet over high. Season chicken with salt and pepper. Add to pan and cook 4 minutes, until browned on bottom. Flip and add tomatoes and garlic to pan. Cover, reduce heat and cook over medium-high 10 minutes. Uncover and remove chicken to a platter; tent with foil. Add ¼ tsp salt to skillet and simmer sauce 5 minutes, stirring often. Remove from heat and stir in basil and mozzarella pearls. Pour sauce over chicken.

PER SERVING 356 **CAL**; 20 g **FAT** (10 g **SAT**); 820 mg **SODIUM**; 3 g **CARB**; 6 g **FIBER**; 2 g **SUGAR**; 40 g **PRO**

Cast-Iron Scallops with Grilled Asparagus

MAKES 4 servings

- 1 lb large scallops, thawed if frozen

  Zest and juice from 1 lemon
- 2 tsp minced garlic
- 1 bunch asparagus, trimmed
- 2 tbsp bottled vinaigrette
- 2 tbsp unsalted butter

  Salt and black pepper to taste

■ Heat grill to medium-high. Pat dry scallops and toss with 2 tsp lemon zest and garlic. Toss asparagus with vinaigrette (split thick spears in half lengthwise for faster grilling). Heat a large cast-iron skillet on grill grate. Spread asparagus on grate next to skillet and grill 8 minutes, turning once. Melt butter in skillet and add scallops; cover grill and cook 4 minutes. Flip scallops and cook 3 minutes. Divide scallops and asparagus among 4 plates and season with salt and pepper. Drizzle with lemon juice and serve with baguette.

PER SERVING 313 **CAL**; 7 g **FAT** (4 g **SAT**); 1,003 mg **SODIUM**; 41 g **CARB**; 4 g **FIBER**; 4 g **SUGAR**; 21 g **PRO**

STEAK FAJITAS

FETTUCCINE WITH
CHICKEN

When you need a meal that's almost speed-of-light fast to put together, consider a sandwich. Our Reuben is tasty and satisfying and there's virtually nothing to clean up.

Fettuccine with Chicken

MAKES 6 servings

- 1 **lb fettuccine**
- 2 **tbsp extra-virgin olive oil**
- 3 **cloves garlic, sliced**
- 4 **cups packed fresh spinach, chopped**
- 2 **cups shredded rotisserie chicken**
- ⅓ **cup oil-packed sliced sun-dried tomatoes, plus 1 tbsp oil from the jar**
- 1 **tsp salt**
- ½ **tsp black pepper**
- ⅓ **cup shredded Asiago cheese, plus more for serving**

■ Bring a pot of salted water to a boil. Add fettuccine and cook al dente, 10 minutes. Drain, reserving 1 cup pasta water. Meanwhile, heat oil in a large nonstick skillet over medium. Add garlic and spinach. Cook 5 minutes, until wilted. Add chicken, sun-dried tomatoes and the oil from the jar; cook 2 minutes. Stir in fettuccine, salt, pepper and ½ cup pasta water. Remove from heat and stir in Asiago cheese, adding more pasta water if desired. Divide among bowls and sprinkle with additional Asiago.

PER SERVING 441 **CAL**; 12 g **FAT** (2 g **SAT**); 611 mg **SODIUM**; 60 g **CARB**; 1 g **FIBER**; 3 g **SUGAR**; 23 g **PRO**

Reuben Sandwiches

MAKES 4 servings

- 8 **slices rye bread**
- 8 **tbsp Thousand Island dressing or Spicy Remoulade (page 213)**
- 32 **slices deli corned beef**
- 2¼ **cups sauerkraut, squeezed dry**
- 8 **slices Swiss cheese**

■ In broiler, toast rye 3 inches from heat 2 minutes. Flip and top each slice with 1 tbsp dressing and ¾ oz thin-sliced deli corned beef (about 4 slices). Divide sauerkraut among toasts. Top each with 1 slice Swiss cheese. Broil 5 minutes, until browned. Serve with carrot and celery sticks, if desired.

PER SERVING 565 **CAL**; 33 g **FAT** (13 g **SAT**); 1,468 mg **SODIUM**; 34 g **CARB**; 4 g **FIBER**; 8 g **SUGAR**; 31 g **PRO**

Coconut Curry

MAKES 4 servings

- 14 **oz Qui extra-firm tofu**
- 1 **tbsp vegetable oil**
- ½ **large sweet onion, sliced**
- 3 **tbsp Thai green curry paste**
- 8 **oz bok choy, chopped**
- 1 **14½-oz can light coconut milk**
- ½ **tsp salt**

■ Place tofu on a paper towel-lined plate; top with more paper towels and a second plate. Let stand 10 minutes. Meanwhile, heat vegetable oil in a large skillet over medium. Add onion; cook 5 minutes. Add curry paste; cook 1 minutes. Add bok choy; cook 3 minutes. Stir in coconut milk. Dice tofu, season with ¼ tsp salt and add to pan; cover and cook 3 minutes. Season with ¼ tsp salt. Serve over cooked rice with lime wedges.

PER SERVING 361 **CAL**; 15 g **FAT** (7 g **SAT**); 918 mg **SODIUM**; 41 g **CARB**; 1 g **FIBER**; 5 g **SUGAR**; 15 g **PRO**

B.L.A.T. Sandwiches

MAKES 4 servings

- **8** slices thick-cut bacon
- **8** slices multigrain bread
- **4** tbsp honey mustard
- **4** small green leaf lettuce leaves
- **1** large beefsteak tomato, cut into 8 slices
- **1** avocado, pitted, peeled and quartered
- Salt
- Black pepper

■ Line a rimmed baking sheet with foil and fit with a rack. Spread bacon on rack. Bake at 400° for 18 minutes, until crisp. Meanwhile, toast bread. Spread 4 slices with 1 tbsp honey mustard each, then top each with 2 slices bacon (broken in half). Add lettuce to sandwiches and 2 slices tomato to each stack. Spread each of 4 remaining bread slices with ¼ of the avocado and sprinkle with salt and pepper. Assemble sandwiches and serve with chips, if desired.

PER SERVING 318 **CAL**; 14 g **FAT** (3 g **SAT**); 708 mg **SODIUM**; 35 g **CARB**; 3 g **FIBER**; 9 g **SUGAR**; 17 g **PRO**

Moroccan Chickpeas

MAKES 4 servings

- **1** box (5.6 oz) pine nut couscous
- **2** tbsp vegetable oil
- **1** tbsp garam masala
- **¾** cup dried apricots, diced
- **2** cans (15 oz each) chickpeas
- **¼** cup chopped fresh parsley
- Zest and juice of 1 lemon
- **½** tsp salt

■ Cook couscous per package instructions. Keep warm. Heat oil in a large lidded skillet over medium-high. Add garam masala to pan and cook 1 minute. Stir in 3 apricots and ½ cup water; cover and cook 4 minutes to plump apricots. Open chickpeas and drain and rinse 1 of the cans; add both

to pan along with lemon zest, parsley, 2 tbsp lemon juice and salt. Cook 3 minutes on high, until thickened slightly. Serve over couscous.

PER SERVING 506 **CAL**; 14 g **FAT** (1 g **SAT**); 1,142 mg **SODIUM**; 82 g **CARB**; 15 g **FIBER**; 19 g **SUGAR**; 19 g **PRO**

Quick Chicken Tacos

MAKES 6 servings

- **1** lb boneless, skinless chicken thighs
- **2** tsp chili powder
- **½** tsp salt
- **2** tbsp vegetable oil
- **1** onion, halved and sliced
- **1** can (14.5 oz) diced tomatoes with garlic
- **24** corn tortillas

■ Sprinkle chicken thighs with chili powder and salt. Heat oil in a large electric pressure cooker on sauté setting. In 2 batches, brown chicken 3 minutes, turning once. Return chicken to pot and stir in onion and diced tomatoes. Secure lid and set to pressure cook 8 minutes on manual. Release pressure and switch to sauté; shred chicken and return to cooker. Warm tortillas (the easiest way: wrap in a damp paper towel and microwave 1 to 2 minutes). For each taco, stack 2 tortillas and top with ¼ cup chicken mixture, some sour cream and shredded leaf lettuce.

PER SERVING 398 **CAL**; 12 g **FAT** (2 g **SAT**); 458 mg **SODIUM**; 50 g **CARB**; 2 g **FIBER**; 7 g **SUGAR**; 20 g **PRO**

Cuban Picadillo

MAKES 6 servings

- **1** tbsp vegetable oil
- **1½** lbs ground meatloaf mix (beef, pork and veal)
- **1** medium onion, diced
- **¾** cup raisins
- **¼** cup tomato paste
- **1½** tsp ground cinnamon

- **¾** tsp salt
- **½** cup pimiento-stuffed olives, sliced
- Prepared yellow rice (optional)

■ Heat oil over medium-high in a large nonstick skillet. Add meatloaf mix, breaking apart with a spoon, and brown about 5 minutes. Add onion; cook 3 minutes. Stir in raisins, tomato paste, cinnamon and salt and cook 2 minutes. Add olives and ¼ cup water. Cover and cook 3 minutes. Serve with yellow rice on the side, if desired.

PER SERVING 398 **CAL**; 9 g **FAT** (3 g **SAT**); 1,172 mg **SODIUM**; 57 g **CARB**; 2 g **FIBER**; 17 g **SUGAR**; 21 g **PRO**

Pesto Tilapia

MAKES 6 servings

- **2** lb russet potatoes, peeled and diced
- **6** tilapia fillets
- **6** tbsp basil pesto
- **½** tsp salt plus more for sprinkling
- Black pepper
- **¼** cup milk
- **¼** cup sour cream
- **3** tbsp butter
- **½** tsp salt

■ Place potatoes in a pot with enough salted water to cover by an inch. Bring to a boil and cook 12 minutes. Drain and return to pot. Meanwhile, coat a rimmed foil-lined baking sheet with nonstick spray and add tilapia fillets. Spread 1 tbsp basil pesto onto each and season with salt and pepper. Bake at 400° for 12 minutes. Mash potatoes in pot with milk, sour cream, butter and ½ tsp salt. Season with pepper and serve with a green vegetable.

PER SERVING 369 **CAL**; 16 g **FAT** (7 g **SAT**); 563 mg **SODIUM**; 29 g **CARB**; 2 g **FIBER**; 3 g **SUGAR**; 29 g **PRO**

Three-Bean Chili

MAKES 6 servings

- 2 **tbsp vegetable oil**
- 1 **large red onion, diced**
- 3 **bell peppers (red, yellow, orange), seeded and chopped**
- 2 **tbsp classic chili powder**
- 2 **tsp chipotle chile powder**
- 1 **can (28 oz) fire-roasted crushed tomatoes**
- 3 **cans (15 oz each) low-sodium chili beans, drained and rinsed**

■ Heat oil in a large stockpot or Dutch oven over medium. Add ½ of the onion (save other half for finished chili) and peppers to pot; cook 5 minutes. Add chili powder and chipotle chile powder; cook 1 minute. Add tomatoes and ½ cup water. Stir beans into pot. Bring to a simmer; cook 18 minutes, stirring occasionally. Season with salt to taste. Serve with remaining chopped red onion and your favorite fixings (such as chopped cilantro, sour cream, diced avocado and shredded cheese).

PER SERVING 275 **CAL**; 5 g **FAT** (0 g **SAT**); 848 mg **SODIUM**; 45 g **CARB**; 4 g **FIBER**; 11 g **SUGAR**; 14 g **PRO**

Steak Frites

MAKES 4 servings

- 3 **tbsp salted butter**
- 4 **beef tenderloin filets (4 to 5 oz each)**
- **Salt and black pepper**
- 1 **shallot, minced**
- 1 **cup beef broth**
- ¼ **cup red wine**
- 2 **tbsp green peppercorns in brine, drained and coarsely chopped**
- ½ **cup heavy cream**

■ Melt 3 tbsp salted butter in a skillet over medium-high. Season beef filets with salt and pepper. Add to pan; cook 8 minutes, turning once, for medium-rare. Remove to a plate; keep warm. Add shallot to pan; cook 1 minute. Add broth and wine. Simmer 5 minutes, until reduced, scraping browned bits from pan bottom. Add peppercorns to pan along with heavy cream. Reduce heat to medium; cook 2 minutes. Spoon over steaks; serve with fries.

PER SERVING 405 **CAL**; 28 g **FAT** (15 g **SAT**); 570 mg **SODIUM**; 4 g **CARB**; 1 g **FIBER**; 2 g **SUGAR**; 33 g **PRO**

Pasta with Sausage and Broccoli

MAKES 6 servings

- 1 **lb rigatoni**
- 2 **tbsp extra-virgin olive oil plus more, if needed**
- 1 **lb fresh bulk pork sausage**
- 4 **cups broccoli florets**
- 1 **cup chicken broth**
- ¼ **tsp red pepper flakes**
- ½ **cup grated Parmesan**
- **Salt and black pepper**

■ Bring a pot of salted water to a boil. Add rigatoni and cook to al dente, 14 minutes. Meanwhile, heat extra-virgin olive oil in a large skillet over high. Add sausage, breaking apart with a spoon; brown 5 minutes. Add broccoli florets and broth. Reduce heat to medium-high, cover and cook 4 minutes. Uncover and stir in red pepper flakes; cook 2 minutes. Drain pasta and add to skillet along with grated Parmesan. Toss to combine, adding a little extra oil if needed. Season with salt and black pepper, to taste.

PER SERVING 559 **CAL**; 23 g **FAT** (6 g **SAT**); 814 mg **SODIUM**; 59 g **CARB**; 1 g **FIBER**; 4 g **SUGAR**; 26 g **PRO**

Sourdough Turkey Burgers

MAKES 6 servings

- ½ **cup packed basil leaves, chopped**
- ¾ **cup light mayo**
- ½ **cup grated Parmesan**
- 2 **lb ground turkey**
- ½ **tsp salt**
- ½ **tsp black pepper**
- 6 **large slices sourdough bread**
- **Arugula**

■ Heat grill or grill pan to medium-high. In a small bowl, whisk chopped basil with mayo and ¼ cup of the Parmesan. In a bowl, mix ground turkey, ⅓ cup basil mayo, remaining ¼ cup Parmesan and salt and pepper. Grill bread 1 minute per side. Oil grill grate. With wet hands, shape turkey mixture into 6 patties. Grill 12 minutes, turning once. Divide remaining basil mayo among bread slices; cut each slice in half. Stack burgers and arugula on bread.

PER SERVING 443 **CAL**; 24 g **FAT** (5 g **SAT**); 870 mg **SODIUM**; 25 g **CARB**; 0 g **FIBER**; 0 g **SUGAR**; 37 g **PRO**

Mushroom Ravioli

MAKES 4 servings

- 2 **pkg (10 oz each) fresh mushroom ravioli**
- ¾ **cup frozen peas**
- 1 **cup crumbled goat or blue cheese**
- ½ **cup heavy cream**
- ½ **cup toasted walnut pieces**

■ Cook mushroom ravioli per package instructions, adding frozen peas during last 2 minutes. (Try this twist: Opt for butternut squash ravioli instead.) Drain and return to pot. Toss with crumbled goat cheese, heavy cream and walnuts. Serve with crusty bread on the side.

PER SERVING 551 **CAL**; 32 g **FAT** (15 g **SAT**); 543 mg **SODIUM**; 48 g **CARB**; 2 g **FIBER**; 5 g **SUGAR**; 20 g **PRO**

4 WAYS TO USE KETCHUP

This beloved condiment can be far more than an accompaniment to fries.

Mini Pizza Meatloaves

Make the meat mixture up to 2 days ahead and refrigerate with plastic wrap pressed on top. You can make the ketchup glaze 2 days in advance as well; store, covered, in fridge.

MAKES 4 servings **PREP** 15 minutes
BAKE 35 minutes

34	slices pepperoni
1	lb ground chuck
¼	cup bread crumbs
¼	cup milk
1	large egg
½	tsp salt
½	tsp black pepper
¾	cup ketchup
2	tsp Italian herb blend
¼	tsp minced onion
¾	tsp garlic powder
¼	tsp crushed red pepper
4	(1 oz each) pieces mozzarella

■ Chop 30 slices of pepperoni; combine with next 6 ingredients. In a small bowl, stir ketchup, Italian herb blend, minced onion, garlic powder and crushed red pepper. Stir half the ketchup mixture into meat. Divide meat into 4 rectangles. Press 1 whole slice pepperoni and 1 piece mozzarella into center of each and shape to close. Top evenly with remaining ketchup mixture. Bake at 350° for 35 minutes.

PER SERVING 512 **CAL**; 22 g **FAT** (10 g **SAT**); 1,375 mg **SODIUM**; 38 g **CARB**; 0 g **FIBER**; 16 g **SUGAR**; 39 g **PRO**

Quick tip: If you like tomato soups a little sweeter, stir in a bit of ketchup.

Blueberry BBQ Wings

Anyone can open a bottle of barbecue sauce: Impress your friends by making your own. Blueberries add a bit of tartness to sweet and savory chicken wings.

MAKES 6 servings **PREP** 10 minutes
COOK 15 minutes

6	oz blueberries
½	cup ketchup
¼	cup blueberry preserves
¼	cup water
½	tsp Worcestershire sauce
½	tsp garlic powder
½	tsp onion powder
½	tsp salt
2	lb just-fried or just-baked chicken wings
	Minced chives

■ In a small pot over medium, combine first 8 ingredients. Cook, stirring occasionally, 15 minutes, until sauce thickens. Toss with chicken wings. Top with chives.

PER SERVING 230 **CAL**; 11 g **FAT** (3 g **SAT**); 473 mg **SODIUM**; 19 g **CARB**; 1 g **FIBER**; 16 g **SUGAR**; 15 g **PRO**

Spicy Remoulade

Mayo and mustard are fine—but with minimal effort, you can elevate your lunches with this creamy, briny spread with a kick. This sauce is also great as a dip for shrimp, crab cakes and crudités.

MAKES 1 cup **PREP** 5 minutes
REFRIGERATE 4 hours

½	cup mayonnaise
2	tbsp ketchup
2	tbsp hot sauce
1	tbsp whole-grain mustard
1	tsp capers in brine, chopped
½	tsp caper brine
¼	cup packed flat-leaf parsley, chopped
1	tbsp minced chives

■ Stir together first 6 ingredients. Fold in parsley and chives. Refrigerate 4 hours, with plastic wrap pressed on top, to marry flavors. Use within 5 days. Makes 1 cup.

PER SERVING 99 **CAL**; 10 g **FAT** (2 g **SAT**); 251 mg **SODIUM**; 1 g **CARB**; 0 g **FIBER**; 1 g **SUGAR**; 0 g **PRO**

Sweet-and-Sour Cauliflower

Use your family's favorite flavors to your advantage: Add sweet-and-sour sauce to side dishes to get your crew to eat more vegetables. This trick also works with eggplant, broccoli and bok choy.

MAKES 6 servings **PREP** 10 minutes
COOK 17 minutes

¼	cup ketchup
3	tbsp rice vinegar
2	tbsp orange juice
2	tbsp light brown sugar
1	tbsp low-sodium soy sauce
2	tbsp vegetable oil
1	head cauliflower, cut into florets
½	tsp salt
2	large ribs celery, peeled and sliced ½ inch thick on the bias
1	red bell pepper, cut into ½-inch pieces
1	tbsp cornstarch
	Celery leaves

■ Combine first 5 ingredients. In a large nonstick pan over medium-high, heat vegetable oil. Add cauliflower and ¼ tsp salt; cook 5 minutes. Add celery, bell pepper and remaining ¼ tsp salt; cook 7 minutes. Stir in ketchup mixture. In a small bowl, stir cornstarch and 1 tbsp water. Increase heat to high, add cornstarch slurry and stir well. Cook until thickened, 3 to 5 minutes. Garnish with celery leaves.

PER SERVING 121 **CAL**; 5 g **FAT** (1 g **SAT**); 351 mg **SODIUM**; 18 g **CARB**; 3 g **FIBER**; 11 g **SUGAR**; 3 g **PRO**

QUICK BREADS

Get your fall baking fix with these simple, satisfying loaves.

PEAR-ROSEMARY
QUICK BREAD

You might be wondering how something that bakes for about an hour can be considered quick. The name refers to the fast-acting leaveners that are used in place of yeast. You don't have to proof and knead these breads before baking.

The Basics:

Checking Doneness Bake until a wooden skewer inserted in the center of the loaf comes out clean. You can also check for an internal temperature of 200°.

After Baking Let cool in pan on a wire rack for 10 to 15 minutes. Remove from pan and let cool completely.

Storing Wrap breads tightly in foil and leave at room temp for up to 3 days. Or freeze foil-wrapped loaves in resealable bags for up to 3 months.

Pear-Rosemary Quick Bread

MAKES 10 servings **PREP** 20 minutes **BAKE** 45 minutes

3	cups all-purpose flour
1	tsp baking powder
1	tsp baking soda
½	tsp salt
1½	tbsp finely chopped fresh rosemary, plus 3 small sprigs
¼	tsp ground cinnamon
1	stick unsalted butter, at room temp
1¼	cups packed light brown sugar
2	large eggs
¾	cup unsweetened applesauce
1	pear

■ Heat oven to 350°. Coat three 5¾ x 3¼ x 2-inch disposable aluminum loaf pans with nonstick spray.

■ Whisk first 6 ingredients.

■ Beat butter and sugar. Beat in eggs, 1 at a time, then applesauce. Gradually beat in flour mixture until evenly moistened.

■ Peel, quarter and core pear. Cut ¾ of the pear into very small dice; stir into batter and transfer to prepared pans.

■ Thinly slice remaining pear; arrange slices over batter. Top each loaf with a small rosemary sprig. Bake 40 to 45 minutes.

PER SERVING 357 **CAL**; 11 g **FAT** (6 g **SAT**); 499 mg **SODIUM**; 61 g **CARB**; 2 g **FIBER**; 30 g **SUGAR**; 5 g **PRO**

CHEDDAR-ZUCCHINI
QUICK BREAD

Quick breads are well-suited to both sweet and savory flavor profiles. Serve the Cheddar-Zucchini Quick Bread with dinner and Banana-Coconut Quick Bread at breakfast or coffee break.

Banana-Coconut Quick Bread

MAKES 10 servings **PREP** 20 minutes
BAKE 1 hour, 20 minutes

- **3** cups all-purpose flour
- **1** tsp baking powder
- **1** tsp baking soda
- **½** tsp salt
- **½** tsp ground cinnamon
- **3** ripe large bananas
- **¾** cup coconut cream
- **1** large egg
- **1** stick unsalted butter, melted
- **⅔** cup plus 2 tbsp packed light brown sugar
- **¾** cup sweetened coconut flakes
- **¼** cup crushed banana chips

■ Heat oven to 350°. Coat a 9¼ x 5¼ x 2¾-inch loaf pan with nonstick spray.

■ Whisk first 5 ingredients.

■ Beat bananas and ½ cup coconut cream until smooth. Beat in egg, then butter, ⅔ cup sugar and ½ cup coconut flakes.

■ Gradually beat in flour mixture until evenly moistened. Transfer batter to prepared pan.

■ Mix remaining coconut cream, sugar and flakes with banana chips; spread over batter. Bake 1 hour, 20 minutes.

PER SERVING 449 **CAL**; 17 g **FAT** (12 g **SAT**); 515 mg **SODIUM**; 71 g **CARB**; 3 g **FIBER**; 36 g **SUGAR**; 6 g **PRO**

Cheddar-Zucchini Quick Bread

MAKES 10 servings **PREP** 20 minutes **BAKE** 1 hour, 10 minutes

- **3** cups all-purpose flour
- **1** tsp baking powder
- **1** tsp baking soda
- **½** tsp salt
- **¼** cup finely grated Parmesan
- **1** tbsp sugar
- **½** tsp salt
- **½** tsp cayenne pepper
- **2** large eggs
- **½** cup vegetable oil
- **2** zucchini, shredded (about 4 cups)
- **1⅓** cups shredded sharp cheddar

■ Heat oven to 375°. Coat a 9¼ x 5¼ x 2¾-inch loaf pan with nonstick spray.

■ Whisk first 8 ingredients.

■ Whisk eggs and oil; stir in zucchini. Stir egg mixture into flour mixture until evenly moistened. (Batter will be dense.) Stir in 1 cup cheddar. Pat batter into prepared pan. Top with remaining cheddar. Bake 1 hour, 10 minutes.

PER SERVING 328 **CAL**; 18 g **FAT** (5 g **SAT**); 560 mg **SODIUM**; 32 g **CARB**; 1 g **FIBER**; 2 g **SUGAR**; 10 g **PRO**

BANANA-COCONUT
QUICK BREAD

THE GAME PLAN

Torch more calories in less time with the perfect workout + meals.

BERRY COCONUT
SMOOTHIE BOWL

WILD SALMON WITH ROASTED VEGETABLES

Outsmart Sugar: A good tip for losing weight is to switch to unsweetened dairy alternatives. Many coconut and almond milk yogurts contain similar amounts of keep-you-full protein without the metabolism-disrupting sugar. And focus primarily on fruits that are low in sugar and high in antioxidants, like berries, and fiber-rich seeds, such as flax and chia.

Berry Coconut Smoothie Bowl

MAKES 2 servings

- **2** **(5.3 oz) cartons coconut yogurt**
- **1** **cup frozen strawberries**
- **¼** **cup raw, unsalted cashews**
- **2** **tbsp ground flaxseeds**
- **1** **tbsp coconut water**
  Fresh berries
  Unsweetened coconut flakes
  Cacao nibs

■ Blend first 6 ingredients on high 1 minute, until smooth, adding a splash more coconut water if necessary. Divide between 2 bowls and garnish with berries of your choice, coconut and cacao nibs.

PER SERVING 262 **CAL**; 15 g **FAT** (7 g **SAT**); 8 mg **SODIUM**; 29 g **CARB**; 5 g **FIBER**; 15 g **SUGAR**; 4 g **PRO**

Wild Salmon with Roasted Vegetables

MAKES 4 servings

- **2** **heads broccoli**
- **2** **sweet potatoes, cut into ¼-inch half-moons**
- **3½** **tbsp extra-virgin olive oil**
- **½** **plus ⅛ tsp fine sea salt**
- **4** **(4 oz each) wild salmon fillets**
- **2** **tbsp whole-grain mustard**
- **1** **tbsp apple cider vinegar**
- **1** **tbsp chopped chives**

■ Cut broccoli into florets; peel stalks and cut into ¼-inch pieces. Toss broccoli and sweet potatoes with 2 tbsp oil and ½ tsp fine sea salt. Arrange in a single layer on 1½ sheet pans. Bake at 425° 25 minutes. Remove half-full sheet from oven. Carefully add salmon to the empty half and drizzle with 1 tbsp oil; sprinkle with ⅛ tsp fine sea salt. Bake 8 to 10 minutes. In a small bowl, combine mustard, vinegar and chives. Drizzle ½ tsp oil over each salmon fillet and top each with 1 tbsp mustard mixture.

PER SERVING 410 **CAL**; 25 g **FAT** (3 g **SAT**); 529 mg **SODIUM**; 22 g **CARB**; 4 g **FIBER**; 7 g **SUGAR**; 26 g **PRO**

HEARTY VEGETABLE
SOUP

Liquids, like soup, are necessary for the body to flush out by-products of fat metabolism.

Greek Herb Burgers

MAKES 5 servings

- 1 **tbsp tahini**
- 2 **tbsp plus ½ tsp freshly squeezed lemon juice**
- ⅛ **tsp garlic powder**
- 1 **Italian eggplant**
- 3 **tbsp extra-virgin olive oil**
- 1 **tsp fine sea salt**
- 1 **lb ground beef**
- ½ **medium onion, chopped**
- ½ **cup chopped mint**
- ½ **cup chopped parsley**
- ½ **cup chopped dill, plus more for serving**
- 1 **clove garlic, minced**
- 10 **pieces Bibb or Boston lettuce**
- **Lemon wedges**

■ Whisk tahini, ½ tsp lemon juice, garlic powder and 2 tbsp water. Set aside. Cut eggplant into ¼-inch rounds. Brush with 2 tbsp olive oil and sprinkle with ¼ tsp salt. Heat grill to medium-high. Grill 5 minutes, then flip and grill 3 minutes. Set aside.

■ Meanwhile, in a large bowl, combine ground beef with onion, mint, parsley, dill, minced garlic, 2 tbsp lemon juice, 1 tbsp olive oil and ½ tsp fine sea salt. Form into 5 patties, about 6 oz each. Sprinkle both sides with ¼ tsp fine sea salt and grill 10 minutes, flipping once for medium. Place an equal amount of grilled eggplant on 2 pieces lettuce. Drizzle with tahini mixture and garnish with chopped dill. Serve with lemon wedges.

PER SERVING 271 **CAL**; 16 g **FAT** (5 g **SAT**); 534 mg **SODIUM**; 11 g **CARB**; 4 g **FIBER**; 5 g **SUGAR**; 21 g **PRO**

Hearty Vegetable Soup

MAKES 6 servings

- 3 **tsp extra-virgin olive oil**
- 8 **oz sliced baby bella mushrooms**
- 1¼ **tsp plus ⅛ tsp fine sea salt**
- 1 **leek, thinly sliced**
- 1 **large bulb fennel, thinly sliced**
- 2 **carrots, sliced**
- 2 **ribs celery, sliced**
- ⅔ **cup pearled barley**
- 1 **sprig fresh thyme**
- 1 **clove garlic, smashed**
- 1 **bay leaf**
- 1 **zucchini**
- 1 **yellow squash**
- 5 **oz baby spinach**
- **Freshly ground black pepper**

■ In a large pot, heat 2 tsp oil over medium-high. Add mushrooms and ⅛ tsp salt. Reduce heat to medium. Cook 8 minutes, stirring once.

■ Add 1 tsp oil. Stir in leek and fennel. Cook 3 minutes. Add carrots, celery, barley, thyme, garlic and bay leaf. Cook 2 minutes. Add 10 cups water. Cover and bring to a boil over high. Reduce heat to medium and cook 20 minutes, until barley is tender.

■ While soup simmers, dice zucchini and yellow squash into ¼-inch cubes; add during last 5 minutes of cooking time. Stir in spinach, remaining 1¼ tsp salt and freshly ground pepper to taste. Discard bay leaf.

PER SERVING 136 **CAL**; 3 g **FAT** (1 g **SAT**); 657 mg **SODIUM**; 24 g **CARB**; 6 g **FIBER**; 5 g **SUGAR**; 5 g **PRO**

GREEK HERB
BURGERS

CAST-IRON-SEARED FILET MIGNON
WITH POTATO AND BUTTERNUT
SQUASH PUREE, BROCCOLINI AND
PARMESAN TUILE, PAGE 225

OCTOBER

229

238

245

MEAT & POTATOES WIN

MasterChef contestants team up to cook for some of the harshest critics around—kids!

PARMESAN
TUILE

POTATO
PUREE

CAST-IRON-
SEARED FILET
MIGNON

BROCCOLINI

BUTTERNUT
SQUASH PUREE

It's not easy cooking for kids of any age. Even more daunting is having to please not only picky palates, but also Michelin-starred chef Gordon Ramsay. He's the king of turning home cooks into restaurant-ready chefs on his show *MasterChef*, which is how 14 contestants found themselves creating 40 plates of food for a dining room full of kids. While this and other challenges mimic what moms face every day (few ingredients, chicken and potatoes), the results are anything but ordinary.

Cast-Iron-Seared Filet Mignon with Potato and Butternut Squash Puree, Broccolini and Parmesan Tuile

SERVES 4   **PREP, BAKE AND COOK** about 1½ hours

PARMESAN TUILE

- 4 tbsp grated Parmesan

BUTTERNUT SQUASH PUREE

- 3 cups diced butternut squash
- 1½ cups heavy cream
- Salt

POTATO PUREE

- 2 large Yukon Gold potatoes
- ½ stick butter
- ½ cup heavy cream
- Salt

FILET MIGNON

- 4 filet mignons (8 oz each)
- Salt and black pepper
- 1 tbsp grapeseed oil
- 2 sticks butter, cubed
- 1 bunch thyme
- 4 cloves garlic, smashed

BROCCOLINI

- 1 tbsp olive oil
- 1 bunch Broccolini, ends trimmed
- 1 lemon
- Salt and black pepper

■ **Parmesan Tuile** Heat oven to 400°. Add 1 heaping tbsp Parmesan to a silicone (highly recommended) or parchment-lined baking sheet and lightly pat down. Repeat with remaining cheese, spacing about ½ inch apart. Bake 3 to 5 minutes, until golden and crisp. Cool.

■ **Butternut Squash Puree** Add squash and cream to a medium pot (if cream doesn't cover all the squash, add more) and bring to a simmer. Add salt to taste and cook until squash is very tender, about 15 minutes. Drain squash, reserving cooking liquid. Transfer to a small bowl or pot and puree with an immersion blender. Add cooking liquid as needed and taste for salt.

■ **Potato Puree** Peel and dice potatoes. Boil in salted water 10 minutes or until soft enough to puree. Heat butter and cream in a small saucepan. Drain potatoes and pass through a ricer. Stir in butter-cream mixture until smooth and season with salt. Keep warm.

■ **Filet Mignon** Let steaks sit at room temp 20 to 30 minutes. Season steaks liberally with salt and pepper.

Heat a large cast-iron skillet and add grapeseed oil. When pan is extremely hot, add steaks. Sear on all sides, about 2 minutes each, until golden brown. Reduce heat slightly and add butter, thyme and garlic. Baste steaks with infused butter, rotating constantly to cook evenly. When steaks reach medium-rare (135°) or just under, remove to a rack and let rest at least 5 minutes before serving.

■ **Broccolini** In a large sauté pan, heat olive oil over medium. Add Broccolini and sauté 5 minutes to bring out color but not char. Deglaze pan with a squeeze of lemon juice and some lemon zest. Season with salt, pepper and if desired, more lemon juice.

■ To serve, add squash to a piping bag or squeeze bottle and squiggle some onto center of each plate. Add 2 spoonfuls of potato puree on top, off to one side. Place steak over potato puree and top with a Parmesan tuile. Lay 2 Broccolini florets across each plate.

PER SERVING 835 **CAL**; 53 g **FAT** (29 g **SAT**); 711 mg **SODIUM**; 31 g **CARB**; 5 g **FIBER**; 5 g **SUGARS**; 60 g **PRO**

CRUNCH TIME

With sugar and spice and everything nice, your favorite snack can go sweet or savory.

Spicy Popcorn Mix

MAKES 11 cups **PREP** 5 minutes

- 8 cups salted popcorn
- 2 tsp Cajun spice blend
- 1 cup pretzel sticks
- 1 cup hot peanuts
- 1 cup spicy crunchy chickpeas, such as Saffron Road Chipotle

■ In a large bowl, toss popcorn with remaining ingredients.

Tip Parmesan crisps and wasabi peas are another way to add a little protein to your mix, which helps move your afternoon treat from mindless to mindful.

Store It Seal in an airtight container; it will keep for up to 3 days.

PER SERVING 216 **CAL**; 11 g **FAT** (1 g **SAT**); 336 mg **SODIUM**; 25 g **CARB**; 5 g **FIBER**; 2 g **SUGARS**; 8 g **PRO**

Sweet Popcorn Mix

MAKES 11 cups **PREP** 5 minutes

- 8 cups kettle corn
- 2 tbsp unsweetened cocoa powder
- 1 cup dried tart cherries
- 1 cup candied nuts
- 1 cup sweet crunchy chickpeas, such as Saffron Road Salted Caramel

■ In a large bowl, toss kettle corn with cocoa powder. Stir in remaining ingredients.

Tip Peanut butter bites are another way to add a little protein to your mix, which helps move your afternoon treat from mindless to mindful.

Store It Seal in an airtight container; it will keep for up to 3 days.

PER SERVING 257 **CAL**; 10 g **FAT** (1 g **SAT**); 138 mg **SODIUM**; 38 g **CARB**; 4 g **FIBER**; 25 g **SUGARS**; 4 g **PRO**

BAKE LIKE A BOSS

Tips and tricks from our test kitchen that will take the fear out of baking.

NEAPOLITAN COOKIES

Rest Your Dough Seriously, do it. Your cookies will be so much better! For our Neapolitan Cookies, the first resting period allows the moisture to evenly distribute throughout the dough and the fat to solidify again, making the dough firm enough to roll out. The second rest sets the layers so they'll be sliceable and hold their shape when baked. Even chocolate chip cookies benefit from resting: A dough that's refrigerated overnight bakes up browner and with a richer flavor thanks to properly hydrated flour and a breakdown in protein and starches. You want to put the dough into the oven cold; this allows the fat to melt evenly, which controls the spread and gives your cookies a nice soft center.

Neapolitan Cookies

MAKES about 2 dozen   **PREP** 30 minutes   **REFRIGERATE** 1 hour   **REST** 4 hour to overnight   **BAKE** 12 minutes

- 2¼ **cups all-purpose flour**
- ½ **cup cornstarch**
- ½ **tsp salt**
- 2¼ **sticks unsalted butter, at room temp**
- 1 **cup confectioners' sugar**
- 2 **tbsp unsweetened cocoa powder**
- ½ **tsp vanilla extract**
- ¼ **tsp almond extract**
- ¼ **tsp cherry extract**
- 8 **to 10 drops red food coloring**
- 1 **egg white, slightly beaten**

■ Sift together first 3 ingredients.

■ Beat butter and sugar until light and fluffy. Gradually beat in flour mixture until soft dough forms. Divide dough into thirds.

■ With plastic gloves on, knead cocoa powder and vanilla into one piece of dough. Knead almond extract into another. Knead cherry extract and red food coloring into third piece. Flatten into disks; wrap each separately in plastic wrap. Refrigerate 1 hour or until firm.

■ Roll each disk between 2 pieces of wax paper to ½ inch thick.

■ Remove top piece of wax paper from chocolate dough. Brush with some egg white. Remove all paper from almond dough; place on chocolate dough and brush top with egg white. Remove wax paper from top of cherry dough; invert onto almond dough. Wrap in plastic wrap. Refrigerate several hours or overnight.

■ Heat oven to 375°.

■ Peel remaining wax paper from dough. Trim edges into even rectangle. Cut dough in half lengthwise and then crosswise into ¼-inch-thick slices. Place slices on baking sheets, spacing slices 1 inch apart.

■ Bake until set, 10 to 12 minutes. Cool on wire racks.

PER SERVING 145 **CAL**; 8 g **FAT** (5 g **SAT**); 1 g **PRO**; 16 g **CARB**; 5 g **SUGARS**; 0 g **FIBER**; 50 mg **SODIUM**

Cookie Tip Cookies with a high fat content, like Neapolitan Cookies, can be baked directly on a sheet pan. But for cookies that might stick to the sheet—like meringues or cookies rolled in sugar—parchment paper and silicone mats are a smart option. You may sacrifice some deep browning on the bottom, but they'll be easier to remove.

Handle with Care The purpose of whipping egg whites is to beat air into them, giving them volume and structure—then you need to be gentle with them so they don't deflate! Follow the folding tips below to keep them fluffy. And FYI, coating the soufflé dish with sugar isn't just for flavor: The sugar granules act as little footholds for the aerated soufflé batter to climb.

Tangerine Soufflé

SERVES 6 **PREP** 25 minutes **BAKE** 40 minutes

- ¾ **cup plus 2 tbsp granulated sugar**
- 2 **tbsp unsalted butter**
- 2 **tbsp all-purpose flour**
- 4 **tangerines, zested (for 2 tsp zest), then squeezed (for ¾ cup juice)**
- 6 **large eggs, separated**
- ½ **tsp cream of tartar**
- ¼ **tsp salt**
- 1 **tbsp confectioners' sugar**

■ With shelf in lowest position, heat oven to 350°.

■ Coat a 6-cup soufflé dish with cooking spray. Add 2 tbsp granulated sugar; shake to coat sides and bottom. Tap out excess.

■ In a small saucepan, melt butter over medium-high. Whisk in flour, then gradually whisk in juice. Boil 3 minutes; remove from heat. Beat yolks until light in color, 3 minutes. Beat in ½ cup granulated sugar until fluffy, 2 minutes. Whisk in zest and 1 tbsp thickened juice mixture. Slowly stir in remaining juice mixture.

■ With clean beaters and bowl, beat egg whites, cream of tartar and salt until foamy. Beat in ¼ cup granulated sugar for medium-stiff peaks. Fold ¼ of whites into yolk mixture, then fold in remaining whites. Transfer to prepared dish.

■ Bake until puffed and browned (do not open oven), 35 to 40 minutes. Dust with confectioners' sugar.

PER SERVING 232 **CAL**; 9 g **FAT** (4 g **SAT**); 7 g **PRO**; 32 g **CARB**; 30 g **SUGARS**; 0 g **FIBER**; 169 mg **SODIUM**

Tempering Tip The trick to tempering egg yolks is to add the hot liquid very gradually, whisking constantly. You want to warm them without cooking them (and ending up with scrambled eggs!).

How to Fold In Egg Whites With a rubber spatula, gently stir about ¼ of your whipped whites into batter (they will deflate but will loosen batter). Add remaining whites in 2 batches, using this technique: Pile on the egg whites. Bisect whites and batter with the spatula. Then, starting from bottom of bowl, scoop up batter and gently flip it on top. Give bowl a quarter turn after each fold. Bisect and flip again. Continue to fold just until there aren't any streaks.

TANGERINE
SOUFFLÉ

CHEESE-STUFFED
PULL-APART
BREAD

Don't Be Afraid of Yeast Yeast is an organism, which tends to make people nervous—you do actually have to determine if it's alive or dead. Put about ¼ tsp yeast and a bit of sugar in a small bowl of warm (not hot) water. Let it sit for about 10 minutes. If it foams up, you're good to go!

Cheese-Stuffed Pull-Apart Bread

SERVES 10   **PREP** 30 minutes   **LET RISE** 3 hours   **BAKE** 35 minutes

- 1½ **cups all-purpose flour**
- 1 **cup bread flour**
- 1 **tsp active dry yeast**
- 1½ **tbsp sugar**
- 1¼ **tsp salt**
- 2 **tbsp unsalted butter, cubed, plus 2 tbsp, melted, and more for bowl and pan**
- 2 **large eggs**
- 4 **logs string cheese, cut into 6 pieces each**
-    **Flaky sea salt**

■ Combine ½ cup all-purpose flour, ½ cup bread flour, yeast, sugar and salt in a large bowl.

■ Heat ½ cup water and cubed butter in a small saucepan until butter melts. Let cool to 120° to 130°. Add to flour mixture; beat until combined.

■ Whisk eggs. Reserve 1 tbsp and beat remaining egg into bowl. Add remaining flours slowly, until dough pulls away from sides of bowl.

■ Transfer to floured work surface. Knead 7 to 9 minutes, until smooth and elastic, adding flour as needed to prevent sticking. Place in a well-greased bowl, turning to coat. Cover with clean kitchen towel. Let rise in a warm place until doubled in volume, 1½ hours.

■ Gently punch dough down. Let rest 5 minutes. Grease a 9x5½x3-inch loaf pan.

■ Divide dough in half. Roll each half into a 12-inch rope. Cut each rope into 12 equal pieces. With floured hands, shape pieces into balls. Insert 1 piece of cheese into each ball.

Arrange balls, touching, in 2 rows in pan. Cover with clean kitchen towel. Let rise until doubled in volume, 1 to 1½ hours.

■ Heat oven to 375°.

■ Brush loaf with reserved egg, being careful not to deflate dough.

■ Bake until golden and hollow-sounding when tapped, 30 to 35 minutes.

■ Remove from pan, running knife around edges if needed. Cool on a wire rack 5 minutes. Brush with melted butter and sprinkle with salt.

PER SERVING 205 **CAL**; 8 g **FAT** (4 g **SAT**); 8 g **PRO**; 26 g **CARB**; 2 g **SUGARS**; 1 g **FIBER**; 418 mg **SODIUM**

Help Yeast Do Its Job Don't shortchange the kneading process: It develops the gluten that ultimately gives your bread its structure. Knead until the dough is smooth and elastic and bounces back when pressed with your thumb. And let the rising process run its course: If your dough doesn't double in size in the time the recipe says, all is not lost! Room temp is likely the culprit—if your kitchen is cool, it's going to take a little longer for the yeast to lift that mass of dough.

Weigh Your Ingredients Yes, we know it sounds like a pain in the butt, but we swear it's the single best thing you can do to improve your baking. (Umm, hello, how do you think pound cake got its name? A pound of each ingredient! Even bakers back in the 1700s knew better.) Here's why it matters: People have a tendency to pack dry ingredients—particularly flour—into their measuring cups, which can lead to dry, dense baked goods. To test yourself, measure your flour as you normally would and then weigh it: 1 cup of flour should come in at 4¼ ounces; a cup of sugar should weigh 7 ounces. Even a little bit more or less than that can impact the texture and flavor of the final product.

Pound Cake

SERVES 12   **PREP** 25 minutes   **BAKE** 1 hour

- ½   **tsp salt**
- 2   **sticks (8 oz) unsalted butter, at room temp, plus more for pan**
- 2¾   **cups (11.7 oz) all-purpose flour, plus more for pan**
- ½   **tsp baking soda**
- 1¾   **cups (12.25 oz) granulated sugar**
- 6   **large eggs**
- 1   **tbsp vanilla extract**
- 1   **cup sour cream**
- ¼   **cup milk**
  Confectioners' sugar, for dusting

■ Heat oven to 350°. Grease an 8-cup Bundt pan generously. Add a little flour; tilt to coat.

■ Whisk flour, baking soda and salt.

■ Beat butter and granulated sugar until fluffy. Beat in eggs, 1 at a time. Add vanilla.

■ Combine sour cream and milk. Beat in half of flour mixture, then sour cream mixture. Beat in remaining flour mixture.

■ Transfer to prepared pan. Bake until cake springs back when pressed, about 1 hour. Cool 10 minutes.

■ Carefully flip pan to release cake; cool completely. Dust with confectioners' sugar.

PER SERVING 429 **CAL**; 21 g **FAT** (12 g **SAT**); 7 g **PRO**; 53 g **CARB**; 31 g **SUGARS**; 1 g **FIBER**; 195 mg **SODIUM**

Tip Most cakes—especially those baked in a faceted, intricate pan—are easier to remove if you grease and flour the pan. And don't be stingy with the fat (butter is common, but shortening and cooking spray work, too). We used a full 2 tbsp of softened butter for our pound cake.

POUND CAKE

FAMILY DINNERS

Because you've gotta get food on the table.

FARRO WITH
CAULIFLOWER AND
HAZELNUT GREMOLATA

Eating a variety of grains such as farro, bulgur, quinoa, barley and rice adds fiber and protein to your diet.

Farro with Cauliflower and Hazelnut Gremolata

MAKES 4 servings   **PREP** 50 minutes

- 1   **cup farro**
- ¾   **tsp salt**
- 1   **large head cauliflower, quartered and any leaves removed**
- ¼   **tsp freshly ground black pepper**
- 5   **tbsp olive oil**
- 1   **packed cup parsley leaves and stems**
- 2   **cloves garlic**
- 1   **large lemon**
- ½   **cup toasted chopped hazelnuts**

■ Bring 1 cup farro plus ½ tsp salt and 2½ cups water to a boil, then simmer 25 to 40 minutes. Drain excess water.

■ On a rimmed baking sheet, toss cauliflower with 3 tbsp olive oil and ¼ tsp each salt and freshly ground pepper. Roast at 450° for 25 minutes, turning halfway through.

■ Meanwhile, finely chop parsley and grate garlic. Zest and juice lemon. Stir parsley, garlic, zest, juice and hazelnuts with 2 tbsp olive oil; season with salt and freshly ground pepper. Serve cauliflower over farro and top with gremolata.

PER SERVING 443 **CAL**; 26 g **FAT** (3 g **SAT**); 679 mg **SODIUM**; 45 g **CARB**; 9 g **FIBER**; 5 g **SUGARS**; 13 g **PRO**

BULGUR WITH SALMON AND CARROTS

Bulgur with Salmon and Carrots

MAKES 4 servings   **PREP** 30 minutes

- 1   **lb peeled carrots, split and cut into 2-inch chunks**
- 2   **tbsp olive oil**
- ¾   **tsp salt**
- ¼   **tsp black pepper**
- 1   **cup coarse bulgur**
- 4   **center-cut salmon fillets (6 oz each)**
- 4   **tsp pomegranate molasses, plus more for drizzling**
- 2   **oz crumbled feta**

■ Toss carrots with 1 tbsp olive oil and ¼ tsp each salt and pepper. Arrange in a single layer on a rimmed sheet pan; roast at 400° for 12 minutes.

■ Meanwhile, bring bulgur plus ½ tsp salt and 2 cups water to a boil, then simmer 10 to 12 minutes.

■ Pat dry salmon fillets. Brush skin sides with 1 tbsp olive oil. Flip and brush each fillet with 1 tsp pomegranate molasses and sprinkle with salt and pepper. Stir carrots and move to one side of pan. Add salmon, skin sides down, and roast 12 minutes more. Let rest 5 minutes, then flake into large pieces.

■ Toss with bulgur, carrots and feta. Drizzle with additional molasses.

PER SERVING 551 **CAL**; 23 g **FAT** (5 g **SAT**); 854 mg **SODIUM**; 41 g **CARB**; 7 g **FIBER**; 10 g **SUGARS**; 46 g **PRO**

Quinoa is often used like a grain, but it is actually a seed and naturally gluten-free. The farro, bulgur and barley in these recipes all contain gluten, so if needed, swap in rice, gluten-free steel-cut oats or buckwheat (despite the name, it does not contain gluten).

Quinoa Salad with Five-Spice Chicken

MAKES 4 servings   **PREP** 30 MINUTES

- **2   tbsp vegetable oil**
- **¾   tsp salt**
- **¾   tsp freshly ground black pepper**
- **1   tsp Chinese five-spice powder**
- **4   bone-in, skin-on chicken thighs (about 1¾ lb total)**
- **2   cups baby spinach**
- **2   cups instant quinoa**
- **½   cup diced English cucumber**
- **Zest and juice of 1 large lemon**

■ Heat oil in a large stainless skillet over medium-high. Combine ½ tsp each salt and freshly ground pepper with Chinese five-spice powder. Rub all over chicken thighs. Place, skin sides down, in pan; cook 12 minutes. Flip thighs, cover pan and cook until temp reaches 165°, about 10 to 12 minutes.

■ Meanwhile, roughly chop baby spinach. Cook quinoa according to package directions. Fold spinach into hot quinoa. Stir in cucumber and ¼ tsp each salt and freshly ground pepper. Add ¾ of lemon zest and juice to quinoa. Serve thighs over quinoa and top with remaining juice and zest.

PER SERVING 547 **CAL**; 36 g **FAT** (9 g **SAT**); 597 mg **SODIUM**; 23 g **CARB**; 4 g **FIBER**; 1 g **SUGARS**; 32 g **PRO**

QUINOA SALAD
WITH FIVE-SPICE
CHICKEN

Store cooked grains in the fridge for up to 4 days. Or spread cooled cooked grains flat in a resealable bag and freeze for up to 2 months.

Dirty Rice-Style Barley

MAKES 4 servings **PREP** 1 hour

- 1 **cup pearl barley**
- ½ **tsp salt**
- 1½ **tsp Cajun seasoning**
- 1 **small onion**
- 1 **red bell pepper**
- 2 **ribs celery, plus leaves for serving**
- 1 **pound bulk spicy sausage**

■ Bring barley, salt and ½ tsp Cajun seasoning and 3 cups water to a boil, then simmer 45 to 60 minutes. Meanwhile, chop onion, bell pepper and celery.

■ When barley has cooked for 40 minutes, cook sausage in a large pot over medium 5 minutes, stirring to break up. Add onion, red pepper and celery to pot and cook, stirring occasionally, 15 minutes.

■ Stir in cooked barley and 1 tsp Cajun seasoning. Serve topped with celery leaves.

PER SERVING 522 **CAL**; 29 g **FAT** (9 g **SAT**); 1,151 mg **SODIUM**; 44 g **CARB**; 9 g **FIBER**; 4 g **SUGARS**; 23 g **PRO**

Basmati with Lamb Kebabs

MAKES 4 servings **PREP** 25 minutes

- ¾ **tsp salt**
- 1 **cup basmati rice**
- 1 **packed cup fresh cilantro**
- 6 **cloves garlic**
- 2 **(2-inch) pieces fresh ginger**
- 3 **tbsp vegetable oil**
- 1 **tsp ground cumin**
- 1 **lb boneless lamb leg, cut into 1½-inch cubes**
- ¼ **tsp freshly ground black pepper**

■ Heat grill to medium-high. In a medium saucepan, bring 1¾ cups water and ¼ tsp salt to a boil. Add basmati rice, reduce heat and simmer 20 minutes.

■ Meanwhile, reserve some cilantro leaves. In blender, pulse remaining cilantro stems and leaves with garlic and ginger. Add oil, cumin and ¼ tsp salt; blend until mostly smooth.

■ Toss lamb with ¼ tsp each salt and freshly ground pepper and ⅔ of garlic mixture. Thread onto metal skewers and grill, turning occasionally, 10 to 11 minutes for medium-rare. Rest 5 minutes.

■ Stir remaining garlic mixture into hot rice and let stand 3 minutes. Top rice with lamb and torn cilantro leaves. Serve with a green salad.

PER SERVING 413 **CAL**; 16 g **FAT** (4 g **SAT**); 519 mg **SODIUM**; 41 g **CARB**; 0 g **FIBER**; 0 g **SUGARS**; 24 g **PRO**

BASMATI WITH
LAMB KEBABS

4 BREAKFASTS WITH CREAM CHEESE

Go beyond bagels.

Strawberry Cheesecake Parfaits

Alternate layers of strawberry sauce and sweetened cream cheese and refrigerate until the a.m. Top with granola just before heading out.

MAKES 4 servings **PREP** 5 minutes **COOK** 15 minutes

- 1 **(14 to 16 oz) pkg frozen strawberries**
- 1 **tbsp cornstarch**
- 5 **tbsp honey**
- 8 **oz softened cream cheese**
- ⅓ **cup sour cream or Greek yogurt**
- 2 **tbsp milk**
- ½ **cup gluten-free granola**

■ In a medium saucepan, toss strawberries with cornstarch. Stir in ¼ cup water and 3 tbsp honey. Cook 15 minutes over medium, breaking up berries with a spoon. Cool, then refrigerate until layering.

■ Meanwhile, beat cream cheese with sour cream, milk and 2 tbsp honey. Layer spoonfuls of strawberry and cream cheese mixtures in 4 small jars. Top each with 2 tbsp gluten-free granola.

PER SERVING 420 **CAL**; 24 g **FAT** (13 g **SAT**); 192 mg **SODIUM**; 46 g **CARB**; 3 g **FIBER**; 32 g **SUGARS**; 8 g **PRO**

Fluffy Biscuits

For the ultimate breakfast upgrade, skip the English muffin and stack a biscuit with sausage and eggs.

MAKES 7 or 8 servings **PREP** 10 minutes **BAKE** 18 minutes

- 2½ **cups self-rising flour**
- ½ **stick cold unsalted butter, cubed**
- 4 **oz cream cheese, cut up**
- ⅔ **cup milk**

■ In a food processor, combine flour, butter and cheese. Pulse until no large pieces of butter or cheese remain. With processor running, add milk. Process until dough comes together and "cleans" side of bowl.

■ Roll out on a floured surface to ¾-inch thickness. Cut into 3-inch rounds, gently rerolling scraps. Bake on parchment at 375° for 15 to 18 minutes.

PER SERVING 287 **CAL**; 13 g **FAT** (8 g **SAT**); 594 mg **SODIUM**; 35 g **CARB**; 1 g **FIBER**; 2 g **SUGARS**; 6 g **PRO**

Cranberry Cinnamon Buns

Give your teens a reason to get out of bed on Saturday! Thaw the frozen bread dough the night before and you'll be ready to roll.

MAKES 12 servings **PREP** 10 minutes **RISE** 45 minutes **BAKE** 30 minutes

- 8 **oz cream cheese**
- ½ **cup confectioners' sugar**
- 1 **tbsp milk**
- ¼ **tsp ground cinnamon**
- 1 **lb thawed frozen bread dough**
- ½ **cup sweetened dried cranberries, chopped**
- ⅓ **cup walnuts, finely chopped**
- 2 **tbsp melted butter**

■ With a hand mixer, beat 4 oz cream cheese, ¼ cup confectioners' sugar, milk and cinnamon.

■ On a floured surface, roll dough to a 15x10-inch rectangle. Spread cream cheese mixture over dough and top with cranberries and walnuts. Starting with a long side, roll up to enclose filling. Pinch seam and trim ends. Slice into 12 pieces and place on a greased baking sheet. Cover with plastic; let rise until doubled, 45 minutes.

■ Brush with melted butter and bake at 350° for 25 to 30 minutes.

■ Beat remaining 4 oz cream cheese with ¼ cup confectioners' sugar and a little water or milk. Drizzle over buns.

PER SERVING 230 **CAL**; 10 g **FAT** (4 g **SAT**); 273 mg **SODIUM**; 30 g **CARB**; 1 g **FIBER**; 12 g **SUGARS**; 5 g **PRO**

B.E.C. Pizza

This take on a bacon, egg and cheese sandwich is ready in under 20 minutes.

MAKES 4 servings **PREP** 5 minutes **BAKE** 13 minutes

- 4 **oz cream cheese**
- 2 **scallions, chopped**
- 2 **tbsp snipped chives, plus more for serving**
- 2 **tbsp grated Parmesan**
- 1 **(10.6 oz) pizza crust**
- 4 **large eggs**
  Salt and black pepper
- 3 **slices cooked bacon, chopped**

■ Combine first 4 ingredients in a mini chopper. Process until blended and smooth. Spread on pizza crust, making a slight lip at edges.

■ Carefully crack eggs onto crust and season with salt and pepper. Bake at 400° for 5 minutes, then scatter bacon on top. Cook 6 to 8 minutes, until eggs are set. Sprinkle with more chives; cut into 4 pieces.

PER SERVING 415 **CAL**; 20 g **FAT** (10 g **SAT**); 777 mg **SODIUM**; 40 g **CARB**; 0 g **FIBER**; 3 g **SUGARS**; 18 g **PRO**

BLACK & WHITE

Halloween party food that does double duty for adults or teens.

**ARUGULA SALAD
WITH BASIC
VINAIGRETTE**

**FARFALLE WITH HAM
AND PEAS**

Black and white snacks for nibbling, then a pasta and salad that go two ways: You make one big batch of each, then split it in half. The kids get the "basic" versions—pasta with ham and peas, salad with croutons. The big difference on the grown-ups' table? More veg! (Oh, and a killer feta dip.) Your version of the pasta gets sautéed leeks and red peppers. Beets and goat cheese are added to the salad.

Farfalle with Ham and Peas

SERVES 12   **PREP** 15 minutes   **COOK** 15 minutes

- 1 **lb black-and-white farfalle**
- ¼ **cup olive oil**
- 6 **cloves garlic**
- 8 **oz diced ham steak**
- 1 **cup frozen peas, thawed**
- ½ **tsp freshly ground black pepper**
- ¼ **tsp salt**
  Grated Parmesan

ADULT VERSION

- 1 **large leek, cleaned and sliced**
- 2 **tbsp olive oil**
- ½ **cup roasted red pepper strips**

■ Bring a large pot of salted water to a boil. Add farfalle and cook per package directions, about 11 minutes.

■ Meanwhile, heat oil in a large skillet over medium. Slice garlic and add to skillet; cook 6 minutes. Stir in ham and peas; cook 3 minutes or until heated through.

■ Drain farfalle and return to pot. Add skillet contents, pepper and salt. Stir until combined, then divide in half. **Adult Version:** Cook leek in oil 4 minutes. Stir in pepper and heat through. Add to half the pasta. Serve both with grated Parmesan.

PER SERVING 238 **CAL**; 7 g **FAT** (2 g **SAT**); 358 mg **SODIUM**; 31 g **CARB**; 2 g **FIBER**; 1 g **SUGARS**; 11 g **PRO**

Basic Vinaigrette

MAKES 24 servings

- ¼ **cup fresh lemon juice**
- ¼ **cup white wine vinegar**
- 2 **tbsp minced shallot**
- 2 **tsp Dijon mustard**
- 2 **tsp honey**
- ½ **tsp salt**
- ¼ **tsp freshly ground black pepper**
- ½ **cup extra-virgin olive oil**

■ Combine first 7 ingredients in a bowl and whisk until smooth. Add oil in a thin stream while whisking. Taste and adjust seasonings. Store in fridge up to 2 weeks.

PER SERVING 116 **CAL**; 12 g **FAT** (2 g **SAT**); 156 mg **SODIUM**; 2 g **CARB**; 0 g **FIBER**; 2 g **SUGARS**; 0 g **PRO**

Party Trays

TEEN

- ☐ **Flavored cheddar**
- ☐ **Jumbo raisins**
- ☐ **Dried Calimyrna figs**
- ☐ **Black grapes**
- ☐ **Salami and/or pepperoni**
- ☐ **Rice crackers**

ADULT

- ☐ **Feta dip with black bread toasts**
- ☐ **Blue cheese**
- ☐ **Black figs**
- ☐ **Purple carrots, jicama**
- ☐ **Cauliflower florets**
- ☐ **Oil-cured olives**
- ☐ **Dry-cured salami**
- ☐ **Rice crackers**

WARM FETA DIP

Teens are going to think this doughnut wall is the coolest thing ever (actually, so will the adults).

Halloween Doughnuts

Two simple elements—store-bought doughnuts and homemade frosting—add up to a high-impact dessert.

MAKES 24 servings

- **4** **oz bittersweet chocolate, chopped**
- **½** **cup heavy cream**
- **Black gel food coloring**
- **2** **cups plus 6 tbsp confectioners' sugar**
- **¼** **cup milk**
- **24** **plain doughnuts, such as Entenmann's Soft'ees**
- **Black decorating sugar**
- **Silver decorating sugar**
- **White jimmies**

■ Place chocolate in a medium bowl. Microwave heavy cream 1 minute, until just steaming. Whisk 1 generous drop black gel food coloring into cream and pour over chocolate. Let stand 2 minutes, then whisk until smooth.

■ Meanwhile, whisk 1 cup plus 2 tbsp confectioners' sugar and 2 tbsp milk in a bowl. Whisk 1¼ cups confectioners' sugar and 2 tbsp milk in another bowl and add 1 drop black gel food coloring.

■ Dip 8 doughnuts in chocolate and sprinkle with black sugar. Dip 8 doughnuts in gray frosting and sprinkle with silver sugar. Dip 8 doughnuts in white frosting and top with jimmies. Let dry.

PER SERVING 281 **CAL**; 15 g **FAT** (7 g **SAT**); 214 mg **SODIUM**; 35 g **CARB**; 0 g **FIBER**; 20 g **SUGARS**; 3 g **PRO**

Warm Feta Dip

SERVES 8 **PREP** 10 minutes **BAKE** 35 minutes

- **8** **oz feta cheese**
- **¼** **cup milk**
- **1** **pkg (12 oz) whipped cream cheese**
- **¼** **cup minced chives**
- **¼** **cup chopped flat-leaf parsley**
- **¼** **cup finely chopped roasted red pepper**
- **1** **tsp chopped thyme leaves**
- **Zest of 1 lemon**
- **¼** **tsp salt**
- **Coarsely ground black pepper**
- **6** **thin slices pumpernickel**

■ Heat oven to 375°. Crumble feta into a large bowl and add milk. Beat with a hand mixer until relatively smooth. Add cream cheese and beat until combined. Fold in next 6 ingredients.

■ Transfer to an oven-safe dish and sprinkle with pepper. Bake 15 minutes.

■ Meanwhile, cut each slice of bread into 8 squares. Place on 1 or 2 baking sheets and add to oven. Bake

10 minutes, flip, then bake 10 minutes more. Remove dip and bread from oven. Serve warm.

PER SERVING 276 **CAL**; 20 g **FAT** (12 g **SAT**); 729 mg **SODIUM**; 16 g **CARB**; 0 g **FIBER**; 3 g **SUGARS**; 10 g **PRO**

DIY Doughnut Wall

measuring tape

pencil

2-ftx3-ft solid wood board

drill fitted with ⅜-inch paddle bit

painters tape

gray spray paint

⅜-inch wooden dowels

rubber mallet

■ Measure and mark where you want the doughnuts to go. We spaced ours 2 inches apart from each other and 2 inches away from the edge of the board. Drill holes where marked all the way through the board. Place a piece of painters tape diagonally across the board and spray one side with gray paint. Once the paint is dry, remove tape and hammer in wooden dowels with the rubber mallet.

HALLOWEEN
DOUGHNUTS

NOVEMBER

251

264

263

FAMILY DINNERS

Because you've gotta get food on the table.

CHICKEN
PUTTANESCA

PORK CHILE VERDE

Although it's not necessary to brown meats and poultry before you place them in the slow cooker, it does make the flavor and texture of the final dish better.

Chicken Puttanesca

MAKES 6 servings   **PREP** 10 minutes   **SLOW COOK** 5½ hours on HIGH

- 2   **tbsp vegetable oil**
- 1¾ **lbs boneless, skinless chicken thighs, cut into large pieces**
- ½   **tsp salt**
- ½   **tsp black pepper**
- 1   **(20 oz) can fire-roasted crushed tomatoes**
- ½   **cup garlic-stuffed green olives, halved**
- 1   **tbsp anchovy paste**
- 1   **tsp packed fresh oregano, minced**
- 1½ **cups orzo**

■ Heat oil in a stainless skillet over medium-high. Season chicken with ¼ tsp each salt and pepper. Add to pan and brown, turning, 4 minutes. Transfer to slow cooker along with tomatoes, olives, anchovy paste, oregano and ¼ tsp each salt and pepper. Cover and cook on HIGH for 5½ hours. During last ½ hour, cook orzo on stovetop per package directions. Serve chicken over orzo.

PER SERVING 341 **CAL**; 13 g **FAT** (2 g **SAT**); 36 g **PRO**; 21 g **CARB**; 5 g **SUGARS**; 2 g **FIBER**; 1,122 mg **SODIUM**

Pork Chile Verde

MAKES 6 servings   **PREP** 15 minutes   **SLOW COOK** 6 hours on HIGH

- 3   **lb boneless pork shoulder, cubed**
- ½   **tsp salt**
- ½   **tsp black pepper**
- ½   **tsp ground cumin**
- 2   **tbsp vegetable oil**
- 6   **cloves garlic, sliced**
- 1   **cup medium salsa verde**
- 1   **tsp dried oregano**
- 1   **(15 oz) can small white beans, drained and rinsed**
-     **Sour cream and cilantro (optional)**

■ Season pork with salt, pepper and cumin. Heat oil in a large stainless skillet over medium-high and brown pork in batches, about 3 minutes per batch. Transfer pork to slow cooker and add garlic, salsa verde, oregano and ½ cup water. Cover and cook on HIGH for 6 hours. Uncover and stir in beans. Serve topped with sour cream and cilantro, if desired.

Tip If you like, opt for boneless chicken thighs instead.

Make It Even Heartier Spoon over white or brown rice and/or add halved small potatoes for an energy-boosting carb hit.

PER SERVING 461 **CAL**; 25 g **FAT** (7 g **SAT**); 42 g **PRO**; 15 g **CARB**; 2 g **SUGARS**; 4 g **FIBER**; 900 mg **SODIUM**

Lacinato kale—also called Tuscan kale (or dinosaur kale, for its nubby textured leaves)—isn't always as readily available as the more common curly-leaf kale. If you can't find it, curly-leaf kale works just fine in the Sausage and Kale Soup.

Sausage and Kale Soup

MAKES 6 servings **PREP** 15 minutes **SLOW COOK** 4½ hours on LOW

- 1 **lb mild sausage links (not precooked)**
- 2 **tbsp vegetable oil**
- 1 **medium onion, diced**
- 4 **large carrots, peeled and diced**
- 1 **tsp fennel seeds**
- 1 **(32 oz) carton low-sodium chicken broth**
- ½ **tsp salt**
- 4 **cups sliced lacinato kale**
   Shaved Parmesan (optional)

■ Brown sausage in oil for 4 minutes, turning once. Transfer to a slow cooker and top with onion, carrots and fennel seeds. Stir in broth, salt and 2 cups water. Cook on HIGH for 4 hours or LOW for 6½ hours. Remove sausages to cutting board and slice into ¼-inch-thick coins. Add back to slow cooker along with kale. Cover and cook 30 minutes. Sprinkle with shaved Parmesan, if desired.

PER SERVING 326 **CAL**; 24 g **FAT** (6 g **SAT**); 16 g **PRO**; 13 g **CARB**; 5 g **SUGARS**; 3 g **FIBER**; 871 mg **SODIUM**

Red Wine-Braised Beef

MAKES 6 servings **PREP** 20 minutes **SLOW COOK** 5 hours on HIGH

- 3 **lbs beef stew meat**
- ¼ **cup plus 2 tsp all-purpose flour**
- ½ **tsp salt**
- ¼ **tsp ground black pepper**
- 3 **tbsp vegetable oil**
- 10 **oz mushrooms, cleaned and quartered**
- 3 **large carrots, peeled and cut into coins**
- 1 **medium onion, diced**
- 1½ **cups red wine**
- 3 **or 4 sprigs fresh thyme**
   Mashed potatoes or polenta

■ Toss beef with ¼ cup flour, ½ tsp salt and ¼ tsp pepper. Brown in oil in 2 batches over high for 3 minutes per batch. Transfer to slow cooker. Toss mushrooms with remaining 2 tsp flour. Add to slow cooker; stir in carrots and onion. Pour wine into same skillet and bring to a simmer, scraping browned bits from bottom of pan. Add to slow cooker along with thyme. Cover and cook on HIGH for 5 hours. Adjust seasoning and serve over mashed potatoes or polenta.

PER SERVING 586 **CAL**; 23 g **FAT** (7 g **SAT**); 76 g **PRO**; 13 g **CARB**; 4 g **SUGARS**; 2 g **FIBER**; 565 mg **SODIUM**

RED WINE-BRAISED
BEEF

SPAGHETTI PIE

Just a handful of ingredients is required to make this family-pleasing saucy pasta pie. Serve it with a crisp green salad or steamed green beans on the side.

Spaghetti Pie

MAKES 6 servings   **PREP** x minutes   **SLOW COOK** 4 hours on LOW

- **1 lb spaghetti**
- **¼ cup seasoned bread crumbs**
- **4 large eggs**
- **3 cups marinara sauce, plus more for serving**
- **1 (12 oz) jar roasted red peppers, drained and chopped**
- **½ cup plus 1 tbsp grated Parmesan**
- **½ tsp salt**
- **½ tsp black pepper**

■ Cook spaghetti for half the time directed on package. Drain. Meanwhile, coat a large slow cooker with cooking spray and dust bottom and halfway up sides with 3 tbsp seasoned bread crumbs. Whisk eggs. Combine spaghetti, marinara, red peppers, Parmesan, salt and black pepper. Fold in eggs and add to prepared slow cooker. Sprinkle with remaining 1 tbsp each grated Parmesan and bread crumbs. Cover and cook on LOW for 4 hours. Serve with additional marinara sauce on the side.

Make Ahead Cook, drain and refrigerate spaghetti. Mix peppers with marinara, Parmesan, salt and black pepper and pop in the fridge.

PER SERVING 479 **CAL**; 10 g **FAT** (4 g **SAT**); 21 g **PRO**; 72 g **CARB**; 11 g **SUGARS**; 2 g **FIBER**; 1,323 mg **SODIUM**

Slow Cooker vs. Pressure Cooker

■ Both use moisture to cook foods.

■ A slow cooker raises the temp over a long period of time, while pressure cookers use steam to quickly cook your food.

■ Both are good for beans and tough cuts of meat.

■ Some people prefer slow cookers because they can see their food while it is cooking and their dinner is ready right when they get home.

Smart and Safe

■ As much as we all want to pile a bunch of ingredients into the crock and leave for work, many foods—like beef or pork—benefit from browning first.

■ Never add still-frozen foods to the crock. They may not reach the proper temperature to cook through and kill harmful bacteria.

■ Use the right-size slow cooker for your dish, filling it no more than two-thirds full (we used a 6-qt crock).

■ Older slow cookers can be inefficient. Newer models have features like auto shut-off and Bluetooth connectivity.

THE ULTIMATE THANKSGIVING SURVIVAL GUIDE

It's kind of like the Super Bowl of holiday hosting—lots of hype (plus some drama and trash talk) before the big game. This year, the order of the day for Thanksgiving is to chill. Everything you need is right here: recipes you can easily adapt for picky preferences.

BASIC ROAST
TURKEY,
PAGE 263

Dealing with Special Diets

DAIRY-FREE Allergies and lactose intolerance (the inability to process sugar in dairy) are the top medical reasons people pass on cheese, milk, butter, chocolate (sadly) and tons of processed foods.

DIABETES Sugar and carbs are practically the pillars of Thanksgiving dinner, which means people with diabetes have to be extra careful. This chronic illness affects how your body processes glucose.

GLUTEN-FREE Bread, pasta and beer can be gut-wrenching if someone at your table has celiac disease or gluten intolerance, both conditions in which the body can't tolerate gluten, a protein found in grains like wheat, barley and rye.

NUT-FREE Nuts are some of the most potent allergenic foods out there. In addition to the real deal, pay attention to oils, candies, sauces and other less obvious foods that could contain them.

VEGAN Vegans won't consume any animal product. This includes not only the obvious turkey but also dairy, eggs, fish and even honey.

PICKY EATER Maybe there's a teen (or even an adult) at your table who refuses to eat anything other than plain rice and chicken or one who just can't stand foods touching. Picky eaters afflict almost every Thanksgiving dinner. Unfortunately, there's not much you can do to accommodate them.

Brussels Sprouts with Bacon

SERVES 8　**PREP** 10 minutes　**ROAST** 35 minutes

- **2 lbs large Brussels sprouts, trimmed and halved**
- **2 tbsp extra-virgin olive oil**
- **1 tsp thyme leaves**
- **½ tsp salt**
- **¼ tsp freshly ground black pepper**
- **6 slices bacon**
- **1½ tbsp balsamic glaze**

■ Heat oven to 400°. On a foil-lined rimmed baking sheet, toss sprouts with oil, thyme, salt and pepper. Roast about 35 minutes.

■ Meanwhile, lay bacon on a rack set in a foil-lined rimmed baking sheet. Roast 18 to 20 minutes. Let cool slightly; crumble.

■ Toss sprouts with two-thirds of the bacon. Top with remaining bacon and drizzle with balsamic glaze.

PER SERVING 167 **CAL**; 12 g **FAT** (3 g **SAT**); 6 g **PRO**; 11 g **CARB**; 4 g **SUGARS**; 4 g **FIBER**; 312 mg **SODIUM**

Make It Vegan: Substitute vegan bacon, such as Lightlife Smart Bacon.

PER SERVING 121 **CAL**; 6 g **FAT** (1 g **SAT**); 8 g **PRO**; 10 g **CARB**; 4 g **SUGARS**; 4 g **FIBER**; 469 mg **SODIUM**

Make It Picky Eater-Proof: Swap in carrots, split and cut into 2-inch chunks; skip the glaze.

PER SERVING 174 **CAL**; 12 g **FAT** (3 g **SAT**); 4 g **PRO**; 13 g **CARB**; 9 g **SUGARS**; 3 g **FIBER**; 344 mg **SODIUM**

Creamed Spinach

SERVES 8　**PREP** 15 minutes　**COOK** 13 minutes

- **20 oz fresh baby spinach, roughly chopped**
- **¼ plus ⅛ tsp salt**
- **2 tbsp unsalted butter**
- **3 cloves garlic, minced**
- **1 small shallot, minced**
- **2 tbsp all-purpose flour**
- **1 cup half-and-half**
- **2 tbsp finely grated Parmesan**
- **⅛ tsp ground nutmeg**

■ In a large stainless skillet over medium-high, cook spinach in 2 batches, 3 to 4 minutes each, adding ⅛ tsp salt to each batch. Drain very well.

■ Wipe out pan and return to heat. Reduce heat to medium and melt butter. Add garlic and shallot. Cook until softened and fragrant, about 3 minutes.

■ Whisk in flour and cook 30 seconds. Whisk in half-and-half, then Parmesan and nutmeg. Stir in ⅛ tsp salt; cook until thickened, about 1 minute.

■ Remove from heat and stir in spinach.

PER SERVING 98 **CAL**; 6 g **FAT** (4 g **SAT**); 3 g **PRO**; 7 g **CARB**; 2 g **SUGARS**; 2 g **FIBER**; 205 mg **SODIUM**

Make It Gluten-Free: Swap the flour and half-and-half for ½ cup milk and 2 oz cubed cream cheese.

PER SERVING 62 **CAL**; 3 g **FAT** (2 g **SAT**); 3 g **PRO**; 5 g **CARB**; 2 g **SUGARS**; 2 g **FIBER**; 216 mg **SODIUM**

Make It Dairy-Free: Opt for extra-virgin olive oil instead of butter. Swap the half-and-half for ¾ cup oat milk and use 1 tbsp nutritional yeast plus ¼ tsp salt instead of the Parmesan.

PER SERVING 146 **CAL**; 5 g **FAT** (1 g **SAT**); 5 g **PRO**; 19 g **CARB**; 1 g **SUGARS**; 4 g **FIBER**; 238 mg **SODIUM**

BRUSSELS SPROUTS WITH BACON

CREAMED SPINACH

SWEET POTATO
CASSEROLE

One potato, two potato. What would Thanksgiving dinner be without a double dose of these creamy tubers? One is sweet and spiked with cinnamon, and the other is buttery and savory and the perfect vehicle for gravy.

Sweet Potato Casserole

SERVES 8 **PREP** 10 minutes **MICROWAVE** 15 minutes **BROIL** 2 minutes

- 2 **lbs sweet potatoes, peeled and cut into 1-inch chunks**
- 1 **tbsp finely grated ginger**
- ¾ **tsp salt**
- 2 **tbsp unsalted butter**
- ¼ **cup packed light brown sugar**
- ¼ **tsp ground cinnamon**
- ⅓ **cup chopped toasted pecans**
- 1 **bag large marshmallows, halved**

■ In a large microwave-safe dish, combine sweet potatoes, ginger and ½ tsp salt with 1 cup water. Cover dish tightly with plastic wrap and poke holes to vent.

■ Microwave at 100% for 15 minutes. Drain potatoes and mash with butter, sugar, cinnamon and ¼ tsp salt.

■ Stir in pecans and spread in a broiler-safe dish.

■ Heat broiler. Top potatoes with marshmallows. Broil until marshmallows are browned, 1 to 2 minutes.

PER SERVING 221 CAL; 6 g FAT (2 g SAT); 2 g PRO; 41 g CARB; 19 g SUGARS; 4 g FIBER; 293 mg SODIUM

Make It Dairy-Free Use coconut oil in place of butter.

PER SERVING 226 CAL; 7 g FAT (3 g SAT); 2 g PRO; 41 g CARB; 19 g SUGARS; 4 g FIBER; 292 mg SODIUM

Make It Diabetic-Friendly Replace the brown sugar with a sugar alternative. Then use about ⅓ cup mini marshmallows to create a single ring along edge of dish.

PER SERVING 162 CAL; 6 g FAT (2 g SAT); 2 g PRO; 26 g CARB; 6 g SUGARS; 4 g FIBER; 283 mg SODIUM

Mashed Potatoes

SERVES 10 **PREP** 10 minutes **COOK** 10 minutes

- 2 **lbs russet potatoes, peeled and cut into 2-inch chunks**
- 1 **tbsp plus ½ to ¾ tsp salt**
- 1 **cup milk**
- 6 **tbsp unsalted butter**

■ Place potatoes in a large pot and cover by 2 inches with cool water. Stir in 1 tbsp salt. Bring to a boil, reduce heat and simmer 10 minutes, until tender.

■ Meanwhile, heat milk and butter over low until butter is melted.

■ Drain potatoes and pass through a ricer into the hot pot. Slowly stir in milk mixture, adding more butter if needed. Stir in ½ tsp salt or to taste.

PER SERVING 143 CAL; 8 g FAT (5 g SAT); 3 g PRO; 17 g CARB; 2 g SUGARS; 1 g FIBER; 186 mg SODIUM

Make It Vegan Swap the milk and butter for ⅔ cup vegetable broth and 4 tbsp extra-virgin olive oil.

PER SERVING 68 CAL; 0 g FAT (0 g SAT); 2 g PRO; 16 g CARB; 1 g SUGARS; 1 g FIBER; 218 mg SODIUM

Make It Diabetic-Friendly Simmer 2 lbs chopped cauliflower for 20 minutes, then drain and puree in a blender. Blend in 2 tbsp unsalted butter; salt to taste.

PER SERVING 45 CAL; 3 g FAT (2 g SAT); 2 g PRO; 5 g CARB; 2 g SUGARS; 2 g FIBER; 203 mg SODIUM

If your turkey is frozen, be sure to allow enough time for it to thaw completely before Thanksgiving Day. You'll need 24 hours in the refrigerator for every 4 to 5 pounds. A 14-pound turkey will take 3 to 4 days. Never thaw a turkey at room temperature.

Basic Roast Turkey

SERVES 12 **PREP** 10 minutes **ROAST** 3 hours, 30 minutes

- 1 **(14 lb) turkey, thawed if frozen**
- 1 **tbsp vegetable oil**
- 1 **tsp salt**
- ½ **tsp freshly ground black pepper**
- 3 **large onions, coarsely chopped**
- 1 **cup chicken broth**

■ Position oven rack in lowest third of oven; heat to 400°F.

■ Remove neck and giblets from the turkey. Rub the turkey with the oil. Sprinkle all over with the salt and pepper. Spread the onions in a large roasting pan. Place the turkey on top. Roast 30 minutes.

■ Lower oven to 350°F. Add the broth to the pan. Tent with foil if browning too quickly Roast 3 to 3½ hours, until internal temperature is 180°F in innermost part of thigh and 170°F in breast. Remove to a platter. Reserve drippings for gravy.

Cranberry Sauce

SERVES 8 **PREP** 5 minutes **COOK** 18 minutes

- 2 **(12 oz) bags fresh or frozen cranberries**
- 1¾ **cups sugar**
- ¾ **cup water**
- 1 **orange slice**
- 1 **tsp freshly grated orange zest**

■ Combine cranberries, sugar, water, orange slice and freshly grated orange zest in medium-size saucepan. Stir over high heat 3 minutes, until sugar melts and water starts to boil. Reduce heat; simmer until thickened, 15 minutes. Discard orange. Pour into serving bowl; cool completely.

Easiest Ever Gravy

SERVES 12 **PREP** 5 minutes **COOK** 4 minutes

- 3 **tbsp butter**
- ½ **cup defatted pan drippings**
- ¼ **cup all-purpose flour**
- 3 **cups turkey or chicken stock**
   Salt and black pepper

■ Melt butter in turkey roasting pan over medium-high. Whisk in pan drippings, scraping up browned bits from bottom of pan.

■ In large measuring cup, whisk flour into stock. While whisking, add in a thin stream to roasting pan. Cook 4 minutes, whisking, until thickened. Season with salt and pepper to taste.

Make It Gluten-Free Replace all-purpose flour with 3 tbsp cornstarch. Check the label on the turkey or chicken stock to make sure it's gluten-free.

Make It Vegan In a clean saucepan, heat 2 tbsp extra-virgin olive oil over medium-high. Whisk ¼ cup all-purpose flour into 3½ cups vegetable broth and whisk into saucepan. Cook 4 minutes or until thickened. Season with salt and pepper to taste.

Sausage Stuffing

SERVES 12 **PREP** 10 minutes **COOK** 9 minutes
BAKE 45 minutes

- 8 **cups (12 oz) stale bread cubes**
- ½ **lb Italian sausage (not precooked)**
- 1 **medium onion, diced**
- 4 **oz mushrooms, diced**
- 2 **ribs celery, diced**
- 1 **tbsp unsalted butter**
- 1½ **tsp chopped fresh rosemary**
- 1½ **tsp chopped fresh sage**
- ¼ **tsp salt**
- ½ **cup chicken or turkey broth**

■ Heat oven to 350°. Place bread cubes in a large bowl. Heat a large nonstick skillet over medium-high. Crumble in sausage and cook 4 minutes, breaking apart with a wooden spoon. Transfer with a slotted spoon to bowl with bread.

■ Reduce heat to medium and add onion, mushrooms, celery and butter. Cook 5 minutes, stirring occasionally.

■ Add onion mixture, rosemary, sage and salt to bowl with bread and stir. Drizzle with broth, tossing to combine.

■ Transfer to a greased 11x7-inch baking dish. Bake uncovered for 45 minutes.

PER SERVING 118 CAL; 4 g FAT (1 g SAT); 6 g PRO; 16 g CARB; 2 g SUGARS; 0 g FIBER; 304 mg SODIUM

Make It Gluten-Free Swap in a multigrain gluten-free bread (such as Udi's), gluten-free sausage and gluten-free broth.

PER SERVING 131 CAL; 5 g FAT (1 g SAT); 6 g PRO; 16 g CARB; 3 g SUGARS; 0 g FIBER; 347 mg SODIUM

Make It Vegan Dice ½ lb Tofurky Italian sausage links and brown in 1 tbsp oil. Sub in vegan bread cubes and vegetable broth. Skip the butter.

PER SERVING 135 CAL; 4 g FAT (0 g SAT); 8 g PRO; 18 g CARB; 3 g SUGARS; 0 g FIBER; 295 mg SODIUM

Cranberry-Walnut Rolls

SERVES 12 **PREP** 20 minutes **LET RISE** 1 hour, 45 minutes **BAKE** 35 minutes

- 1 **tsp sugar**
- ⅔ **cup warm milk**
- 1 **(0.25 oz) envelope yeast**
- 3 **cups all-purpose flour**
- 1½ **tsp salt**
- ½ **tsp ground cinnamon**
- ½ **cup sour cream**
- ½ **cup sweetened dried cranberries, chopped**
- ½ **cup chopped walnuts**
- 1 **tbsp unsalted butter, melted**

■ Sprinkle sugar over milk. Add yeast and let sit until foamy, about 5 minutes. Meanwhile, in a large bowl, whisk flour, salt and cinnamon.

■ Stir sour cream into yeast mixture, then stir into flour mixture until dough forms.

■ Scrape dough onto a lightly floured surface and knead in cranberries and walnuts. Continue to knead until they are well distributed and dough is elastic, about 5 minutes.

■ Place dough in a greased bowl; turn to coat. Cover with plastic wrap and let rise 1 hour, until almost doubled.

■ Punch dough down. Coat a 9-inch square pan with nonstick spray. Divide dough into 12 equal pieces. Shape into balls and place in prepared pan. Cover and let rise 45 minutes.

■ Heat oven to 350°. Uncover rolls and bake 20 minutes. Brush with melted butter and bake 15 minutes, until rolls sound hollow when tapped. Remove from pan to a rack; cool slightly.

PER SERVING 175 CAL; 4 g FAT (2 g SAT); 4 g PRO; 31 g CARB; 6 g SUGARS; 1 g FIBER; 313 mg SODIUM

Make It Picky Eater-Proof Replace cinnamon with garlic powder. Skip the cranberries and nuts and knead ¼ cup grated Parmesan into dough instead.

PER SERVING 167 CAL; 4 g FAT (3 g SAT); 5 g PRO; 26 g CARB; 1 g SUGARS; 1 g FIBER; 353 mg SODIUM

Make It Nut-Free Swap in ⅓ cup coarsely chopped salted pumpkin seeds (pepitas) for the walnuts.

PER SERVING 203 CAL; 6 g FAT (2 g SAT); 6 g PRO; 32 g CARB; 6 g SUGARS; 2 g FIBER; 325 mg SODIUM

CRANBERRY SAUCE, PAGE 263

CRANBERRY-WALNUT ROLLS

SAUSAGE STUFFING

MASHED POTATOES, PAGE 261

EASIEST EVER GRAVY, PAGE 263

BASIC ROAST TURKEY, PAGE 263

APPLE-CRANBERRY
LATTICE PIE, PAGE 271

APRICOT-ALMOND
TART, PAGE 271

CARAMELIZED
PEAR TART,
PAGE 271

WINTER CITRUS
TART, PAGE 270

TART CHERRY
SPOKE PIE,
PAGE 269

APPLE STREUSEL
PIE, PAGE 270

APPLE BLOSSOM
PIE, PAGE 268

SIMPLY PECAN PIE,
PAGE 269

CLASSIC PUMPKIN
PIE, PAGE 268

Classic Pumpkin Pie

SERVES 8 **PREP** 20 minutes **BAKE** 55 minutes

- 1 **prepared refrigerated pie crust (from a 15-oz pkg)**
- ½ **cup granulated sugar**
- ¼ **cup packed dark brown sugar**
- 1 **can (15 oz) solid pack pumpkin**
- 1¼ **tsp pumpkin pie spice**
- ½ **tsp salt**
- 2 **large eggs**
- 1 **can (12 oz) evaporated milk**

■ Heat oven to 425°. Fit crust into a 9-inch deep-dish pie plate. In a medium bowl, whisk granulated sugar and next 4 ingredients. Whisk eggs and stir into pumpkin mixture. Whisk in evaporated milk and pour into pie crust.

■ Bake 15 minutes, then lower oven to 350°. Bake 40 minutes, until center is set. Cool completely on a wire rack.

Make It Diabetic-Friendly Replace the granulated sugar with a sugar alternative, increase pumpkin pie spice to 1½ tsp and add 1 tsp vanilla.

Make It Dairy-Free Replace the evaporated milk with 1 cup vanilla soy milk.

Apple Blossom Pie

SERVES 12 **PREP** 35 minutes **BAKE** 40 minutes

- 4 **tbsp melted butter**
- 4 **large Red Delicious apples**
- 1 **cup cranberry juice cocktail**
- ⅓ **cup sugar**
- 1 **tbsp ground cinnamon**
- 1 **tsp ground cardamom**
- 1 **prepared refrigerated pie crust (from a 15-oz pkg)**

■ Coat a shallow 9-inch pie pan with some of the melted butter; reserve the rest.

■ Core but do not peel apples and slice them thinly, top to bottom.

■ In a shallow skillet, bring juice to a simmer. Add apple slices, working in batches and turning once, and simmer just until they begin to soften, about 10 minutes. Remove to a baking sheet. Simmer juice until reduced to ¼ cup and add reserved butter. Keep warm.

■ Heat oven to 400°.

■ Combine sugar, cinnamon and cardamom and place on a large plate. With a sharp knife, cut pie crust into 1-inch-wide strips. Coat 1 rounded (outer) strip with spiced sugar and press it onto side of pan. Press overlapping apple slices along face of dough strip, rounded side up. (For how-to photos, visit *familycircle.com/pie-time.*)

■ Continue with more dough strips and more apple, working your way around in a spiral until you've used all apples and dough and you have one large flower filling pan. Brush apples with juice-butter mixture and bake on a lower oven rack for 10 minutes. Reduce temp to 350° and bake 30 minutes, until apples are curled and beginning to crisp.

Tart Cherry Spoke Pie

SERVES 12 **PREP** 10 minutes **STAND** 30 minutes
BAKE 50 minutes

- 1 **cup sugar**
- 3 **tbsp cornstarch**
- 6 **cups pitted sour cherries, frozen or jarred**
- ¼ **tsp pure almond extract**
- 2 **prepared refrigerated pie crusts (one 15-oz pkg)**

  Egg wash and turbinado sugar, to decorate

■ Mix sugar and cornstarch and toss with cherries and almond extract. Set aside for about 30 minutes, until cherries release some of their juice.

■ Heat oven to 400°.

■ Line a 9-inch pie pan with one of the pie crusts. Unroll the other crust onto a cutting board and with a sharp knife or pizza cutter (wheel), cut into ¼-inch strips.

■ Scrape the filling into the lined pan. Place one of the longer strips of dough across the center of the pie, pressing it into the bottom crust at the edges. Continue placing strips in the same manner, spacing them ½ inch apart, around the entire pie. You may have some of the smaller strips left over.

■ Brush crust carefully with egg wash and give it a good sprinkling of turbinado sugar. Bake for 15 minutes, turn oven down to 350° and continue to bake until the filling is bubbly and crust is brown, about 30 to 35 minutes.

Simply Pecan Pie

SERVES 12 **PREP** 10 minutes **BAKE** 55 minutes

- 1 **prepared refrigerated pie crust (from a 15-oz pkg)**
- 4 **large eggs**
- 1 **cup light corn syrup**
- ½ **cup granulated sugar**
- ½ **cup packed dark brown sugar**
- 1 **tsp vanilla extract**
- 2 **cups pecan halves**
- ⅓ **cup mini chocolate chips**

TART CHERRY SPOKE PIE

■ Heat oven to 350°. Fit the pie crust into a 9-inch pie plate.

■ In a large bowl, lightly beat eggs. Stir in corn syrup, granulated and dark brown sugars and vanilla until combined. Stir in 1½ cups of the pecans and the chocolate chips. Pour into pie shell and arrange the remaining ½ cup pecans over the top.

■ Bake at 350° for 55 minutes or until knife inserted between center and rim tests clean. Cool on rack to room temperature.

Winter Citrus Tart

SERVES 12 **PREP** 15 minutes **BAKE** 40 minutes

- 1 **prepared refrigerated pie crust (from a 15-oz pkg)**
- 1 **small thin-skinned lemon**
- 1 **thin skinned clementine or small tangerine**
- 1 **cup sugar**
- 1 **tsp vanilla extract**
  Pinch of salt
- 4 **large eggs**
- 1 **stick butter, melted**
- 4 **small oranges, ruby grapefruit, tangerines or blood oranges, or any combination**

■ Heat oven to 375°.

■ Line a 10-inch tart pan with removable bottom with the pie crust. Line crust with aluminum foil; bake 20 minutes.

■ Quarter but do not peel the lemon and clementine. Remove any seeds and place the fruit in a high-speed blender. Add sugar, vanilla, salt and eggs and blitz until smooth. Add the butter and blitz again until smooth. Pour into the baked tart pan and bake on a lower rack of the oven for 10 minutes. Lower oven temp to 350° and continue to bake until tart is just set in the center, 10 minutes. Cool completely.

■ Peel 4 remaining fruits, carefully removing all of the white pith with a sharp knife. Slice crosswise into ¼-inch rings and place decoratively atop cooled tart.

Apple Streusel Pie

SERVES 10 **PREP** 30 minutes **BAKE** 1 hour, 20 minutes

- 1 **prepared refrigerated pie crust (from a 15-oz pkg)**
- 1½ **cups packed light brown sugar**
- 1 **tsp ground cinnamon**
- ½ **tsp salt**
- ¼ **tsp ground nutmeg**
- 1¾ **cups all-purpose flour**
- 1½ **sticks cold unsalted butter, cubed**
- ⅔ **cup chopped walnuts**
- 2 **lbs Golden Delicious apples, peeled, cored and thinly sliced**

■ With a rimmed sheet pan on lowest rack, heat oven to 400°. Press pie crust into a 9-inch pie plate (not deep-dish); crimp or pleat crust. Line crust with foil, place on hot sheet pan and bake 20 minutes. Reduce oven to 375°.

■ Combine sugar, cinnamon, salt and nutmeg. Combine half the sugar mixture (about ¾ cup) with 1½ cups flour, the butter and walnuts. Rub butter into flour mixture until chunky crumbs form. Combine remaining sugar mixture with apples and ¼ cup flour.

■ Remove foil from crust and fill with apple mixture, mounding in center; top evenly with crumb mixture. Bake until browned and bubbly, 55 minutes to 1 hour.

Make It Nut-Free Add ½ cup old-fashioned oats in place of walnuts.

Make It Dairy-Free Choose a crust made with shortening or lard. Swap the streusel for 12 oz granola mixed with 2 tbsp honey; add topping during last 15 minutes of baking.

Apple-Cranberry Lattice Pie

SERVES 12 **PREP** 25 minutes **BAKE** 45 minutes

- **5** large Granny Smith apples, peeled, cored and cut into thick slices
- **1** bag (12 oz) fresh or frozen cranberries
- **1½** cups sugar
- **2** tbsp cornstarch
- Grated zest and juice of half a lemon
- Grated zest and juice of half an orange
- Pinch of salt
- **4** tbsp melted butter
- **2** prepared refrigerated pie crusts (one 15-oz pkg)
- Egg wash and more sugar, to decorate

■ In a large bowl, combine apples, cranberries, sugar, cornstarch, zests, juices, salt and butter and let sit until the fruit begins to release its juice.

■ Heat oven to 400°.

■ Line a 9-inch deep-dish pie pan with one of the pie crusts. Place it on a baking sheet to catch any spills. Fill with apple mixture. Cover loosely with foil and bake on a lower rack in oven for 10 to 15 minutes or until fruit is hot and beginning to steam. Meanwhile, unroll second pie crust onto a cutting board and with a sharp knife, cut it into 1½-inch strips. You should have 6 strips. Brush with egg wash and sprinkle generously with sugar.

■ Remove pie from oven, discard foil and working quickly, place pie dough strips crisscross on the pie to form a lattice. You don't have to weave the strips; just lay them across one another and press onto the edge of the bottom crust.

■ Return to oven and bake another 25 to 30 minutes or until filling is bubbly and crust is nicely browned.

Caramelized Pear Tart

SERVES 12 **PREP** 15 minutes **COOK** 10 minutes **BAKE** 35 minutes

- **4** oz salted butter
- **6** ripe but firm Bosc pears, peeled, cored and cut in quarters
- **4** tbsp dark rum
- **½** cup sugar
- **1** prepared refrigerated pie crust (from a 15-oz pkg)

■ In a large skillet, melt butter over medium until it sizzles. Quickly add pears and saute, turning once or twice, until beginning to soften, about 10 minutes. Add rum and swirl pan to cook off alcohol. Add sugar and swirl pan until the sugar dissolves, turning the pears carefully to coat with the caramel.

■ Heat oven to 400°.

■ Transfer pears, cut sides up, to a 9-inch oven-safe skillet with any caramel remaining in the pan. Heat until sizzling. Unroll pie crust and place on top of the pears in skillet. Roll edges toward the center so they just fit inside the lip of the pan and immediately transfer to oven.

■ Bake for 10 minutes, then reduce heat to 350° and continue to bake another 20 to 25 minutes or until crust is a deep brown. Remove from oven, cool 5 minutes, then turn over onto a 10-inch rimmed plate (to catch any excess caramel). Remove pan and serve warm.

Apricot-Almond Tart

SERVES 8 **PREP** 5 minutes **BAKE** 40 minutes

- **1** prepared refrigerated pie crust (from a 15-oz pkg)
- **8** oz apricot jam
- **¾** cup sugar
- **2** tbsp melted butter
- Few drops pure almond extract
- **3** large eggs
- **1** cup sliced almonds

■ Line a 9-inch pie pan with the pie crust, crimping the edges. Chill while you prepare filling.

■ Heat oven to 400°. Warm apricot jam in a small saucepan to liquefy. Transfer to a mixing bowl and whisk in sugar, butter, extract and finally eggs, until smooth. Pour into pie crust and top with almonds, pressing them gently into filling.

■ Bake for 10 minutes, then reduce heat to 350° and continue to bake for 25 to 30 minutes or until center is just set. Remove from oven and cool to room temp before serving.

3-D TREES,
PAGE 290

DECEMBER

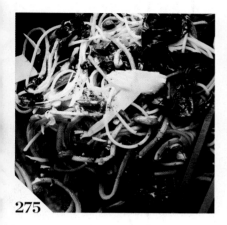

275

283

294

FAMILY DINNERS

Because you've gotta get food on the table.

PASTA WITH
BUTTERNUT
SQUASH AND KALE

A combination of spiralized butternut squash and a small amount of spaghetti provides bulk to this dish but cuts the amount of carbs it would have if it called for twice the amount of spaghetti. And the squash gives it an additional flavor and nutritional boost as well!

Pasta with Butternut Squash and Kale

MAKES 5 servings **PREP** 20 minutes **COOK** 15 minutes

- **1** medium butternut squash, peeled and spiralized
- **½** lb spaghetti
- **3** tbsp extra-virgin olive oil
- **¾** lb lacinato kale, tough ribs removed and leaves chopped
- **½** tsp salt
- **1** tbsp chopped fresh sage
- **½** tsp sherry or white wine vinegar
- **⅔** cup chopped toasted almonds
- **¾** cup shaved Parmesan
  Freshly ground black pepper

■ Place butternut squash in a large colander. Bring salted water to a boil in a large pot. Add spaghetti; cook to al dente per package directions. Drain over squash; return pasta and squash to pot.

■ Meanwhile, in a large stainless skillet over medium-high, heat 2 tbsp olive oil. Add kale and ¼ tsp salt; cook until tender, 7 minutes. Stir in sage, vinegar, half the almonds and ½ cup shaved Parmesan.

■ Drizzle pasta and squash with remaining 1 tbsp olive oil and add ¼ tsp salt. Top with kale mixture; toss well. Serve topped with remaining ¼ cup shaved Parmesan and remaining almonds. Sprinkle with pepper.

PER SERVING 480 **CAL**; 23 g **FAT** (5 g **SAT**); 18 g **PRO**; 54 g **CARB**; 4 g **SUGARS**; 6 g **FIBER**; 514 mg **SODIUM**

Tuna with Roasted Niçoise Vegetables

MAKES 4 servings **PREP** 10 minutes **COOK** 35 minutes

- **¾** lb tricolor baby potatoes, halved
- **5½** tbsp vegetable oil
- **¾** tsp plus ⅛ tsp salt
- **¾** lb green beans, trimmed
- **10½** oz cherry tomatoes
- **2** hard-boiled eggs, quartered
  Zest of 1 to 2 lemons
- **3** tbsp lemon juice
- **⅛** tsp black pepper
- **4** (4 to 5 oz) 1-inch-thick tuna fillets

■ Heat oven to 425°. On one side of a rimmed baking sheet, toss potatoes with 1 tbsp oil and ¼ tsp salt. Roast 10 minutes.

■ Toss green beans and tomatoes with 1 tbsp oil and ¼ tsp salt. Add to baking sheet next to potatoes. Roast until browned and tender, 25 minutes.

■ Meanwhile, in mini food processor, pulse next 4 ingredients to finely chop. Add 1½ tbsp oil; blend until smooth.

■ Heat remaining 2 tbsp oil in a large stainless skillet over high. Pat tuna dry. Season with ¼ tsp salt. Cook about 3 minutes per side, until temp reaches 130°. Top veggies with tuna and drizzle with dressing.

PER SERVING 508 **CAL**; 29 g **FAT** (4 g **SAT**); 40 g **PRO**; 24 g **CARB**; 6 g **SUGARS**; 6 g **FIBER**; 603 mg **SODIUM**

If your family likes our Instant Pot Shepherd's Pie, try it again with tweaks: Swap in ground turkey or lamb, switch to mashed sweet potatoes or stir in other frozen veggies.

Instant Pot Shepherd's Pie

MAKES 6 servings **PREP** 10 minutes
COOK 20 minutes

- 2   **tbsp tomato paste**
- 1   **small onion, diced**
- 8   **oz frozen peas and carrots**
- ½   **tsp salt**
- ¼   **tsp black pepper**
- ¼   **tsp dried thyme**
- 1   **lb ground beef**
- 2   **tbsp Worcestershire sauce**
- 1   **(24 oz) package prepared mashed potatoes**

■ In an electric pressure cooker, whisk tomato paste with ¼ cup water. Stir in onion, peas and carrots, salt, pepper and thyme. Top with ground beef and Worcestershire sauce.

■ Seal and cook on Manual for 8 minutes. Carefully quick-release the steam. Heat broiler.

■ Heat mashed potatoes per package instructions. Break up cooked beef. Stir 1 cup potatoes into beef mixture to thicken sauce. Transfer to a 1-qt soufflé dish. Top beef mixture with remaining potatoes and broil until browned, 3 to 5 minutes.

PER SERVING 291 **CAL**; 14 g **FAT** (6 g **SAT**); 18 g **PRO**; 23 g **CARB**; 4 g **SUGARS**; 2 g **FIBER**; 683 mg **SODIUM**

INSTANT POT
SHEPHERD'S PIE

CREAMY CAULIFLOWER
SOUP WITH CHORIZO

Both the soup and the cooked sausage will keep up to 5 days in the fridge. Store them separately and just heat servings as needed. This recipe makes a big batch. Let soup cool, then freeze a portion for up to 6 months.

Creamy Cauliflower Soup with Chorizo

MAKES 8 servings **PREP** 20 minutes **COOK** 15 minutes

- 2 **tbsp vegetable oil**
- 2 **heads cauliflower, broken into small florets**
- 1 **tsp salt**
- 8 **cups vegetable broth**
- 4 **cloves garlic, smashed**
- 1 **lb crumbled chorizo (not precooked)**
- ½ **tsp white wine vinegar**
- 1 **to 2 cups seasoned croutons, chopped if large**
- **Chopped parsley**

■ Heat oil in a large pot over high. In 2 batches, cook cauliflower with ¼ tsp salt per batch until browned, about 4 minutes.

■ Return all cauliflower to pot. Add broth, garlic and ½ tsp salt. Bring to a boil, then simmer, covered, 7 minutes. Let cool slightly.

■ Meanwhile, cook chorizo in a medium stainless skillet over medium-low until cooked through, 7 to 8 minutes. Transfer to a paper towel-lined plate. With an immersion blender, blend soup until smooth. Blend in vinegar; season to taste.

■ Serve topped with chorizo, croutons and chopped parsley.

PER SERVING 361 **CAL**; 28 g **FAT** (7 g **SAT**); 13 g **PRO**; 18 g **CARB**; 6 g **SUGARS**; 5 g **FIBER**; 1,306 mg **SODIUM**

Make-Aheads, Shortcuts and Swaps

Instant Pot Shepherd's Pie Prep beef up to 2 days ahead; reheat and continue recipe. Use individual ramekins if you want to store completed servings.

Pasta with Butternut Squash and Kale Skip the spiralizing and go for packaged butternut squash noodles. If you don't want to chop the kale, swap in a box of baby kale.

Sheet Pan Pesto Chicken with Polenta Opt for boneless, skinless breasts and adjust total roasting time to 18 to 20 minutes. Mix it up with sun-dried-tomato pesto.

Tuna with Roasted Niçoise Vegetables Swap in Yukon gold or red-skinned potatoes you've cut into 1½-inch pieces.

Prepared pesto comes in both shelf-stable and refrigerated containers. If you can find it, get the refrigerated stuff—it has much better flavor and a nice bright green color.

Sheet Pan Pesto Chicken with Polenta

MAKES 4 servings **PREP** 10 minutes
ROAST 40 minutes

- **4** **bone-in, skinless chicken breasts (about 3 lbs)**
- **3** **tbsp vegetable oil**
- **½** **tsp salt**
- **1** **lb broccoli rabe, trimmed**
- **1** **(18 oz) tube prepared polenta**
- **2** **tbsp finely grated Parmesan**
  Freshly ground black pepper
- **¼** **cup prepared pesto**

■ Heat oven to 400°. Arrange chicken on one side of a rimmed baking sheet. Drizzle with 1 tbsp oil and sprinkle with ¼ tsp salt. Roast 20 minutes.

■ Meanwhile, toss broccoli rabe with 2 tbsp oil and ¼ tsp salt. Arrange on a second rimmed sheet pan. Trim ends of polenta and slice lengthwise into 4 planks. Sprinkle with Parmesan and add pepper to taste.

■ Remove chicken from oven. Spoon 1 tbsp prepared pesto over each breast. Add polenta to pan. Return chicken to oven along with broccoli rabe. Roast until chicken is cooked through, 20 minutes more. Serve chicken with polenta and broccoli rabe.

PER SERVING 607 **CAL**; 25 g **FAT** (4 g **SAT**); 69 g **PRO**; 24 g **CARB**; 2 g **SUGARS**; 3 g **FIBER**; 1,043 mg **SODIUM**

SHEET PAN PESTO
CHICKEN WITH
POLENTA

SUGAR & SPICE

Have a DIY holiday brunch with batch waffles and a simple-but-yummy toppings bar.

If you don't mind manning the waffle iron and waiting to eat, you can keep cranking out the waffles and serving them straight from the waffle maker. Or you can use up all of the batter and keep the cooked waffles warm in a single layer (to keep them from steaming and getting soggy) on a large rimmed baking sheet in a 200° oven.

Orange-Spice Waffles

MAKES 5 servings **PREP** 10 minutes
COOK 3 minutes per batch

- 2 cups all-purpose flour
- 2 tbsp sugar
- 2 to 3 tsp pumpkin pie spice
- 2 tsp baking powder
- ½ tsp salt
- ¼ cup orange zest (from about 3 oranges)
- 2 eggs
- 1 cup milk
- ½ cup orange marmalade
- ⅓ cup vegetable oil

■ In a large bowl, stir together flour, sugar, pumpkin pie spice, baking powder, salt and orange zest. In a medium bowl, whisk egg yolks, milk, marmalade and oil. Blend into flour mixture.

■ Beat egg whites to soft peaks and fold into batter. Heat and fill a waffle iron per manufacturer's instructions. Cook to desired doneness, 3 to 5 minutes.

PER SERVING 472 **CAL**; 19 g **FAT** (4 g **SAT**); 9 g **PRO**; 69 g **CARB**; 27 g **SUGARS**; 2 g **FIBER**; 497 mg **SODIUM**

Brown Sugar Whipped Cream

MAKES 5 servings **PREP** 5 minutes

- ¾ cup heavy cream
- 2 tbsp dark brown sugar

■ Beat cream with sugar until light and fluffy.

PER SERVING 143 **CAL**; 13 g **FAT** (8 g **SAT**); 1 g **PRO**; 6 g **CARB**; 6 g **SUGARS**; 0 g **FIBER**; 11 mg **SODIUM**

Syrup-Glazed Bacon

MAKES 5 servings **PREP** 5 minutes
BAKE 16 minutes

- 10 slices bacon
- 2 tbsp maple syrup

■ Arrange bacon on a rack over a foil-lined pan. Bake at 375° for 16 to 18 minutes, rotating pan halfway through. Brush with syrup; broil about 1 minute.

PER SERVING 127 **CAL**; 11 g **FAT** (4 g **SAT**); 4 g **PRO**; 3 g **CARB**; 2 g **SUGARS**; 0 g **FIBER**; 188 mg **SODIUM**

Rum-Marmalade Sauce

MAKES 5 servings **PREP** 5 minutes
COOK 4 minutes

- ½ cup orange marmalade
- ⅛ tsp salt
- 2 tbsp + ½ tsp spiced rum

■ In a small saucepan over medium, bring marmalade, salt and 2 tbsp each spiced rum and water to a simmer. Cook 4 minutes or to desired consistency. Remove from heat; stir in ½ tsp spiced rum. Serve warm.

PER SERVING 93 **CAL**; 0 g **FAT** (0 g **SAT**); 0 g **PRO**; 21 g **CARB**; 19 g **SUGARS**; 0 g **FIBER**; 76 mg **SODIUM**

Citrus Relish

MAKES 5 servings **PREP** 10 minutes

- 2 oranges
- 2 pink grapefruits
- 1 vanilla bean
  Flaky sea salt

■ Slice tops and bottoms from oranges and grapefruits. Peel fruit. Working over a bowl to collect juices, cut segments from between membranes. Stir in seeds scraped from vanilla bean. Season with salt.

PER SERVING 64 **CAL**; 0 g **FAT** (0 g **SAT**); 1 g **PRO**; 17 g **CARB**; 5 g **SUGARS**; 2 g **FIBER**; 60 mg **SODIUM**

THINK BIG

Super-sized cookies put the happy in your holiday.

HOLIDAY WREATHS, PAGE 293

ALMOND
CHECKERBOARDS,
PAGE 289

Luster dust is a type of decorating powder that adds sparkle and shine to decorated baked goods. It comes in an array of shimmery colors. Look for brands that are labeled "Food Grade" or "FDA Approved" wherever cake decorating supplies are sold.

Chocolate Ornaments

MAKES 8 cookies; 16 servings **PREP** 20 minutes **MICROWAVE** 1 minute **REFRIGERATE** 1 hour **BAKE** 14 minutes

- 1 **oz unsweetened chocolate**
- 1½ **sticks unsalted butter, softened**
- 1¼ **cups sugar**
- 1 **large egg, at room temp**
- 2 **tsp corn syrup**
- 1 **tsp vanilla extract**
- 3¾ **cups all-purpose flour**
- ½ **cup unsweetened cocoa powder**
- ½ **tsp salt**

■ Place chocolate in a small microwave-safe bowl. Microwave at 50% for 1 minute, stirring once halfway through. Stir until smooth and melted. Let cool 5 minutes.

■ Meanwhile, combine butter and sugar in a mixer bowl; beat until light and fluffy, about 3 minutes. Add 3 tbsp water, egg, corn syrup and vanilla; beat until well combined. Scrape down sides of bowl. With mixer on low, add flour, cocoa and salt; beat until combined. Stir in melted chocolate and mix until well blended.

■ Divide dough into 2 disks, wrap in plastic and refrigerate 1 hour or up to 2 days.

■ Heat oven to 350°. Line baking sheets with parchment. On a sheet of wax paper, roll dough to ⅛- to ¼-inch thickness. Cut into 6- or 7-inch circles, using a salad plate as a guide (make your own template at *familycircle .com/cookie-templates*). Place on prepared baking sheets, 1 inch apart, and bake until edges are just lightly browned, about 14 minutes. Cool on baking sheet for 2 minutes. Transfer cookies to a wire rack and cool completely. Repeat with any remaining dough. Follow directions at right for icing and decorating.

PER SERVING 393 **CAL**; 11 g **FAT** (6 g **SAT**); 5 g **PRO**; 71 g **CARB**; 46 g **SUGARS**; 2 g **FIBER**; 89 mg **SODIUM**

Royal Icing with Luster Dust

MAKES 8 cookies

- 4 **cups confectioners' sugar**
- 2 **tbsp meringue powder (powdered egg whites)**
- **Assorted colors food-grade luster dust**
- **Lemon extract**

■ Place confectioners' sugar and meringue powder in a standing mixer bowl. Beat in ¼ cup water; increase speed to high and beat until stiff peaks form, about 3 minutes. Add 2 tbsp water and beat until light and fluffy.

■ To decorate, dilute icing with 1 tbsp water at a time until it has the consistency of thick heavy cream. Spread 1 to 2 tbsp icing over each cooled cookie with an offset spatula. Let dry at least 3 hours or overnight.

■ Paint with luster dust: For each color, mix dust with 1 tsp lemon extract until smooth. Brush over dry iced cookies; let each color dry before brushing on more luster dust.

CHOCOLATE
ORNAMENTS

ALMOND
CHECKERBOARDS

These eye-popping oversized cookies are almost too pretty to eat—almost. Their buttery, almondy flavor may prove to be too much temptation. Each cookie serves 4, so be sure to share! (It is the holidays, after all!)

Almond Checkerboards

MAKES 5 cookies; 20 servings **PREP** 20 minutes **REFRIGERATE** 2 hours **BAKE** 20 minutes

3⅓	**cups all-purpose flour**
½	**cup almond flour**
½	**tsp salt**
2	**sticks cold unsalted butter, cut up**
1½	**cups sugar**
1	**large egg, separated**
⅓	**cup milk**
1	**tsp almond extract**
	Sparkling sugars

■ In a food processor, combine flours and salt. Pulse to blend. Add butter and sugar and pulse until well combined. Add egg yolk, milk and extract; process until dough comes together.

■ Divide dough in half, wrap and refrigerate 2 hours.

■ Heat oven to 350°. Roll out each piece of dough between sheets of wax paper to a 15x9-inch rectangle.

■ Cut dough into 6-inch squares (use the bottom of a tart pan or make your own template at *familycircle.com/cookie-templates*). Transfer squares to a large parchment-lined baking sheet. Reroll scraps, chilling if dough is soft.

■ Brush dough squares with egg white. Sprinkle with sparkling sugar to coat. Roll out scraps and cut more 6-inch squares. Cut each square into 16 squares. Brush smaller squares with egg white; sprinkle with sugars. Place 9 squares on top of each sugar-topped square at a 45° angle to form a checkerboard pattern, trimming as needed. Bake 20 minutes or until edges just turn golden.

PER SERVING 258 **CAL**; 11 g **FAT** (6 g **SAT**); 3 g **PRO**; 37 g **CARB**; 20 g **SUGARS**; 1 g **FIBER**; 66 mg **SODIUM**

Gotta-Have Gear

Use **heavy-duty rimless baking sheets** so that cookie-packed parchment can slide on and off with ease.

Speaking of which, **recipe-ready parchment sheets** are a baker's best friend.

Hit up crafts stores for **food-safe paint brushes** and keep them in a kitchen drawer (so they aren't "borrowed" for other household projects).

To achieve a saturated green on the Holiday Wreaths, opt for **gel food coloring**; visit *michaels.com* for colors.

For Chocolate Ornaments, buy **a range of sheer, shiny luster dusts**. Check out *bakell.com* for options.

Tree Tip: To ensure a smooth edge on cut cookies, use a Microplane to shave down any bumps. Instead of buying a cutter, make your own tree template at familycircle. com/cookie-templates.

3-D Trees

MAKES 5 large or 8 small cookies; 20 servings **PREP** 20 minutes **REFRIGERATE** 2 hours **BAKE** 13 minutes **ASSEMBLE** 1 hour

2¾ **cups all-purpose flour**

¼ **tsp baking soda**

1 **tbsp ground ginger**

1 **tsp ground cinnamon**

½ **tsp ground cloves**

¼ **tsp salt**

1 **stick unsalted butter, softened**

½ **cup packed dark brown sugar**

1 **large egg**

½ **cup unsulphured molasses (such as Grandma's Original)**

2 **cups confectioners' sugar, plus more for dusting**

1 **tbsp meringue powder (powdered egg whites)**

Desiccated coconut

■ In a bowl, whisk first 6 ingredients. Set aside.

■ In a large bowl, beat butter and brown sugar until smooth. Beat in egg, then molasses. Stir flour mixture into butter mixture. Divide dough in half. Wrap and refrigerate 2 hours.

■ Heat oven to 350°. On a well-floured surface, roll half the dough to ⅛-inch thickness. Cut tree shapes with 7½-inch and 5-inch cookie cutters (or make your own template at familycircle.com/cookie-templates); transfer to parchment-lined baking sheets. Reroll scraps and cut. Repeat with remaining dough. With a sharp knife, slice half the cookies in half vertically, but do not pull halves apart. Bake 13 minutes.

■ Recut split cookies and transfer all cookies to racks to cool.

■ Combine confectioners' sugar with meringue powder and 2 tbsp water to make a royal icing glue. Place in a disposable piping bag and snip off a ¼-inch point.

■ Smooth out cut edges of trees (see Tree Tip, above). Pipe a thick bead of icing glue along long side of 1 tree half. Press onto 1 whole cookie and stand it up to make sure trunk is level. Repeat with second tree half and let dry 30 minutes. (You may have to brace it with something, like a ball of foil.) Repeat with all trees. Pipe icing along edges, dust with confectioners' sugar or sprinkle with coconut "snow."

PER SERVING 201 **CAL**; 5 g **FAT** (3 g **SAT**); 2 g **PRO**; 37 g **CARB**; 23 g **SUGARS**; 1 g **FIBER**; 63 mg **SODIUM**

HOLIDAY WREATHS

You'll want to overlap each holly leaf by at least ¼ inch so the wreath is solid enough to hold together. If dough seems soft, refrigerate after cutting out but before arranging.

Holiday Wreaths

MAKES 3 large or 9 small cookies; 15 servings   **PREP** 25 minutes   **REFRIGERATE** 2 hours or overnight   **BAKE** 16 minutes per batch

- **3** **cups all-purpose flour**
- **½** **tsp baking powder**
- **¼** **tsp salt**
- **2** **sticks unsalted butter, softened**
- **1¼** **cups sugar**
- **1** **egg**
- **2** **tsp vanilla extract**
- **1** **tbsp milk**
  Green gel food coloring
- **1** **beaten egg white**
  Sparkling sugar or edible pearls

- In a medium bowl, combine flour, baking powder and salt.

- In a large bowl, beat butter and sugar on medium-high for 3 minutes, until smooth. Beat in egg and vanilla.

- On low, beat flour mixture and milk into butter mixture just until combined. Tint dough with food coloring. Divide dough into thirds and shape each third into a disk. Wrap in plastic and refrigerate 2 hours or overnight.

- Heat oven to 325°. Roll 1 disk of dough to ¼-inch thickness between sheets of wax paper. Remove top sheet. Cut dough into leaf shapes with a 3¾-inch cookie cutter (you'll need 15 leaves for each wreath).

- Draw a 6-inch circle on a sheet of parchment paper. Flip over parchment and place on a baking sheet. Arrange 15 slightly overlapping cookies on top of circle to make a 9½-inch-wide wreath. Brush with egg white and sprinkle with sparkling sugar or pearls. For smaller wreaths, cut dough into leaf shapes with a 2½-inch cookie cutter. (You'll still need 15 or even 16 cookies for each wreath, and you'll draw a 4-inch circle on parchment.)

- Bake 16 minutes or until shiny. Cool completely on pans on a rack, then carefully remove. Repeat with all dough, chilling between batches.

PER SERVING 283 **CAL**; 13 g **FAT** (8 g **SAT**); 3 g **PRO**; 39 g **CARB**; 19 g **SUGARS**; 1 g **FIBER**; 68 mg **SODIUM**

Make 'Em Mini

Any of our oversized options can be made much smaller. Check all cookies for doneness after baking 8 to 10 minutes.

ORNAMENTS AND TREES Go with a 2-inch cookie cutter. Opt for simple decorations—otherwise, they may look super busy.

CHECKERBOARDS AND WREATHS Pick up a fluted cookie cutter set. For Almond Checkerboards, cut out dough with the 1½-inch cutter. Cut 1-inch centers out of half the cookies. Sprinkle base cookies with colored sugars, then stack cutouts on top before baking. For Holiday Wreaths, use 1½-inch and 1-inch cutters to form a wreath shape.

QUICK NIBBLES & SIPS

When time is short and it's time to celebrate.

Have a Ball Cheese balls: easy, delicious, make-ahead-friendly and inexpensive.

Feta-Dill Cheese Ball

MAKES 12 servings **PREP** 10 minutes **CHILL** 2 hours, 30 minutes

- 8 oz cream cheese, softened
- 1½ cups crumbled feta cheese
- 2 tsp lemon zest
- 1 tsp cracked black pepper
- ⅛ tsp salt
- ½ cup chopped fresh dill

■ Beat cream cheese and feta cheese. Stir in lemon zest, pepper and salt. Shape into a ball and chill 30 minutes. Roll in dill. Wrap in plastic and refrigerate at least 2 hours before serving.

PER SERVING 116 **CAL**; 11 g **FAT** (7 g **SAT**); 4 g **PRO**; 2 g **CARB**; 1 g **SUGARS**; 0 g **FIBER**; 256 mg **SODIUM**

Spicy Pimento Cheese Ball

MAKES 12 servings **PREP** 10 minutes **CHILL** 2 hours, 30 minutes

- 8 oz cream cheese, softened,
- 1½ cups shredded cheddar cheese
- ¼ cup chopped pimentos
- 2 tbsp finely chopped pickled jalapeños
- 1 tsp garlic powder
- ⅛ tsp salt
  Dash black pepper
  Hot sauce

■ Beat cream cheese and 1 cup of the shredded cheese. Beat in pimentos, jalapeños, garlic powder, salt, pepper and hot sauce to taste. Shape into a ball and chill 30 minutes. Chop remaining ½ cheddar cheese. Roll in chopped cheese. Wrap in plastic

and refrigerate at least 2 hours before serving.

PER SERVING 145 **CAL**; 13 g **FAT** (7 g **SAT**); 6 g **PRO**; 2 g **CARB**; 1 g **SUGARS**; 0 g **FIBER**; 222 mg **SODIUM**

Pistachio-Fig Cheese Ball

MAKES 12 servings **PREP** 10 minutes **CHILL** 2 hours, 30 minutes

- ½ cup chopped dried figs
- 8 oz cream cheese, softened
- 4 oz goat cheese
- ⅛ tsp salt
- ½ cup chopped salted pistachios

■ Pour 1 cup boiling water over figs. Let steep for 5 minutes; drain. Beat cream cheese with goat cheese and salt. Fold in figs. Shape into a ball and chill 30 minutes. Roll in pistachios. Wrap in plastic and refrigerate at least 2 hours before serving.

PER SERVING 136 **CAL**; 11 g **FAT** (6 g **SAT**); 4 g **PRO**; 6 g **CARB**; 4 g **SUGARS**; 1 g **FIBER**; 128 mg **SODIUM**

Trio of Twists Puff pastry feels fancy, even though you just have to fill and twist. These are particularly impressive because they're almost a foot long!

Brown Sugar–Cardamom Twists

MAKES 12 servings **PREP** 15 minutes **BAKE** 17 minutes

- 2 sheets thawed frozen puff pastry
- 1 beaten egg
- ½ cup light brown sugar
- 1 tbsp ground cardamom or cinnamon
- 1 tsp salt

■ Brush 1 side of each sheet puff pastry with egg. Stir together brown sugar, cardamom and salt. Sprinkle evenly over 1 sheet. Place second sheet egg side down on first sheet. Cut stack into 12 strips and pinch all sides of each to seal; twist. Divide twists between 2 parchment-lined baking sheets.

■ Bake 17 minutes at 400°. Swap position of sheets halfway through baking.

PER SERVING 195 CAL; 29 g FAT (5 g SAT); 3 g PRO; 29 g CARB; 10 g SUGARS; 1 g FIBER; 335 mg SODIUM

Miso-Sesame Twists

MAKES 12 servings   PREP 10 minutes
BAKE 7 minutes

   1   tbsp miso paste
   2   tbsp boiling water
   2   sheets thawed frozen puff pastry
   3   tbsp toasted sesame seeds

■ Stir together the miso paste and boiling water. Brush 1 side of each sheet puff pastry with miso mixture. Sprinkle 1 sheet with sesame seeds. Place second sheet miso side down on first sheet. Cut stack into 12 strips and pinch all sides of each to seal; twist. Divide twists between 2 parchment-lined baking sheets.

■ Bake 17 minutes at 400°. Swap position of sheets halfway through baking.

Gruyère-Cayenne Twists

MAKES 12 servings   PREP 10 minutes
BAKE 17 minutes

   2   sheets thawed frozen puff pastry
   1   beaten egg
   2   cups finely grated Gruyère
   ½   tsp cayenne
   ¼   tsp salt

■ Brush 1 side of each sheet puff pastry with egg. Press Gruyère evenly over 1 sheet; sprinkle with cayenne and salt.

■ Place second sheet egg side down on first sheet. Cut stack into 12 strips and pinch all sides of each to seal; twist. Divide twists between 2 parchment-lined baking sheets.

■ Bake 17 minutes at 400°. Swap position of sheets halfway through baking.

PER SERVING 214 CAL; 14 g FAT (8 g SAT); 7 g PRO; 20 g CARB; 1 g SUGARS; 1 g FIBER; 235 mg SODIUM

Batch Drinks Because who has time to fuss with individual cocktails?

Pomegranate French 75

MAKES 12 servings   PREP 10 minutes

   16   oz gin
   8   oz pomegranate juice

   4   oz freshly squeezed lemon juice
   2   oz simple syrup
       Chilled sparkling wine

■ In an ice-filled pitcher, combine the first 4 ingredients. Stir until chilled and pour into 12 champagne flutes. Top each with chilled sparkling wine.

PER SERVING 180 CAL; 0 g FAT (0g SAT); 0 g PRO; 10 g CARB; 7 g SUGARS; 0 g FIBER; 3 g SODIUM

Slow Cooker Triple-Chocolate Cocoa

MAKES 16 servings   PREP 5 minutes
SLOW COOK 3 hours on LOW

   1   qt whole milk
   1   pt half-and-half
   1   cup semisweet chocolate chips
   ½   cup chocolate syrup
   ½   cup sifted confectioners' sugar
   ½   cup sifted unsweetened cocoa powder
       Bourbon, Baileys or mint schnapps (optional)

■ In a 6-qt slow cooker, whisk the first 6 ingredients. Cook 3 hours on LOW. For adults, serve with a shot of bourbon, Baileys or mint schnapps, if desired.

PER SERVING 172 CAL; 9 g FAT (5 g SAT); 4 g PRO; 23 g CARB; 18 g SUGARS; 2 g FIBER; 53 mg SODIUM

INDEX